THE WAR AND DEMOCRACY

MACMILLAN AND CO., Limited
LONDON · BOMBAY · CALCUTTA
MELBOURNE

THE MACMILLAN COMPANY
NEW YORK · BOSTON · CHICAGO
DALLAS · SAN FRANCISCO

THE MACMILLAN CO. OF CANADA, Ltd.
TORONTO

THE WAR AND DEMOCRACY

BY

R. W. SETON-WATSON, D.Litt.

J. DOVER WILSON

ALFRED E. ZIMMERN

AND

ARTHUR GREENWOOD

MACMILLAN AND CO., LIMITED

ST. MARTIN'S STREET, LONDON

1915

TO

The Workers' Educational Association

When wilt Thou save the people ?
O God of mercy, when ?
Not kings and lords, but nations !
Not thrones and crowns, but men !
Flowers of Thy heart, O God, are they ;
Let them not pass, like weeds, away—
Their heritage a sunless day.
God save the people !

EBENEZER ELLIOTT.

" To remake the map of Europe, and to rearrange the
peoples in accordance with the special mission assigned to
each of them by geographical, ethnical and historical conditions—this is the first essential step for all."

MAZZINI (1832).

PREFACE

FOR many years past the prospect of universal war has haunted the dreams of pacificists and militarists alike. Many of us, without denying its growing menace, hoped against hope that it might be averted by the gradual strengthening of international goodwill and mutual intercourse, and the steady growth of democratic influences and political thought. But our misgivings proved more prophetic than our hopes; and last August the great war came upon us like a thief in the night. After four months of war we feel that, in spite of the splendid response of the nation at large, in spite of a unanimity which has no parallel in our previous history, there are still large sections of the community who fail to realise the vastness of the issues at stake, the formidable nature of the forces ranged against us, and the true inner significance of the struggle. And yet all that is worth living for depends upon the outcome of this war—for ourselves the future of the democratic ideal in these islands and in the British Empire at large, for the peoples of Europe deliverance from competing armaments and the yoke of racial tyranny. But before our future can be secured, sacrifices

vii

will be required of every citizen, and in a free community sacrifice can only spring from knowledge. Moreover, if we are to put an end to the intolerable situation of an unwilling Europe in arms, public opinion must think out very carefully the great problems which have been thrown into the melting-pot and be prepared for the day of settlement.

The present volume has been written as a guide to the study of the underlying causes and issues of the war. It does not pretend to cover the whole of so vast a field, and it will have attained its aim if it provides the basis for future discussion. It originated in the experience of its five writers at the Summer Schools for working-class students held in connection with the Workers' Educational Association. In the early days of August, at the outbreak of the war, Summer Schools were in full swing at Oxford, Cambridge, Eton, Bangor, and Durham, and it at once became apparent, not merely that the word " citizen " had suddenly acquired a new depth and significance for the men and women of our generation, but also that for the individual citizen himself a large new field of study and discussion had been opened up on subjects and issues hitherto unfamiliar. This book was planned to meet the need there expressed, but it is hoped that it may be found useful by a wider circle of readers.

We have called the book *The War and Democracy*, because our guiding idea throughout has been the sense of the great new responsibilities, both of thought and action, which the present situation lays upon British Democracy and on believers in democracy throughout the world.

In devoting one chapter to a survey of the issues raised for settlement by the war, we must disclaim most emphatically all idea of dividing the lion's skin before the animal has been killed. Our object has not been to prophesy, but merely to stimulate thought and discussion. The field is so vast and complicated that unless public opinion begins to mobilise without further delay and to form clear ideas as to how the principles laid down by our statesmen are to be converted into practice, it may find itself confronted, as it was confronted in 1814, with a situation which it can neither understand nor control, and with a settlement which will perpetuate many of the abuses which this war ought to remove. Our best excuse is supplied by the attitude of many leaders of German political thought—men like Franz von Liszt, Ostwald, and Paul Rohrbach—who are already mapping out the world according to their victorious fancies.

R. W. S.-W.

December 1914.

J. D. W.

A. E. Z.

A. G.

CONTENTS

CHAPTER I

CHAPTER II

CHAPTER III

CHAPTER IV

AUSTRIA–HUNGARY AND THE SOUTHERN SLAVS

By R. W. SETON-WATSON, D.Litt., New College, Oxford, author of *Racial Problems in Hungary, The Southern Slav Question*, etc.

CHAPTER V

RUSSIA

By J. DOVER WILSON

CHAPTER VI

FOREIGN POLICY

[*Contributed*]

CONTENTS xiii

CHAPTER VII

The Issues of the War

By R. W. Seton-Watson

CHAPTER VIII

Social and Economic Aspects of the War

Arthur Greenwood, B.Sc., Lecturer in Economics at the University of Leeds

CHAPTER IX

GERMAN CULTURE AND THE BRITISH COMMONWEALTH

By ALFRED E. ZIMMERN

MAPS

CHAPTER I

INTRODUCTORY

" It seems to me that the amount of lawlessness and crime, the amount of waste and futility, the amount of war and war possibility and war danger in the world are just the measure of the present inadequacy of the world's system of collective organisations to the purpose before them. It follows from this very directly that only one thing can end war on the earth, and that is a subtle mental development, an idea, the development of the idea of the world commonweal in the collective mind."—H. G. WELLS in 1908.

THIS is a testing time for Democracy. The people of Great Britain and the Dominions, to whom all the world looks as the trustees, together with France and America, of the great democratic tradition, are brought face to face, for the first time, with their full ultimate responsibility as British citizens. Upon the way in which that responsibility is realised and discharged depends the future of the democratic principle, not only in these islands, but throughout the world.

Democracy is not a mere form of government. It does not depend on ballot boxes or franchise laws or any constitutional machinery. These are but its trappings. Democracy is a spirit and an atmosphere, and its essence is trust in the moral instincts of the people. A tyrant is not a democrat, for he believes in government by force ; neither is a demagogue a democrat, for he believes in government by flattery. A democratic country is a country where the government has confidence in the people and

1   B

the people in the government and in itself, and where all are united in the faith that the cause of their country is not a mere matter of individual or national self-interest, but is in harmony with the great moral forces which rule the destinies of mankind. No form of government is so feeble as a democracy without faith. But a democracy armed with faith is not merely strong: it is invincible; for its cause will live on, in defeat and disaster, in the breast of every one of its citizens. Belgium is a living testimony to that great truth.

British Democracy has carried this principle of confidence to the furthest possible point. Alone among the States of Europe, Great Britain relies for her existence and for the maintenance of her world-wide responsibilities upon the free choice of her citizens. Her privileges are extended to all: her active obligations are forced upon none. Trusting in the principle of individual freedom, and upon the sound instinct and understanding of her people, she leaves it to each citizen to make his choice whether, and in what manner, he shall serve his country. Never have responsibilities so arduous and so urgent been laid upon the citizens of any community: and never have the citizens been so free to choose or to decline the burden. The world will judge Great Britain, and judge Democracy, according to the measure of our free response.

What is the nature of the responsibility cast upon us at this crisis?

It is threefold. It concerns the present, the past, and the future. There are three questions which every citizen must needs ask, and try to answer, for himself. The first and most urgent is a matter of present decision: What is my duty here and now? The second involves a judgment of past events: Why is it that we are at war? Are we fighting in a just cause? The third involves an estimate of the future and of the part which British public opinion can and should play in shaping it : What are the issues involved in the various belligerent countries ? What should be the principles of a just settlement ? How can Great Britain best use her influence in the cause of human progress and for the welfare of the peoples involved in the war ?

It is with the second and especially with the third of these responsibilities that this volume is concerned.

" What is the war about ? " " Are we fighting in a just cause ? " Every one by now has asked himself this question, and most people have studied some at least of the evidence, and tried to satisfy themselves as to the answer. The Foreign Office White Paper and numberless books and pamphlets have enlightened the public on many of the questions at issue. Yet the fact remains that the necessity of this educative campaign involves a confession of failure —or at least of grave neglect—on the part of British democracy. Under our democratic constitution the people of Great Britain have assumed the responsibility for the management of their own affairs. One great department of those affairs, the most vital of all, they and their representatives have systematically neglected. Deeply engaged and interested in domestic problems, they have left the control of their foreign relations in the hands of expert advisers. And so it was with something like stupefaction that they discovered, one day in August, that they were called upon to honour the obligations contracted in their name.

There has been no desire to evade those obligations. But there has been a very real desire to understand them, and also a fixed determination never again to allow such a lack of contact, on vital issues, between the mind of the people and the activities of their ministers.

But no mere changes in the machinery of democratic control can avail to save the people from the consequences of their own ignorance and neglect. There is only one way in which we can achieve full Democracy in this country, and that is through Education.

In the sphere of domestic affairs, particularly in connection with social and industrial questions, the people have slowly realised this hard truth. After a generation or more of attempts and failures and disillusionments many thousands of workpeople have learnt the lesson that power without knowledge is not power at all, and that knowledge, whether for public affairs or for any other purpose, cannot be gained without effort and discipline. They have come to realise that Democracy needs, for its full working, not only schools in which to train its young, but also—what no Democracy save those of the ancient world has ever possessed—such facilities for the education for its adult citizens, engaged in the active work of the community, as will enable them to maintain unimpaired their intellectual freshness and vigour, and to face with wisdom and courage the problems for which, as citizens, they have assumed responsibility. They have come to think of Education, not as a time of tutelage or training, but as a part of active life itself, woven of the same texture and concerned with the same issues, as being, in fact, the effort to understand the world in which they live. But they have naturally tended to confine those issues within the limits of their own domestic interests and experience. They are called upon now to widen their horizon, and to apply the democratic conception of education to the new problems which have arisen owing to the part which Great Britain is now playing in the affairs of Europe.

It is never easy to think things out clearly and coldly. But it is hardest of all in the crisis of a great war, when men's minds are blurred by passionate emotions of sorrow, anxiety, and indignation. Hence a time of war is the heyday of fallacies and delusions, of misleading hopes and premature disillusionments : men tend to live in an unreal world of phrases and catchwords. Yet never is it more necessary than at such a period, in the old Greek phrase, "to follow the argument whithersoe'er it leads," to look facts squarely in the face, and, particularly, the great ugly outstanding fact of war itself, the survival of which democrats, especially in Great Britain and the United States, have of recent years been so greatly tempted to ignore.

People speak as if war were a new sudden and terrible phenomenon. There is nothing new about the fact of war. What is new about this war is the scale on which it is waged, the science and skill expended on it, and the fact that it is being carried on by national armies, numbering millions, instead of by professional bodies of soldiers. But war itself is as old as the world : and if it surprises and shocks us this is due to our own blindness. There are only two ways of settling disputes between nations, by law or by war. As there is as yet no World-State, with the power to enforce a World-law between the nations, the possibility of war, with all its contingent horrors, should have been before our eyes all the time. The *occasion* of this war was no doubt a surprise. But that it could happen at all should not be a surprise to us, still less a disillusionment. It does not mark a backward step in human civilisation. It only registers the fact that civilisation is still grievously in-complete and unconsolidated. Terrible as this war is in its effect on individual lives and happiness, it ought not to depress us—even if, in our blindness, we imagined the world to be a far better organised place than it actually is. The fact that many of the combatants regard war as an anachronism adds to the tragedy, but also to the hope, of the struggle. It shows that civilised opinion is gathering strength for that deepening and extension of the meaning and range of citizenship which alone can make war between the nations of the world as obsolete as it has become between the nations of the British Empire or between the component parts of the United States.

It was perhaps inevitable that British citizens in particular, removed from the storm centres of Continental Europe, and never very logical in their thinking, should have failed to realise the possibility of another great war, similar to the Napoleonic struggle of a hundred years ago. For nearly half a century the great European States had been at peace : and we had come to look upon their condition, and the attachment of their peoples, as being as ancient and as stable as our own. We had grown used to the map of Europe as it had been left by the great convulsions between 1848 and 1871. Upon the basis of that map and of the governments represented on it, and in response to the growing needs of the world as a whole, we had embarked on every kind of international co-operation and cosmopolitan effort. The Hague Congress, convened by the Tsar of Russia, looked forward to the day when war, and the causes of war, should be obsolete. The Socialist Movement, a growing force in all industrial communities, stood for the same ideal, and for the international comradeship of the working class. Law and medicine, science and scholarship followed suit ; and every summer, in quest of health and change, thousands of plain citizens have crossed international frontiers with scarcely greater sense of change than in moving from province to province in a single State. Commerce and industry, the greatest material forces of our time, have become inextricably international, and in the palpable injury in which a war would involve them some thinkers of clear but limited vision saw the best hope of averting a European conflagration.

And yet, throughout these two generations of economic and social development, the fear of war has never been absent from the mind of Europe. Her emperors and statesmen have talked of peace; but they have prepared for war, more skilfully and more persistently than ever before in the history of Europe or of the world. Almost the entire manhood of every European nation but England has been trained to arms; and the annual war budget of Europe rose, in time of peace, to over 300 million pounds. The States of Europe, each afraid to stand alone against a coalition of possible rivals, formed themselves into opposing groups; and each of the groups armed feverishly against the other, fearful lest, by any change in the diplomatic or political situation, they might be caught unawares and suffer loss. Thus, it ought not to have surprised us that finally, through the accident of a royal murder, the spark should be fired and the explosion ensue, and that merchants and manufacturers, propagandists and philanthropists, scholars and scientists, should find the ground shaken beneath their feet and the projects patiently built up through years of international co-operation shattered by the events of a few days.

Now that the war has come it is easy to see that they were mistaken. They had built up the structure of a cosmopolitan society without looking to the foundations. The economic activities of mankind have indeed brought a World-Society and a World-Industry into being; but its political analogue, a World-State, can only be formed, not through the co-operation of individuals or groups of individuals, but through the union of nations and the federation of national governments. The first task of our time for Europe, as we shall try to show in the next chapter, is to lay firm the foundations of those nations by carrying to victory the twin principles of Nationality and Democracy—

to secure that the peoples of Europe shall be enabled to have governments corresponding to their national needs and responsible to their own control, and to build up, under the care and protection of those governments, the social institutions and the civilisation of their choice. So long as there are peoples in Europe under alien governments, curtailed in the use of their own language,[1] in the propagation of their literature and ideas, in their social intercourse, in their corporate life, in all that we in Great Britain understand by civil liberty, so long will there be men who will mock at the very idea of international peace, and look forward to war, not as an outworn instrument of a barbarous age, but as a means to national freedom and self-expression. Englishmen sometimes forget that there are worse evils than open war, both in political and industrial relations, and that the political causes for which their fathers fought and died have still to be carried to victory on the Continent. Nationality and their national institutions are the very life-blood of English people. They are as natural to them as the air they breathe. That is what makes it sometimes so difficult for them to understand, as the history of Ireland and even of Ulster shows, what nationality means to other peoples. And that is why they have not realised, not only that there are peoples in Europe living under alien governments, but that there are governments in Europe so foolish as to think that men and women deprived of their national institutions, humiliated in their deepest feelings, and forced into an alien mould, can make good citizens, trustworthy soldiers, or even obedient subjects.

The political causes of the present war, then, and of the

---

[1] The German official *communiqué* on August 26, 1914, reports as follows: "All the newspapers in Belgium, with the exception of those in Antwerp, are printed in the German language." This, of course, is on the model of the Prussian administration of Poland. The Magyars are more repressive even than the Germans. See pp. 132 ff. below.

half century of Armed Peace which preceded it are to be found, not in the particular schemes and ambitions of any of the governments of Europe, nor in their secret diplomacy, nor in the machinations of the great armament interests allied to them, sinister though all these may have been, but in the nature of some of those governments themselves, and in their relation to the peoples over whom they rule.

" If it were possible," writes Prince Bülow, who directed German policy as Imperial Chancellor from 1900 to 1909, " for members of different nationalities, with different language and customs, and an intellectual life of a different kind, to live side by side in one and the same State, without succumbing to the temptation of each trying to force his own nationality on the other, things on earth would look a good deal more peaceful. But it is a law of life and development in history that where two national civilisations meet they fight for ascendancy. In the struggle between nationalities one nation is the hammer and the other the anvil; one is the victor and the other the vanquished." [1] No words could indicate more clearly the cause that is at stake in the present war. They show us that there are still governments in Europe so ignorant as to believe that the different nationalities of mankind are necessarily hostile to one another, and so foolish and brutal as to think that national civilisation, or, as the German Professors call it, "culture," can and indeed must be propagated by the sword. It is this extraordinary conception which is at the back of protests like that of Professor Haeckel and Professor Eucken (men whom, in the field of their own studies, all Europe is proud to honour) against " England fighting with a half-Asiatic power against Germanism." [2]

[1] *Imperial Germany*, by Prince Bernhard von Bülow, English translation, 1st ed. pp. 245-6 (London, 1914).

[2] Protest of Professors Ernst Haeckel and Rudolf Eucken of Jena, quoted in *The Times* from the *Vossische Zeitung* of August 20, 1914.

There are not only half-Asiatics, there are real Asiatics side by side with England ; and England is not ashamed of it. For she does not reckon the culture of Europe as higher than the culture of Asia, or regard herself as the hammer upon the anvil of India.

Prince Bülow's words, and the theory of policy underlying them, really go to the root of the whole trouble in European politics. They explain the Balance of Power, the competition in armaments, the belief in the inevitability and the moral value of war, and all those common European shibboleths which seem so inexplicable to citizens of the more modern-minded States and communities of the world. Why should Germany and Austria arm against France and Russia when Canada does not arm against the United States ? Why should a Balance of Power be necessary to the maintenance of European Peace when we do not consider the preponderance of a single Power, such as the United States in North, Central and South America, or Great Britain in the Pacific or Southern Asia dangerous to the peace of the whole world ? Why, finally, to press Prince Bülow's logic home, if members of different nationalities cannot live side by side without playing the game of Hammer and Anvil together, are not the English spending the whole of their energy fighting the Welsh, the Scotch, and the Irish in the United Kingdom, the Dutch in South Africa, and the French in Canada, not to speak of the Jews in every part of the British Empire ? The fact is that the statesmen of Germany and Austria-Hungary, and of Russia also, have missed the chief lesson of recent history and politics : that in the growing complexity of world-relations power is falling more and more, of necessity, into the hands of States which are not Nations but Commonwealths of Nations, States composed, like the British Empire and the United States, of a variety of nationalities and " cultures," living peacefully, each with its own institutions, under a single law and a single central government.

But the time is not ripe yet for a Commonwealth of Europe. The peoples of Europe have yet to win their liberties before they can be free to dream of a United States of Europe. So long as the Emperors and statesmen of Central Europe believe, like the Mahomedans of old, that propaganda can be imposed by the sword, they can only be met by the sword, and controlled by the sword. Not till they have been conquered and rendered harmless, or displaced by the better mind of the peoples whom they have indoctrinated, can Europe proceed along the natural course of her development.

So far we have been concerned—as we shall be concerned throughout this book—with the *political* causes underlying the war. But it would not be right to ignore the fact that there are other deeper causes, unconnected with the actions of governments, for which we in this country are jointly responsible with the rest of the civilised world.

This war is not simply a conflict between governments and nations for the attainment of certain political ends, Freedom and Nationality on the one side and Conquest and Tyranny on the other. It is also a great outburst of pent-up feeling, breaking like lava through the thin crust of European civilisation. On the *political* side, as we have said just now, the war reveals the fact that civilisation is still incomplete and ill-organised. But on the *moral* side it reveals the fact that modern society has broken down, that the forces and passions that divide and embitter mankind have proved stronger, at the moment of strain, than those which bind them together in fellowship and co-operation. " What we are suffering from," says one of the greatest of living democrats,[1] " is something far more widespread than

[1] *The War and the Church*, by Charles Gore (Oxford, Mowbray, 1914).

the German Empire. Is it not the case that what we are in face of is nothing less than the breakdown in a certain idea and hope of civilisation, which was associated with the liberal and industrial movement of the last century? There was to be an inevitable and glorious progress of humanity of which science, commerce, and education were to be the main instruments, and which was to be crowned with a universal peace. Older prophets like Thomas Carlyle expressed their contempt for the shallowness of this prevailing ideal, and during this century we have been becoming more and more doubtful of its value. But we are now witnessing its downfall. Science, commerce, and education have done, and can do, much for us. But they cannot expel the human spirit from human nature. What is that? At bottom, love of self, self-interest, selfishness individual and corporate. As a theory, the philosophy of selfishness has often been exposed. But, to an extent that is difficult to exaggerate, it has been the motive, acknowledged and relied upon without shame or apology in commerce, in politics and in practical life. Our civilisation has been based on selfishness, our commerce on competition and the unrestricted love of wealth, our education on the motive of self-advancement. And science and knowledge, made the instrument of selfishness and competition, have armed man against man, class against class, and nation against nation, with tenfold the power of destruction which belonged to a less educated and highly organised age."

The civilised world has been shocked during the past months at the spectacle of the open adoption by a great Power of this philosophy of selfishness. Men had not realised that the methods and principles underlying so much of our commercial and industrial life could be transferred so completely to the field of politics or so ruthlessly pressed home by military force. But it is well for us to remember that it is not Prussia, even in the modern world, who invented the theory of Blood and Iron or the philosophy of Force. The Iron Law of Wages is a generation older than Bismarck : and " Business is Business " can be no less odious a watchword than " War is War." Treitschke and Nietzsche may have furnished Prussian ambitions with congenial ammunition ; but Bentham with his purely selfish interpretation of human nature and Marx with his doctrine of the class-struggle—the high priest of Individualism and the high priest of Socialism— cannot be acquitted of a similar charge. If the appeal has been made in a less crude and brutal form, and if the instrument of domination has been commercial and industrial rather than military, it is because Militarism is not the besetting sin of the English-speaking peoples. Let us beware, therefore, at this moment, of anything savouring of self-righteousness.

" Some of us," says Bishop Gore, " see the chief security " against this disease which has infected our civilisation " in the progress of Democracy—the government of the people really by the people and for the people. I am one of those who believe this and desire to serve towards the realising of this end. But the answer does not satisfy me. I do not know what evils we might find arising from a world of materialistic democracies. But I am sure we shall not banish the evil spirits which destroy human lives and nations and civilisations by any mere change in the methods of government. Nothing can save civilisation except a new spirit in the nations."

The task before Europe, then, is a double one—a task of development and construction in the region of politics, and of purification and conversion in the region of the spirit. " For the finer spirits of Europe," says the great French writer, Romain Rolland, who is none the less a patriot because he is also a lover of Germany, " there are two dwelling-places : our earthly fatherland, and that other, the City of God. Of the one we are the guests, of the other the builders. To the one let us give our lives and our faithful hearts ; but neither family, friend, nor fatherland, nor aught that we love has power over the spirit which is the light. It is our duty to rise above tempests and thrust aside the clouds which threaten to obscure it ; to build higher and stronger, dominating the injustice and hatred of nations, the walls of that city wherein the souls of the whole world may assemble." [1]

Internationalism as a political theory has broken down : for it was based on a false conception of the nature of government and of the obligations of citizenship. The true internationalism—a spirit of mutual understanding and fellowship between men and nations, to replace the suspicions, the competition, and the watchful selfishness of the past generation—is the moral task that lies before Europe and America to-day. If Great Britain is to lead the way in promoting " a new spirit between the nations " she needs a new spirit also in the whole range of her corporate life. For what Britain stands for in the world is, in the long run, what Britain is, and, when thousands are dying for her, it is more than ever the duty of all of us to try to make her worthier of their devotion.

---

[1] Article in the *Journal de Genève*, translated in the *Cambridge Magazine* and reprinted in *Public Opinion*, Nov. 27, 1914.

Those who hold that Christianity and war are incompatible would seem to be committed to a monastic and passively anarchist view of life, inconsistent with membership in a political society. But whatever the relation between Christianity and war, there can be no question of the relation between Christianity and *hatred*. Hatred (which is not the same thing as moral indignation) is a poison which corrodes and embitters, and so degrades, and thereby weakens, the national spirit. It is a pity that some of our most prominent newspaper-proprietors do not understand this.

CHAPTER II

THE NATIONAL IDEA IN EUROPE, 1789–1914

Europe, what of the night ?—
  Ask of heaven, and the sea,
  And my babes on the bosom of me,
Nations of mine, but ungrown.
There is one who shall surely requite
  All that endure or that err :
She can answer alone :
  Ask not of me, but of her.

Liberty, what of the night ?—
  I feel not the red rains fall,
  Hear not the tempest at all,
Nor thunder in heaven any more.
All the distance is white
  With the soundless feet of the sun.
Night, with the woes that it wore,
  Night is over and done.

A. C. SWINBURNE, *A Watch in the Night.*

SIXTY-TWO years ago reaction reigned supreme in Europe after the great national and social uprisings of 1848, and England looked on passively while the hopes of freedom were crushed in Bohemia, Hungary, and Italy. Mazzini, the noblest of Italian patriots, the most prophetic soul among nineteenth-century nationalists, selected this moment of profound despair to publish an essay, entitled *Europe, Its Condition and Prospects*, which, burning with the passion of an inextinguishable faith, pierced the veil of the future

15

and foreshadowed in an almost miraculous fashion the situation which faces Europe and England to-day. Nothing printed in this country since the war broke out expresses more clearly the real issues of the mighty conflict and the part our country is called to play in it than the following words, in reference to the unredeemed peoples of Europe, uttered by the great Italian more than half a century ago :

" They struggled, they still struggle, for country and liberty ; for a word inscribed upon a banner, proclaiming to the world that they also live, think, love, and labour for the benefit of all. They speak the same language, they bear about them the impress of consanguinity, they kneel beside the same tombs, they glory in the same tradition ; and they demand to associate freely, without obstacles, without foreign domination, in order to elaborate and express their idea, to contribute their stone also to the great pyramid of history. It is something moral which they are seeking ; and this moral something is in fact, even politically speaking, the most important question in the present state of things. It is the organisation of the European task. In principle, nationality ought to be to humanity that which division of labour is in a workshop— the recognised symbol of association ; the assertion of the individuality of a human group called by its geographical position, its traditions, and its language, to fulfil a special function in the European work of civilisation.

" The map of Europe has to be re-made. This is the key to the present movement ; herein lies its initiative. Before acting, the instrument for action must be organised ; before building, the ground must be one's own. The social idea cannot be realised under any form whatsoever before this reorganisation of Europe is effected ; before the peoples are free to interrogate themselves, to express their vocation, and to assure its accomplishment by an alliance capable of substituting itself for the absolute league which now reigns supreme.

" If England persist in maintaining a neutral, passive, selfish part, she will have to expiate it. A European transformation is inevitable. When it shall take place, when the struggle shall burst forth at twenty places at once, when the old combat between fact and right is decided, the peoples will remember that England stood by, an inert, immovable, sceptical witness of their sufferings and efforts. The nation must rouse herself and shake off the torpor of her government. She must learn that we have arrived at one of those supreme moments in which one world is destroyed and another is to be created ; in which, for the sake of others and for her own, it is necessary to adopt a new policy."

England to-day has adopted this " new policy " ; she has responded to Mazzini's appeal by stepping into the arena and declaring herself ready to take part in " the organisation of the European task " ; her sons are dying on the Continent in defence of the principle of nationality, in support of the rights of other nations to that liberty which her insular position has secured for herself for many centuries, the liberty " to associate freely, without obstacles, without foreign domination, in order to elaborate and express their idea." She is fighting, moreover, not only on behalf of the threatened freedom of Belgium, France, and Serbia, on behalf of the unborn freedom of Poland, Alsace-Lorraine, and the subject races of the Austro-Hungarian and Ottoman Empires, but also on her own behalf. It is not merely that she recognises that her Empire is in danger ; she recognises also that she is unable to work out her own

C

salvation, unable to carry on her industrial development and her schemes for the betterment of her people in security, while the Continent at her doors remains in constant peril of change. " The social idea cannot be realised under any form whatsoever before this reorganisation of Europe is effected."

§ 1. *Nation and Nationality.*—The social idea and the national idea have been for a century past the twin pivots of European development. The political structure of the Continent has oscillated this way and that according as these ideas have in turn assumed ascendancy over men's minds; and when, as in 1848, both claimed attention at the same time, the whole edifice was shaken to its very foundations. In England, on the other hand, it is the social idea alone which has been a motive force in the nineteenth century, although she has always had to reckon with the national idea across the St. George's Channel. Owing to her fortunate geographical situation, she acquired national unity many centuries ago and has always been able to defend it successfully against the danger of external aggression. The national idea, therefore, has long ceased to be an aspiration, and consequently a revolutionary force, among us; it has been realised in actual fact, we have grown as accustomed to it and as unconscious of it as of the air we breathe. Thus Englishmen, as their attitude towards Ireland has shown, find it difficult to understand exactly what the principle of nationality means to those who have never possessed national freedom or are in constant danger of losing it. This is perhaps especially true of the English working classes, who grew to the full stature of political consciousness some fifty years after the last serious threat to our national existence was made by Napoleon, and upon whom the burden of the social idea presses with peculiar weight.

And yet, unless the significance of the principle of nationality and the part which it has played in the history of modern Europe be realised, it is impossible to enter fully into the true meaning of the present tremendous conflict.

What then is nationality? The question is more difficult to answer than appears at first sight. A nationality is not quite the same thing as a nation. For example, there is a German nation, ruled by the Kaiser Wilhelm II., but this does not include twelve million people of German nationality who are the subjects of the Emperor of Austria; or again, there is the Swiss nation, which is made up of no less than three distinct nationalities. Still less are the terms state and nationality synonymous; for, if they were, then the natives of India might claim to be of the same nationality as ourselves, or, *vice versa*, the United States would be regarded as part of the British Empire because a large proportion of their inhabitants happen to be of British descent. The word " race " brings us somewhat nearer to the point, but even this will not satisfy us when we remember that the Slavonic race, for example, consists of a large number of nationalities, such as the Russians, the Poles, the Czechs, the Serbs, the Montenegrins, etc., or that the English (as distinguished from the other three nations of the United Kingdom) belong to the same Teutonic race as the Germans. Nevertheless, a belief, whether well grounded or not, in a common racial origin is one of the root principles of the idea of nationality.

" What is a nation? " the great Magyar nationalist, Kossuth, asked a Serb representative at the Hungarian Diet of 1848. The reply was : " A race which possesses its own language, customs, and culture, and enough self-consciousness to preserve them." " A nation must also have its own government," objected Kossuth. " We do not go so far," explained his interlocutor; " one nation can live under several different governments, and again several nations can form a single state." [1] Both the Magyar and the Serb were right, though the latter was speaking of " nationality " and the former of " nation." The conversation is in fact instructive in more ways than one. It would be difficult to find a better definition of *nationality* than that given by the Serb speaker. A common language, a common culture, and common customs : these are the outward and visible signs which make a people conscious of its common race, which make it, in other words, a nationality.

The element of "consciousness" is all-important. There are, for example, members of the Finnish race scattered all over northern Russia, but they evince no consciousness of any kind that they are allied to the nationality which inhabits the country of Finland. Again, it is only within recent years that the Serbs and the Croats in the south-west corner of the Austro-Hungarian Empire have begun to realise that the only things which divide them one from the other are a difference of religion and a difference of alphabet ; and now that the realisation of this fact has spread from the study to the market-place, we see the formation of a new nationality, that of the Serbo-Croats. The researches of historians and other learned men have done an immense deal to stimulate the development of nationalities during the past century, but they are unable of themselves to create them. The fact of kinship is not enough; community of language, customs, and culture is not even enough ; to be a real nationality a people must be conscious of all these things, and not merely conscious, but sufficiently conscious to preserve them and, if need be, to die for them.

[1] R. W. Seton-Watson, *The Southern Slav Question*, p. 46.

Now the interesting thing for us about a nationality is that it is always striving to become a *nation*. A nation, as we have seen, may be composed of several nationalities; but such cases are rare, and are due to peculiar geographical conditions, as for example in Switzerland and Great Britain, or to external pressure, as in Belgium, which have as it were welded together the different racial elements into a single whole. In general, therefore, a nation is simply a nationality which has acquired self-government; it is nationality *plus* State. "Ireland a nation," the warcry of the Irish Nationalist party, is a claim, not a statement of fact; Ireland will become a nation when its desire for self-government is satisfied. The case is instructive because it shows that it is not necessary for a nationality to become a *sovereign* State in order to be in the full sense of the word a nation. It is perfectly possible, as our Serb remarked, for several nations to form a single sovereign state; but as a general rule all such nations will be allowed to manage their own internal affairs. The self-governing Dominions of the British Empire and the Magyars of Hungary are nations, though they are subordinate to their respective imperial governments in questions of peace and war, treaty obligations, etc.

The real test of national existence is ultimately a sentimental one. Does the nationality inhabiting a given country regard the government under which it lives as a true expression of its peculiar genius and will? Does the State, of which it forms a part, exist by its consent, or has it been imposed upon it by some alien authority or nationality? Is it a territorial unity, or has it been split up into sections by artificial frontiers? All these questions must be answered before we can say of any nationality that it is also a nation. The "national idea," therefore, which has been one of the chief factors in modern history, is essentially an idea of development. Its root is the conception of nationality, that is of a people consciously united by race, language, and culture ; and from this springs the larger conception of nationhood, that is of a nationality possessing its own political institutions, governed by its own consent, and co-extensive with its natural boundaries. As we shall see later, political development does not always stop at the Nation-State. Further growth, however, is extra-national in character ; it may either take the parasitical form of one nation imposing its will and its " culture " upon other nations, or it may assume the proportions of that highest type of polity yet known to mankind, a commonwealth of nations freely associating together within the confines of a single sovereign State.[1]

§ 2. *The Birth of Nationalism : Poland and the French Revolution.*—With these general principles in mind let us now consider the national idea at work in the nineteenth century. Nations, in the sense just defined, have of course long existed in Europe. England, Scotland, and Switzerland are nations whose life-histories date right back to the Middle Ages. Joan of Arc was a nationalist, and France has been a nation since the end of the Hundred Years' War in 1453. Spain became a nation a few years later by the expulsion of the Moors and the union of Castille and Aragon under Ferdinand and Isabella. Holland, again, acquired her national freedom in her great struggle against Spain in the sixteenth century. But it was not until the end of the eighteenth century that nationalism became a real force in Europe, an idea for which men died and in whose name monarchies were overthrown. " In the old European system," writes Lord Acton, " the rights of nationalities were neither recognised by govern-

[1] See Chapter IX. for further treatment of this.

ments nor asserted by the people. The interest of the reigning families, not those of the nations, regulated the frontiers, and the administration was conducted generally without any reference to popular desires. Where all liberties were suppressed, the claims of national independence were necessarily ignored, and a princess, in the words of Fénelon, carried a monarchy in her wedding portion." [1] The State was, in short, regarded as a purely territorial affair; it was the property, the *landed* property, of the monarch, who in his capacity of owner controlled the destinies of the people who happened to live upon that territory. Conquest or marriage might unite in the hands of a single monarch the most diverse peoples and countries, the notorious case of the kind being that of the Emperor Charles V., who in the sixteenth century managed to hold sway over Germany, Spain, the Netherlands, Naples, and a large part of the New World.

The golden age of the dynastic principle was, however, the eighteenth century, and the long and tedious wars of that period were nearly all occasioned by the aggrandisement of some royal house. The idea of a nation as a living organism, as something more than a collection of people dwelling in the same country, speaking the same language and obeying the same ruler, had not yet dawned upon the world. Apart from England, Scotland, Switzerland, and Holland, no European nation had really become conscious of its personality as distinct from that of its hereditary monarch. And as we have seen, until nationality becomes keenly self-conscious, the national idea remains unborn. Only some great internal cataclysm or an overwhelming disaster inflicted by a foreign power could evoke this consciousness in a nation ; and fate ordained that the two methods should be tried simultaneously at opposite ends of Europe. France,

[1] *History of Freedom*, p. 273.

"standing on the top of golden hours," and Poland, crushed, dismembered, downtrodden—it would be difficult to say which of these contributed the more to the great national awakening in Europe.

Poland was the first and greatest martyr of the nationalist faith. By its constitution, which was that of an oligarchical republic with an elective king, Poland was placed beyond the pale of a Europe ruled upon dynastic principles. Its very existence was an insult to the accepted ideals of legitimacy and hereditary monarchy, and it was impossible for any particular house to acquire it in the honest way of marriage. This was particularly annoying to its immediate neighbours, Prussia, Russia, and Austria, all of whom had grown into great powers while Poland, torn by internal dissension, sank lower and lower in the political scale. It is significant that the earliest suggestion of partition came from Frederick the Great of Prussia, who was obliged to take Russia and Austria into his counsels, as he knew that they would never allow him to annex the whole country himself. Indeed, from first to last, the story of the Polish partitions is a good example of Prussian *Realpolitik*. At length, after much hesitation on the part of Russia and Austria, the Powers agreed among themselves in 1772 to what is known as the First Partition, whereby the three monarchs enriched their respective territories by peeling, as it were, the unfortunate republic on all its frontiers. Perhaps the most remarkable fact about the whole disgraceful concern is that it did not appear in the least disgraceful, either morally or politically, to the public opinion of the age. Meanwhile Poland by a heroic effort converted herself in self-defence into a hereditary constitutional monarchy on the model of England. Prussia, playing the part of Judas, pretended to welcome these reforms at first and lent the Poles its encouragement; but when Russia took up arms on behalf of the Polish reactionary party, and the country turned to Prussia to aid it in defending the constitution, the treacherous Frederick William not only declined to do so, but began to send his troops to occupy Polish territory. The upshot was the further dismemberment of Poland known as the Second Partition (1793). " No sophistry in the world," writes Mr. Nisbet Bain, " can extenuate the villainy of the Second Partition. The theft of territory is its least offensive feature. It is the forcible suppression of a national movement of reform, the hurling back into the abyss of anarchy and corruption of a people who, by incredible efforts and sacrifices, had struggled back to liberty and order, which makes this great political crime so wholly infamous. Yet here again the methods of the Russian Empress were less vile than those of the Prussian King. Catherine openly took the risk of a bandit who attacks an enemy against whom he has a grudge ; Frederick William II. came up, when the fight was over, to help pillage a victim whom he had sworn to defend." [1] After this the end came rapidly. The heroic patriot Kosciuszko headed a popular rising against Russia; but after a remarkable resistance to the combined forces of the three partitioning powers, the insurrection was finally suppressed in torrents of blood. The crowned bandits nearly quarrelled between themselves over the booty, but eventually in 1795 Austria, Russia, and Prussia signed a treaty which left nothing of Poland on the map at all.

The effect upon the subsequent history of the world of this crime against humanity, carried out by the three most absolute dynasties in Europe, was incalculable. " The annihilation of the Polish nationality has probably done more to endanger the monarchies of Europe than any one

[1] *Slavonic Europe*, p. 404.

political act accomplished since the monarchies of Europe were first founded. To trace its effects in all their various ramifications would lead us a long way. It is sufficient here to notice that the destruction of Poland, like the destruction of Jerusalem, produced a "dispersion," and

Present State Boundaries —
THE PARTITION OF POLAND.

that as the Jews of the dispersion have discharged a peculiar office in the economy of the world as usurers and financiers, so, too, have the Poles of the dispersion as agents and vectors of revolution. In all the republican movements of the Continent the Poles have taken a leading part. They are to be found in the Saxon riots of '48;

in the Berlin barricades ; in the struggle for the Republic
in Baden ; in the Italian and Hungarian wars of liberation ;
in the Chartist movement, and in the French Commune.
Homeless and fearless, schooled in war and made reckless
by calamity, they have been the nerve of revolution
wherever they have been scattered by the winds of mis-
fortune." [1] And what Mr. Fisher, in this passage, puts in
a concrete fashion, Lord Acton has expressed with equal
emphasis, if more abstractly. " This famous measure,"
he writes of the final partition, " the most revolutionary
act of the old absolutism, awakened the theory of nationality in Europe, converting a dormant right into an aspiration, and a sentiment into a political claim. ' No wise or
honest man,' wrote Edmund Burke, ' can approve of that
partition, or can contemplate it without prognosticating
great mischief from it to all countries at some future date.'
Thenceforward there was a nation demanding to be united
in a State—a soul, as it were, wandering in search of a body
in which to begin life over again ; and for the first time a
cry was heard that the arrangement of States was unjust—
that their limits were unnatural, and that a whole people
was deprived of its right to constitute an independent
community. Before that claim could be efficiently asserted
against the overwhelming power of its opponents—before
it gained energy, after the last partition, to overcome the
influence of long habits of submission, and of the contempt
which previous disorders had brought upon Poland—the
ancient European system was in ruins, and a new world
was rising in its place." [2]

The last sentence reminds us that, while in the East the
dynastic principle was displaying with cynical indifference

[1] *The Republican Tradition in Europe*, pp. 212-213.
[2] *History of Freedom*, p. 276.

its true character to the world, events were occurring in the West which threatened to shake its very foundations. If Poland was the first martyr of the national idea, Revolutionary France was its first evangelist, for the new gospel which France preached was the gospel of Liberty, and nationalism is an extension, a variant of this gospel. In France itself, at the time of the Revolution, the doctrine of Liberty was interpreted in its individual and constitutional sense, which involved the abolition of class privileges and of political institutions that conflicted with or did not adequately express what Rousseau called the "general will." There was no national question to be settled in France, and she could therefore devote herself exclusively to the development of the "social idea," the establishment of democratic government, the foundation of a republic, and in general the determination of what should be the relations between the individual and the State, a question which in course of time led on to the problem of Socialism.

But indirectly the French Revolution did an enormous deal to promote the national idea in Europe. In the first place, the execution of Louis XVI. and the proclamation of the Republic administered a blow to the theory of legitimacy upon which the dynastic principle rested, from which it never recovered. If the French nation could rise and abolish its native dynasty, was there not hope that some day the Italian, Hungarian, and Polish nations might also rise and throw off the still more objectionable yoke of their foreign rulers? In the second place, the Revolution in and for itself produced a tremendous effect upon the rest of Europe, and in every country men awoke from the long sleep of feudalism to the desire of sweeping away antiquated constitutions and rebuilding them upon a democratic basis.

It is, however, sufficient to glance at a map of Europe at

the end of the eighteenth century to see why these dreams could not be at once realised. Of what real value were ideals of democratic reform to the peoples dwelling in Italy, Germany, or the Austrian Empire ? Look, for example, at Germany, split up like a jig-saw puzzle into over three hundred different States, each with its petty prince or grand-duke. Her poets and philosophers might sing of liberty and dream Utopian dreams, and here and there an experiment in popular government might be tried by some princeling who had caught the liberal fashion ; but her political fabric, together with the rivalry between Prussia and Austria, kept her disunited and strangled all real hopes of reform. In short, the first and most crying need of Europe was not the abolition of antiquated constitutions, but the redrawing of anomalous frontiers.

The doctrine of the sovereignty of the people proclaimed in France presupposed the doctrine of the solidarity of the people proclaimed by the dismembered nations of Europe. France could set its house in order ; but Belgium, Germany, Italy, Bohemia, Hungary, etc., had as yet no house of their own. The house had to be built before it could be furnished on the latest democratic lines ; and before it could be even built, the ground had to be wrested from the hands of absentee landlords or cleared of the little dynastic State-shanties which cumbered it. The Polish nationalists became the backbone of the republican movement in Europe ; the French republicans proclaimed the independence of nations as one of their cardinal principles. Thus the social idea and the national idea were originally intimately connected. They were the twin children of Poland and the French Revolution, and in their cradle it was hard to tell them apart, so strongly were the features of each stamped with the likeness of Liberty.

For a time it seemed that the new ideas would carry all before them. Even before France had herself abolished the monarchy, Belgium threw off the Austrian rule and declared for a republic. And when in 1792 France found herself at war with the Austrian and Prussian governments, and in the following year with practically all the governments of Europe, her victorious armies were everywhere greeted as saviours by the subject peoples. But the old dynastic states proved to be of tougher material than was expected. Moreover, it was not long before France found herself in conflict with the national aspirations which she had called into existence. The various republics which France set up all over Europe soon discovered that they were nothing but tributary states of their " deliverer " ; and when Napoleon began his career of undisguised conquest, he unwittingly did even more than the Revolution to strengthen the national idea in Europe, for the nationalities had now become thoroughly hostile to France and fought in alliance with their old dynasties to throw off the yoke of the hated foreign tyrant.

This strange change in France from liberator to despot is worthy of some attention. It is not good for a nation, any more than for an individual, to be too successful. Moreover, the doctrine of liberty, whether in the individualist or nationalist sense, if carried to extreme, is liable to abuse. All to-day are aware that sheer individualism in the economic sphere is an almost unmitigated evil ; sheer individualism in the political sphere and sheer nationalism are equally evil. France at the beginning of last century was suffering from too much success, too much political liberty, too much nationalism. Having overthrown the old *régime* within the State quickly and easily, she began to think she could do without the State altogether : the result was anarchy, for which the only remedy is despotism. Having, again, suddenly become conscious of her power and mission as a nation, she began to send her armies across her frontiers to carry the gospel of her peculiar "culture" to other and more benighted nations: the result was occupation, which degenerated into conquest. Despotism within and conquest without, both being summed up in the one word Napoleon—such was the fate of the Mother of Liberty, who had loved her child "not wisely but too well." Yet Napoleonism was a very necessary stage in the development of modern Europe. It was the tramp of the invader which did more than anything else to awake sleeping nationalism all over the Continent; it was before the roar of Napoleon's cannon that the artificial boundaries which had divided peoples crumbled to dust. Napoleon cleared the ground, and even did something toward laying the foundations of the great modern Nation-States, Germany and Italy. What Napoleon did for Europe at the beginning of the nineteenth century, Germany, the Napoleon-State among nations to-day, is doing for Europe at the beginning of the twentieth century.

§ 3. *The Congress of Vienna and the International Idea.*— The overthrow of Napoleon was due in a large measure to the spirit of nationalism which his conquests had evoked against him among the various peoples of Europe; the rewards of that overthrow, however, were reaped not by the peoples, but by the dynasties and State-systems of the old *régime*. The Congress of the Powers which met at Vienna in 1814 to resettle the map of Europe, after the upheavals and wars of the previous twenty-five years, was a terrible disappointment; and we, who are now hopefully looking forward to a similar Congress at the end of the present war, cannot do better than study the great failure of 1814, and take warning from it. The phrases which heralded the approaching Congress were curiously and disquietingly similar to those on the lips of our public men and journalists to-day when they speak of the " settlement " before us.   " The Parliament of Man, the Federation of the World," which had become a remote dream when Tennyson first coined the expression in 1842, seemed in 1814 on the eve of accomplishment. The work of the Congress was to be no less than " the reconstruction of the moral order," " the regeneration of the political system of Europe," the establishment of " an enduring peace founded on a just redistribution of political forces," the institution of an effective and a permanent international tribunal, the encouragement of the growth of representative institutions, and, last but not least, an arrangement between the Powers for a gradual and systematic disarmament. " It seemed," writes Sir A. W. Ward, " as if the states composing the European family, free once more to take counsel together on terms of independence, were also free to determine their own destinies." [1] The Congress of Vienna was to inaugurate a New Era. Such of these views, however, as pointed in a democratic or nationalistic direction represented the expectations of the peoples, not the intentions of the crowned heads and diplomatists who met at the Austrian capital. Among the members of the Congress the only man who at first voiced these aspirations of the world at large was the Russian Tsar, Alexander I., and such concessions to popular opinion as were made were due to what the English plenipotentiary, Lord Castlereagh, described as the " sublime mysticism and nonsense " of the Emperor.

Instead, therefore, of establishing a new era, the Congress did its utmost to restore the old one. Everything which had happened in Europe since the out-

[1] *Cambridge Modern History*, vol. ix. p. 577.

break of the French Revolution was regarded as a bad
dream, the principles of popular freedom and national
liberty were completely ignored, and an attempt was made
to rivet again on the limbs of Europe the shackles of the
antiquated frontiers which had been struck off by the
hammer of Napoleon. Everywhere the "national idea"
was trampled upon. Germany and Italy were put back
again into the eighteenth century, Austria's territory in
the latter country being largely increased ; Norway was
unwillingly yoked with Sweden, and Belgium with Holland ;
Switzerland was made to surrender her democratic constitution and to return to the aristocratic cantonal system
of the past ; and, lastly, Poland remained dismembered.

The Allies, while fighting Napoleon, had issued the following proclamation to the world, couched in language almost
identical with that used by the Allies who are now fighting
Germany : " Nations will henceforth respect their mutual
independence ; no political edifices shall henceforth be
erected on the ruins of formerly independent States ; the
object of the war, and of the peace, is to secure the rights,
the freedom, and the independence of all nations." [1] The
Congress of Vienna failed to redeem these pledges : firstly,
because its members had not grasped the principle of
nationality, and used "nation" and "State" as if they
were synonymous terms ; secondly, because they did not
represent the peoples whose destinies they took it upon
them to determine, and made no attempt whatever to
consult the views of the various masses of population which
they parcelled out among themselves like so much butter.
They honestly tried to lay the foundations of a permanent
peace ; but their method of doing so was not to satisfy
the natural aspirations of the European nations and so

[1] Alison Phillips, *Modern Europe*, p. 8.

leave them nothing to fight about, but to establish such an exact equipoise among the great States, by a nice distribution of the aforesaid butter in their respective scales, that they would be afraid to go to war with each other, lest they might upset the so-called " balance of power." The " settlement " of 1814, therefore, left a heritage of future trouble behind it which has kept Europe disturbed throughout the nineteenth century, and is directly responsible for the present war. The real settlement is yet to come ; and if we of this generation are to make it a final one we must avoid the errors committed by the Congress of a hundred years ago.

Yet, when all is said, the Congress of Vienna represents an important milestone along the road of progress. It is a great precedent. As a disillusioned contemporary admitted, it " prepared the world for a more complete political structure ; if ever the powers should meet again to establish a political system by which wars of conquest would be rendered impossible and the rights of all guaranteed, the Congress of Vienna, as a preparatory assembly, will not have been without use." [1] There is a prophetic ring about this, very welcome to us of the twentieth century. We cannot think altogether unkindly of our great-grandfathers' ill-judged attempt to avert the calamity which has now broken over us.

Nor was the Congress altogether barren of positive result ; for it gave birth to that conception of a " Confederation of Europe," which, though never realised, has been one of the guiding ideas of nineteenth-century politics. As this solution of the world's problems is likely to be urged upon us with great insistency at the conclusion of the present war, it will be well to look a little more closely into it and to see why it failed to secure the allegiance of Europe

[1] Friedrich von Gentz, quoted in *Camb. Mod. Hist.* vol. x. p. 2.

a hundred years ago. The Congress had met at Vienna and settled all outstanding questions, to the satisfaction of its members ; why should it not meet periodically, and constitute itself a supreme international tribunal ? The question had only to be asked to receive the approbation of all concerned. The dreamer, Alexander I., at once saw the destinies of the world entrusted to a Holy Alliance, which would rule according to " the sacred principles of the Christian religion " ; and even the more practical mind of Castlereagh conceived that a council of the great powers, " endowed with the efficiency and almost the simplicity of a single State," was a possibility.

Yet, it is quite clear to-day that, at that time and under those conditions, the establishment of a permanent and effective Confederation of Europe would have proved disastrous to the world. The Congress of Vienna was followed by further congresses in 1818, 1819, 1820, and 1822 ; and each succeeding conference revealed to Europe more clearly the true character of the new authority into whose hands the power was slipping. Certain very dangerous tendencies became, for example, apparent. The first conference had assembled to confer the blessings of order upon a continent ravaged by the revolutionary and Napoleonic wars of France. Hence the Confederation of Europe started life as a kind of anti-Jacobin society, whose main business it was to suppress revolution, whether it took the nationalistic or democratic form. Furthermore, the interference with the internal affairs of France in 1814 and 1815 tended to establish a precedent for interference with the internal affairs of any country. The Holy Alliance, therefore, soon assumed the character of a " Trust " of absolute monarchs, determined to aid each other when threatened by risings or agitations among their

peoples, and to crush liberal aspirations wherever they were
to be found in other parts of Europe. The popular desire
for peace was exploited in the interests of unpopular
government ; settlement by conference in regard to international matters was extended to settlement by a cabal
of irresponsible crowned heads in regard to internal constitutional and national questions ; a clique of despots
threatened the liberties of the world and proposed to back
up their decisions by using their armies as police. One
government, however, even in that period of reaction,
refused to lend its countenance to such proceedings.
England at first protested and at length took up an attitude
of complete opposition, and it is due to her that the
Confederation never became really effective. She had to
choose between peace and liberty, and she chose the latter.[1]

The truth is that there were three ideas in the air at the
beginning of the nineteenth century, all excellent in themselves, but quite impossible to be realised at one and the
same period. Two of these, the social or democratic idea
and the national idea, were made, as we have seen, living
issues by the French Revolution ; the third, which may
be called the international idea, was raised by the Congress
of Vienna. It was an old idea, of course, for it had been
embodied in that shadowy " Holy Roman Empire " which
was the medieval dream of Rome the Great ; but its form
was new, and now for the first time it became a dream of
the future rather than a dream of the past. What men did
not see then, and still for the most part fail to see, is that
the human race can only work out these three ideas properly

---

[1] See Alison Phillips, *The Confederation of Europe*, together with
his chapter on " The Congresses, 1815–1822 " in vol. x. of the
Cambridge Modern History. The whole subject of the Concert of
Europe, which can only be touched upon here, is of great importance.
It is again referred to in Chap. VIII. ; see pp. 374 ff.

in a certain order. Democracy and nationhood may, as in the case of Italy, be acquired by a people at the same moment; but without the realisation of the national idea it is hardly possible to conceive of democratic government for any country. The national idea, therefore, precedes the social idea, as Mazzini rightly insists. Still more must it precede the international idea. By this it is not meant that every nation in the world must have grown to self-consciousness and have possessed itself of freedom before we come within sight of a world-concert and world-peace. But certainly in Europe itself the national question had to be settled before there could be any chance of establishing an international tribunal. It is equally certain that the social idea also ¦claims preference of the international idea. The great danger of setting up " an effective machine for regulating the affairs of Europe " is that the machine may get into the wrong hands. The Holy Alliance is a warning, which should not be forgotten. It became an obstruction to progress, a strait-waistcoat which threatened to strangle the liberties of Europe, because it got into the hands of a " vested interest," the dynastic interest, which was hostile both to nationalism and democracy.

Since 1814, however, there have been great strides along the paths both of democracy and of nationalism. And if Germany loses this war, the congress of the settlement will meet in a very different atmosphere from that in which its predecessor assembled at Vienna. It will be a conference of powers victorious over Reaction not Revolution, and pledged to the support of a liberal programme. And yet if such a conference became a permanent feature of European life, if, in other words, a new attempt were made to set up an international tribunal, it might easily become as dangerous to the liberties of the people as ever was the Holy Alliance. The dynastic principle, it is to be hoped, will never again threaten the world's peace or progress ; but there are other vested interests besides the dynastic one. During the nineteenth century economic development has given an enormous impetus to international movements and cosmopolitanism generally. Unfortunately political development, though great, has not by any means kept pace with the economic ; in other words, it is still possible in most countries, and in some more possible than in others, for a small oligarchy to gain control of the political machine.

Again, if there is one thing in the world more international than Labour, it is Capital ; and, as Mr. Norman Angell has shown, it is the capitalist who is hardest hit by international war and who stands to gain most from its abolition. European capital is almost certain to have a large say in the settlement, and considerable influence in the counsels of any new Concert of Europe that might come into existence. Now suppose—a not impossible contingency—that a ring of capitalists gained complete control of some politically backward country like Russia, and suppose a grave crisis arose in the Labour world in England or France, what would be easier than for arrangements to be made at the international conference for the transference of Russian troops to the west, " to preserve the sacred rights of property and the peace of Europe " ? This may seem a somewhat fantastic supposition, yet it was precisely in this way and on grounds like these that the Holy Alliance interfered with the internal affairs of European countries during the second and third decade of last century, and even as late as 1849 we have Russia, still faithful to the principles of thirty years before, coming to the assistance of Austria in her suppression of the liberties of Hungary. It was a healthy instinct in the English people that led them to break up the Concert of Europe in 1818—" a system which not only threatened the liberties of others, but might, in the language of the orators of the Opposition, in time present the spectacle of Cossacks encamped in Hyde Park to overawe the House of Commons " ; [1] and, if the prevailing " internationalism " has not quite blinded their eyes to-day, they will scrutinise with the greatest possible care any new proposals to re-erect the Concert of Europe as a permanent and authoritative tribunal. What the world needs at present is more nationalism and more democracy. And it is only after these two great nineteenth-century movements have worked themselves out to the full, at least on the continent of Europe, that mankind will be able safely to make experiments towards the realisation of the third and crowning principle, the principle of a European Commonwealth.

The national problems which the Congress of Vienna bequeathed to posterity may be seen at a glance by looking at a political map of Europe in 1815. The entire centre of the Continent from Ostend to Palermo, and from Königsberg to Constantinople, was left a political chaos. And it is not too much to say that the history of Europe from 1814 to 1914 is the history of the settlement of this vast area. The only State whose frontiers have not altered during this period is Switzerland, and even that country seized the opportunity which a disturbed Europe offered her in 1848, to substitute a unified federal system for the constitution imposed upon her in 1815. The rest of the area falls into six sections : (1) The kingdom of the Netherlands, containing the two distinct and often antagonistic nations, Belgium and Holland ; (2) the German nationality split up into no less than thirty-eight [2] sovereign States, loosely held together

---

[1] *Cambridge Modern History*, vol. x. p. 16.
[2] Napoleon had succeeded in reducing the number from 360 to 38.

EUROPE IN 1815

in a " confederation "; (3) the Italian nationality, distributed under eight independent governments, including four duchies, two kingdoms, the Papal States, and the provinces under Austrian rule ; (4) the Polish nationality, divided up between the three Powers, Prussia, Russia, and Austria ; (5) the Austrian Empire, comprising a dozen distinct nationalities ; and (6) the Ottoman Empire, in which at least five different Christian peoples groaned beneath the sway of the Mohammedan Turk. Thus, if we may regard the inhabitants of the southern Netherland provinces, for the moment, as of one nationality, there were roughly ten great nationalities, the Germans, the Italians, the Belgians, the Poles, the Bohemians, the Hungarians, the Southern Slavs, the Rumanians, the Bulgarians, and the Greeks, all left with national aspirations unsatisfied, all hampered by State frontiers which had no correspondence with their natural boundaries. Can we wonder that there have been wars in the nineteenth century ? Should we not rather wonder that those wars have not been greater and more numerous ? For the Congress of the Powers in 1814 having failed to give the nationalities what they wanted, nothing remained for them but to seize it for themselves. The only alternative to settlement by conference is " blood and iron," and it is with " blood and iron " that nearly every nationality which has attained nationhood in the last hundred years has cemented the structure of its State.

It is not our purpose in the present chapter to deal with the whole of this vast area ; the three eastern sections, Poland, the Austrian Empire, and Turkey, present special problems of their own, and therefore need special treatment. Still less do we intend to write a history of the nineteenth century, or even to adhere to a chronological treatment. Rather our object is to exemplify the principle of nationality by watching it at work in the three western sections of the central European area; to show how the national idea has been moulded in Belgium, Italy, and Germany, by the various problems which the nationalities in these countries have had to face, and the forces which they have overcome; and, lastly, to indicate the part which an over-developed nationalism in Germany has played in bringing about the war of 1914.

§ 4. *The National Idea in Belgium and the Problem of Small Nations.*—The problem of the Netherlands, which it will be convenient to deal with first, introduces us to an aspect of nationhood which we have hitherto not touched upon. " The chief forces which hold a community together and cause it to constitute one state," wrote Sir John Seeley, " are three,—common nationality, common religion, and common interest. These may act in various degrees of intensity, and they may also act singly or in combination." [1] In the Low Countries religion has up to the present been a stronger nation-making force than nationality. Three nationalities, each with its own language, live there side by side,—the Dutch, the Flemings, and the Walloons; but of these the Dutch and the Flemings are very closely allied racially, Flemish being only a slight variant of the Dutch language. It would therefore seem natural on the face of it that these two sections would amalgamate together, leaving the Walloons to attach themselves to their French cousins. That it is not so is due to the fact that the Flemings and the Dutch are adherents of two different and mutually hostile creeds, and that this distinction in their faith has been stamped upon the national memories by the whole history of their past. Holland, the stronghold of

[1] *Expansion of England*, p. 59.

Calvinism, had at the end of the sixteenth century thrown off the yoke of Catholic Spain and asserted its independence, while the Belgic provinces, after Alva had cruelly crushed out such Protestantism as existed among their peoples, returned to the faith and the allegiance of their fathers, and remained part of the Hapsburg inheritance until the Congress of Vienna. Thus the cleavage between Protestantism and Catholicism has made two nations out of one Low German nationality in the Netherlands, as it threatens to do with one Celtic nationality in Ireland. On the other hand, their common Catholic faith has welded Flemings and Walloons together, making one nation out of two nationalities far more racially distinct than the Flemings and the Dutch, and this amalgamation has acquired a certain flavour of common nationality from the fact that the language of the upper classes is French.

It is obvious therefore that the attempt of the diplomatists in 1814 to ignore both historical and religious differences and to combine Holland and Belgium into a single State was doomed at the outset. Fifteen years of constant friction were followed in 1830 by a rising in Brussels against " Dutch supremacy," which quickly spread to the rest of Belgium. The Great Powers, recognising the inevitable, interfered on behalf of Belgium, she was declared a neutral State, separate from Holland, and took to herself a king in the person of Leopold I. It is, however, highly significant that directly the Dutch menace was removed from Belgium the internal cleavage of nationality began to be felt. " In 1815 the differences between Flemish and Walloon were to a large extent concealed beneath a veneer of French culture and French manners. Among the upper and commercial classes no language but French was ever spoken ; and in their dislike of Dutch supremacy the

Flemish Belgians took a sort of patriotic pride in their borrowed speech, and for a time relegated their native tongue to the level of a rustic *patois*." [1] And yet, on the other hand, " the separation of Belgium from Holland had no sooner taken place than the newly aroused national spirit began to show itself among the Flemish-speaking part of the people by a revival of interest in their ancestral Teutonic language. . . . King William I.'s attempt to make Dutch the official language had met with universal opposition ; but as early as 1840 a demand was put forward for the use of the Flemish tongue (which is closely akin to the Dutch) on equal terms with French in the Legislature, the Law Courts, and the Army. As the years passed by, the movement gathered ever-increasing numbers of adherents, and the demand was repeated with growing insistence." [2] In 1897 the Flemish party attained its ambition, and Flemish became the official language of the country, side by side with French. The remarkable thing about this Teutonising movement is that its mainstay has always been the extreme Catholic party, which on religious grounds had been the most violent opponent of the attempted Teutonification by the Dutch. The opposition between Flemish and Walloon, indeed, became so marked in recent years that many feared that the Belgian nation was about to split into two. Germany has, however, postponed this national calamity for generations if not for ever, and the Belgium which arises like a phoenix from the ashes of this third attempt at Teutonification will, we cannot doubt, be a Belgium indissolubly knit together by common memories of a glorious struggle for freedom and cemented by the blood and tears of the whole population. Germany, like Napoleon

---

[1] *Cambridge Modern History*, vol. x. p. 521.
[2] *Ibid.* vol. xi. p. 693.

a century ago, will call many nations into being; the first and not the least of her creations is a transfigured and united Belgium.

As a frontier State, a link between the Latin and Teutonic races to both of which her peoples are akin, Belgium offers an extremely interesting study of the national idea at work. The peoples of Germany and France, which have been perpetually at war with each other since the times of Julius Caesar, have almost always met on her fair and prosperous plains to fight their battles, since she is geographically the gateway from one to the other. Neither could afford to let the other occupy her territory, and so she has won her independence as a State; both have constantly threatened her existence in times past, and so have forced upon her bi-lingual population that consciousness of common interests which if strong enough may become as firm a basis for national unity as actual community of nationality.

It should be noticed further that it has become the practice in recent times to guarantee the neutrality of small frontier States like Belgium which lie at the mercy of their greater neighbours, a practice intended not only to preserve the integrity of such States but also to prevent the frequent occurrence of war by closing, as it were, the military gate between the hostile countries.[1] It remains to be seen whether the violation of these principles by Germany has the effect of strengthening them in the future, rather than the reverse. In any case, we may expect to see attempts to apply the same principles to other parts of Europe. Already the northern and southern ends of the frontier between Germany and France are neutralised by the existence of Belgium and Switzerland; why, it

[1] The neutralisation of sovereign States is very recent in origin. Switzerland and Luxembourg are the only other instances. The former was neutralised in 1815, the latter in 1867.

may be asked, should not the whole frontier be treated in the same way by neutralising the disputed territory of Alsace-Lorraine ? Perhaps, too, a neutral Poland would form a useful buffer between Germany and Russia. Such neutralisation, it should be noted, need not necessarily carry with it independence. Poland and Alsace-Lorraine might form part of Russia and France respectively, and still be neutralised by a guarantee of other powers. A precedent exists for this in the terms of the cession of the Ionian Islands to Greece in 1864, while Savoy, though a province of France, is technically neutralised territory.[1] Cases like these, however, it must be admitted, are extremely anomalous and could hardly stand the strain of a serious war. But, then, as recent experience has shown us, not even independent neutralised States are safe when all Europe is aflame. The truth is that the whole conception of neutrality implies the existence of some power above and beyond the State, it may be simply a group of powerful States who are able to impose their will upon the rest of Europe, it may be a general Congress, like the Congress of Vienna. Since the Concert of Europe disappeared and gradually gave place to the two opposing alliances of great powers, there has been no such authority in the civilised world. The results are before us in the ruined cities and starving population of violated Belgium.

As independent States, therefore, small nations can only survive, in the long run, if their neutrality is permanently guaranteed by some international authority, which is itself permanently capable of enforcing its decrees upon recalcitrant States. Sovereignty and independence, how-

---

[1] *Cambridge Modern History*, xi. 642. See for the whole question of neutralised States, Lawrence, *Principles of International Law*, §§ 246-248.

ever, are not, as we have seen, essential to full nationhood, provided the nation possesses a certain amount of " home-rule " and regards the government under which it lives as a true expression of its genius and will. For example, from 1809 till the setting in of Russian reaction in 1899, the Finnish nation enjoyed all the privileges of complete nation-hood except actual sovereignty. There is, therefore, a future for small nations, either as autonomous protégés of great powers, like Russia, or as partners in some common-wealth of nations, like the British Empire.

But there is yet another consideration to be faced. Why, it is asked, should we trouble ourselves about the preserva-tion of small nationalities at all ?   " The State is power," and it is only the really powerful State, therefore, that can and ought to survive. There is something laughable in the idea of a small State ; it is weakness trying to pose as strength. And as for nations which have lost their inde-pendence and have bowed to the yoke of the conqueror, their fate is incorporation. How can they hope or expect to retain their separate existence and their peculiar culture when they have surrendered the power upon which these privileges depend ?   " No nation can permit the Jews to have a double nationality " ; and the same applies to Poles, Finns, Alsatians, Irishmen, and Belgians.[1]   This is the point of view of Bernhardi, Treitschke, and the German Government. This is the theory which is said to justify the practice of Prussianisation, Russianisation, Magyarisation, and so on. It raises the whole question of the value and significance to civilisation of the existence of small nations. Treitschke, of course, and his school are convinced that they possess neither value nor significance. In small States

[1] See *Selections from Treitschke*, translated by A. L. Gowans, pp. 17-20, 58-61.

there is developed that beggarly frame of mind which
judges the State by the taxes that it raises; there is completely lacking in small States the ability of the great State
to be just; all real masterpieces of poetry and art arose
upon the soil of great nationalities—such are a few of
Treitschke's dogmatic utterances on this subject.[1] But it
is not merely the Germans who think small beer of
small nationalities. Listen to Sir John Seeley: "The
question whether large states or small states are best is
not one which can be answered or ought to be discussed
absolutely. We often hear abstract panegyrics upon
the happiness of small states. But observe that a small
state among small states is one thing, and a small
state among large states quite another. Nothing is more
delightful to read of than the bright days of Athens and
Florence, but those bright days lasted only so long as the
states with which Athens and Florence had to do were
states on a similar scale of magnitude. Both states sank
at once as soon as large country states of consolidated
strength grew up in their neighbourhood. The lustre of
Athens grew pale as soon as Macedonia arose, and Charles V.
speedily brought to an end the great days of Florence.
Now if it be true that a larger type of state than any
hitherto known is springing up in the world, is not this a
serious consideration for those states which rise only to the
old level of magnitude?"[2] The answer to which is, "Yes,
indeed, if   the good old plan
            That he should take who has the power,
            And he should keep who can

is to be the guiding principle in European politics of the

[1] See *Selections from Treitschke*, pp. 17-20, 58-61.
[2] *The Expansion of England*, p. 349. See also p. 1, "Some
countries, such as Holland and Sweden, might pardonably regard
their history as in a manner wound up."

future." But surely Sir John Seeley's argument, though undoubtedly telling as regards the sovereign independence of small *States*, tells for and not against the preservation of small *nations*. Was it to the interest of the world as a whole that Athens and Florence should be crushed ? Is it not true, in spite of Treitschke, that the great things of earth have been the product of small peoples ? We owe our conceptions of law to a city called Rome, our finest output of literature and art to small communities like Athens, Florence, Holland, and Elizabethan England, our religion to an insignificant people who inhabited a narrow strip of land in the Eastern Mediterranean. And small nations are as valuable to the world to-day as they have ever been. Denmark has enriched our educational experience by the establishment of her famous high schools, which we can hardly imagine her doing had she been a province of Prussia ; Norway has given us the greatest of modern dramatists, Henrik Ibsen ; and Belgium has not only produced Maeterlinck and Verhaeren, but is industrially the most highly developed country on the continent. The world cannot afford to do without her small peoples, who must be either independent or autonomous if they are to find adequate expression for their national genius, if they are to obtain proper conditions in which " to live, think, love, and labour for the benefit of all." Can we guarantee to them this freedom ? That is one of the great questions which this war will settle.[1]

§ 5. *The National Idea in Italy : The Ideal Type.*—Let us now turn to Italy, a country which has in the past been

[1] See J. M. Robertson, *Introduction to English Politics*, pp. 251-390; Mr. H. A. L. Fisher's pamphlet on *The Value of Small States*, in which, however, the distinction between *states* and *nations* is not made clear ; and the article on "Nationalism and Liberalism" in *The Round Table*, December 1914.

as much of a European Tom Tiddler's ground as Belgium, though for rather different reasons. Italy is inhabited by a race speaking a common language and observing a common religion, she has historical memories as glorious as those of any other country in the world, and her natural boundaries are almost as well-defined as those of Great Britain ; yet it was not until the latter half of the nineteenth century that she managed to become a nation. The chief reason why she remained a " geographical expression " long after England, France, and Spain had acquired national unity was the fact that she was until comparatively recent times an example of the less containing the greater. Throughout the Middle Ages she was a suburb, not a country. Rome was the capital of the world, Italy only its environs. Moreover, since all roads lead to Rome, and the lord of Rome was the master of Europe, the roads Romeward were worn by the tramp of the armies of all nations. Thus Italy was constantly subject to invasion, and the state-systems with which the Congress of Vienna resaddled her in 1814 were little more than relics of past military occupations of her soil by foreign armies. The main problem, therefore, in the making of modern Italy was how to get rid of the heavy burden of the past, how to deal with Rome and all that Rome stood for.

The problem would have been insoluble had not the prestige of Rome declined considerably since the Middle Ages, a prestige which sprang from the fact that she was the capital of two Empires—the spiritual Empire of the Papacy, and the secular Empire founded by Charles the Great. The former had suffered from the Reformation and the rise of the great Protestant nations, the latter had been growing feebler and feebler for centuries, until it was abolished as an institution by Napoleon. Yet Italy in 1814 still lay helpless and divided at the feet of

Rome. The Pope held under his immediate sway a large zigzag-shaped territory running across the centre from sea to sea, and, as spiritual leader of half Europe, he could at any moment summon to his assistance the Catholic chivalry of the world. " The Roman emperor " no longer existed, but " the Austrian emperor " was another title for the same man, holding much the same territory ; and the fact that he had renounced his vague suzerainty over the rest of Europe did not prevent him exercising a very real suzerainty in Italy, not merely over the eastern half of the Lombard Plain which definitely belonged to Austria, but also over the other States of the peninsula which were, in theory at least, independent. The kingdom of the two Sicilies in the South, the grand duchy of Tuscany on the West, and the smaller duchies of Parma, Modena, and Lucca were only stable in so far as Austria bolstered up their corrupt and unpopular governments. Even the Papal States themselves, equally undermined with corruption and unpopularity, ultimately rested upon the same support. Thus Austria represented for Italy all that evil past of which she wanted to be rid : the foreign yoke against which her newly conscious spirit of nationality revolted, the dynastic frontiers which were abhorrent to her desire for unity, the absolute *régime* under which her soul, after feeding on the principles of the French Revolution, lay gagged and bound. The first step to be taken towards the creation of Italy was the expulsion of the Austrians.

This fact in itself purified the struggle for Italian freedom and raised Italian nationalism to heights of nobility and heroism almost unparalleled in history. The nation had not merely to be unified, but *delivered*, and delivered from the oppression of that power which was the mainstay of reaction in Europe. Nor was it simply a question of national freedom ; Austria had declared war upon individual and constitutional liberty also, and used all her power to suppress them wherever they dared to raise their head. From beginning to end of her fight for national existence, Italy never forgot that she was also fighting for individual liberty, or ceased to be conscious that the downfall of Austria in Italy would mean the downfall of reaction in Europe. The banner which Mazzini raised in 1831 had the words " Unity and Independence " on the one side and " Liberty, Equality, and Humanity " on the other. Italy was indeed greatly blessed, inasmuch as in seeking her own deliverance she could not help bursting the bands of brass which bound the whole world in captivity.

It is not possible here to tell the glorious story of the resurrection of Italy, or even to say anything of the three heroes at whose hands she received her freedom—Cavour who gave her the service of his brain, Mazzini who devoted to her the love and passion of his great heart, and Garibaldi who fought for her with the strength of his own right arm. It must suffice to indicate very briefly the various stages in the development of her national idea, and the manner in which she finally realised it. Liberal principles took root in Italy at the time of the French Revolution, and the first glimmerings of nationalism were due to Napoleon, who bundled the princes out of the peninsula and even for a time exiled the Pope himself. But it was constitutional rather than national freedom which seemed most urgent to the generation which succeeded Napoleon. The Carbonari, as the early Italian revolutionaries were called, confined themselves almost entirely to the demand for a constitution in the various existing States, and though they eagerly desired the expulsion of Austria, they did so not because she prevented Italian unity, but because she forbade political reform. Their risings, therefore, local and disunited in character, were bound to fail; the first fifteen years after the Congress of Vienna were occupied by a series of attempts to substitute a constitutional for an absolute *régime* in different parts of Italy, attempts which Austria crushed with a heavy hand.

The period which followed, 1830–1848, belongs to Mazzini and his " Young Italy " party. His task was to fire Italy for the first time with the ideal of national unity and independence. The conception of unity was a difficult one for Italians to grasp; all history seemed to fight against it. There were, for example, not only the traditions connected with Rome to be reckoned with, but there was also the difference between north and south, and, perhaps most important of all, the local spirit of independence associated with the great cities like Venice, Milan, Florence, Naples, etc. Thus, over against Mazzini's ideal of a single unified State there arose the counter-ideal of a federal system. In this, however, later events proved Mazzini to be right. Where he failed in foresight was in regard to the constitutional character of the State he dreamed of. He wished not only to abolish all existing frontiers in Italy, but to do away with all existing state-systems. The only Italy he could conceive was a republic, and Italy was not ripe for a republic, which was, for the rest, a form of government too much bound up with the disruptive traditions of the City-States to be acceptable.[1] But if Italy was not to be a republic, she must be a monarchy, and where could she find a prince to put at the head of her united State ? Clearly, she would accept no one who was not the declared enemy of Austria

[1] It is noticeable that Greece also played with the idea of a republic at first and eventually selected a monarchical form of government. As a matter of fact, not a single nation-State, formed in Europe since the Congress of Vienna, has adopted the republican principle.

and the declared friend of constitutional reform. For a month or so in 1846 it seemed that the Pope himself might be prevailed upon to undertake the rôle ; and the elevation of Pius IX. to the Chair of St. Peter was greeted with wild enthusiasm in Italy because he was believed to be a Liberal. These hopes proved illusory, however, and so the eyes of all patriots turned more and more in the direction of Piedmont.

This principality, which was part of the kingdom of Sardinia, ruled over by the semi-French house of Savoy, shared the northern plain of Italy with Austria, and at first showed neither anti-Austrian nor Liberal proclivities. Victor Emmanuel came back smiling in 1814, saying that he had been asleep for fifteen years ; the old *régime* was restored as though the Revolution had never been ; and a rising of the Carbonari in 1821 was suppressed with the aid of Austrian troops. But in 1831 a king, Charles Albert, came to the throne, who realised that it was the mission of his house to drive the Austrians from Italy, and who was enlightened enough to begin to institute reforms, as unostentatiously as possible, so as not to attract the unwelcome attention of Vienna. Then came the great outburst of 1848, which was the culmination of Mazzini's propaganda for the past sixteen years. At first all went well. The Austrian army was almost expelled from the peninsula ; constitutions were granted in Rome, Naples, Tuscany, and Piedmont ; Venice and Rome declared themselves republics. But no real scheme for all Italy emerged ; the Mazzinians were heroic but unpractical ; and next year Austria returned once more, dealt as before piecemeal with the revolted provinces, and finally crushed the hopes of Italy again at the battle of Novara. Yet all was not lost. The republican dreams of Mazzini were, it is true, at an end. But Piedmont had stepped into Mazzini's shoes; she had championed the cause of freedom against Austria; and, when the latter reasserted her sway, she alone of the various States refused to abrogate the newly-acquired constitution.

Thus began the third period in the emancipation of Italy, the period of Cavour, who became head of the Piedmontese cabinet in 1850. His aim was first to make Piedmont the model State and champion of all Italy. He believed fervently in liberty—" Italy," he said, " must make herself by means of liberty, or we must give up trying to make her "—and he was at the same time one of the ablest and most practical statesmen who have ever guided the destinies of a nation. In ten years he made the State of the north-west an oasis of freedom and good government which attracted the best intellects of Italy to its service, and henceforth Piedmont became the centre of Italian aspirations. A new propaganda movement was set on foot, called the National Society, which rejected both federalism and republicanism and declared in favour of a united Italy under the crown of Victor Emmanuel of Savoy; and when the chance of French support came in 1858, Cavour felt it was time to act. This time the end crowned the work. Austria was deprived of everything but Venice; Tuscany and Romagna declared for incorporation by plebiscite; Garibaldi conquered Sicily and the south; and by the end of 1860 the King of Sardinia was king of practically the whole of Italy. All that still remained to be won was Venice, which Austria ceded in 1866; Rome, which the French had occupied in the name of the Pope, and were forced to evacuate in 1870; and the Italia Irredenta of to-day, viz. the Trentino, Trieste, and Istria, which may be recovered as a result of the present war. It is worthy of note also that the trans-Alpine provinces, Savoy and Nice, which had been part of the dominions of the Sardinian kingdom, were ceded to France in 1858–1859 as a return for her aid, thus rounding off the western frontier of the new kingdom of Italy so as to correspond fairly closely with the boundary of nationality.

The foundation of modern Italy shows us the " national idea " at its best; it was accomplished by noble means and by noble minds; and the latter, in their perpetual struggle against the forces of reaction, were never allowed to forget the claims of individual as well as of national freedom. Three tests of true nationhood, it will be remembered, were suggested at the beginning of this chapter : a state-frontier co-extensive with the nationality-frontier, a unitary state-system, and a form of government recognised by the inhabitants as an expression of their general will. Italy fulfils all these conditions; for, though the first has not yet been perfectly realised as regards Italia Irredenta, the exception is after all a trifling one. Thus the development of the national idea in Italy is almost a model of what such a development should be, and we have dwelt some-what at length upon it for that very reason. The work of Mazzini and Cavour provides us with a standard of comparison which should be found very useful in dealing with the national idea in other countries.

§ 6. *The National Idea in Germany : a Case of Arrested Development.*[1]—Nothing, for example, could be more instructive, both as a study in nationalism and as an aid to the understanding of the present situation in Europe, than a comparison between the making of modern Italy and the making of modern Germany. At first sight the German Empire, with its marvellous progress, its vast

[1] The student is advised to read the chapter on Germany before beginning this section.

resources, and its world-wide ambitions, would appear to be an even more successful example of national development than the kingdom of Italy. Its demand for " a place in the sun," its hustling diplomacy, its military spirit, its obvious intention to expand territorially, if not in Europe itself then in Asia or Africa, are all taken as symptoms of this success. No doubt there is a certain amount of truth in this view. The truculence of German foreign policy is to be partly attributed to that form of swollen self-consciousness and self-complacency to which all nations are subject more or less, and which is most likely, one would suppose, to be found in countries where a nationality had recently succeeded in making itself into a nation. The natural instinct to regard one's own nation as the peculiar people of God and to look down on other nations as " lesser breeds without the law " is a phenomenon which must be constantly reckoned with in any comprehensive treatment of nationalism. Every nation has its own variety of it ; in England it is Jingoism, in France Chauvinism, in Italy Irredentism, in Russia Pan-Slavism, and so on. These are instances of over-development of the national idea, due either to some confusion between race and nationality, or to simple national megalomania, which usually subsides after a healthy humiliation, such as we suffered in England, for example, in the Boer War or as Russia suffered in her struggle with the Japanese.

Yet a careful examination of the German body-politic will reveal symptoms unlike those to be found in any other nation. German nationalism is over-developed in one direction because it is under-developed and imperfect in other directions. Apply our three tests to the German nation, and it will be found to fail in them all. National boundary and State frontier do not coincide because there are still some twelve million Germans living outside Germany, in Austria-Hungary ; [1] Germany is a State, but not a unitary State, for she still retains the obsolete "particularism" of the eighteenth century, with its petty princes and dynastic frontiers ; and lastly, the government of Germany cannot claim to express the general will, while more than a third of the voters in the empire are sworn to overthrow the whole system at the earliest opportunity. The German nation, in fact, is suffering from some form of arrested development, and arrested development, as the criminologists tell us, is almost invariably accompanied by morbid psychology. That Germany at the present moment, and for some time past, has been the victim of a morbid state of mind, few impartial observers will deny. It has, however, not been so generally recognised that this disease—for it is nothing less—is due not to any national depravity but to constitutional and structural defects, which are themselves the result of an unfortunate series of historical accidents. Let us look a little closer into this matter, considering the three defects in German nationalism one by one, and using the story of Italy as an aid to our investigation.

First, then, why was it that, while the unification of Italy led to the inclusion of the whole Italian nationality within the State frontiers, with the trifling exceptions above referred to, the unification of Germany was only brought about, or even made possible, by the *exclusion* of a large section of the nationality ? Germany, like Italy, was hampered by traditions inherited from the mediaeval Roman Empire, represented by an ancient capital which stood in the path of unity. Why was it that, while Italy

[1] There are also Germans living in Switzerland, the Baltic Provinces of Russia, and the United States of America ; but these may be regarded as lost to the German nation as the French Canadians are lost to France.

could not and would not do without Rome, Germany was compelled to surrender Vienna and to exclude Austria ? The answer is : because the unification of Germany was only possible through the instrumentality of Prussia, which would not brook the rivalry of Austria, and therefore the latter had to go. The problem of the making of Germany as it presented itself to the mind of Bismarck was first of all a problem as to which should be *supreme* in Germany, Prussia or Austria ; in other words Bismarck cared more for the aggrandisement of Prussia than for the unity of Germany.[1] To the mind of Cavour the problem of the unification of Italy presented itself in a totally different light. For him there was no question of the aggrandisement of Piedmont, though he no doubt felt pride in the thought that the House of Savoy was to possess the throne of Italy. Austria was expelled from Italy in 1860, not that Piedmont might take her place as ruler of the peninsula, but that Piedmont might disappear in the larger whole of an emancipated Italy. Austria was expelled from Germany in 1866 in order that Prussia might rule undisturbed. Thus, though the Austro-Prussian War of 1866 was an essential step in the foundation of the modern German State, its motives and results were not in the least comparable to those which inspired and followed the Italian War of Liberation in 1859–60. In the first place the Austrians were not foreigners but Germans, whom it was necessary for reasons of State not of nationality to place outside the rest of Germany. Germany had, in fact, to choose between national unity and State unity ; and she chose the latter, partly because Prussia really decided the matter for her, partly because she realised that the establish-

---

[1] Perhaps it would be fairer to say that he was incapable of distinguishing between them. See his *Reflections*, i. pp. 315, 316.

ment of a strong German State was the essential prelude to the creation of a strong united nation. Austria had to be shut out in 1866 in order that she might be received back again at some later date on Germany's own terms. In the second place Austria was in no sense the oppressor of Germany as she had been of Italy. She was simply the presiding member of the German Confederation who, as the rival of Prussia, as the inheritor of the mediaeval imperial tradition, as the ruler of millions of non-Germanic people, would have rendered the problem of German unification almost insoluble. It was therefore necessary to get rid of her as gently and as politely as possible. After the crushing victory at Königgrätz, Bismarck treated Prussia's ancient foe with extraordinary leniency; for he had already planned the Dual Alliance in his mind, knowing as he did that, though in Germany Austria might be an inconvenient rival to Prussia, in Europe she was the indispensable ally of Germany. And so, though the ramshackle old German imperial castle was divided in two, and the northern portion, at any rate, brought thoroughly up to date, the neighbours still lived side by side in a " semi-detached " kind of way.

It would be a mistake then to call the war of 1866 a war of deliverance. Indeed, since the defeat of Napoleon at Leipzig, Germany has had no such war. That is in a great measure her national tragedy. Italian nationalism was spiritualised by the very fact that it had to struggle for decades against a foreign oppressor, and the foundations of her unity were laid on the heroic memories of her efforts to expel the intruder. This spiritualisation, these heroic memories were Germany's also in 1813–14, but the opportunity of unification was allowed to slip by, and when the task was performed fifty years later it was through quite other means and in a very different spirit. And yet, though there was no one to expel, Germany could only hope to attain unity by fighting. In 1848 she made an attempt to do so by peaceable means, and a national Parliament actually assembled at Frankfurt to frame a constitution for the whole country. But the attempt, noble as it was in conception, proved a dismal failure, and it became clear that national unity in Germany was to be won " not by speeches and majority resolutions, but by blood and iron." The words are Bismarck's, and the task was his also. Set them beside the words of Cavour about Italy and liberty, quoted above, or compare the harsh unscrupulous spirit of the great German master-builder with the spirit of Mazzini, Cavour, and Garibaldi, and you get a measure of the difference between the developments of the national idea in Germany and in Italy. Yet Bismarck's famous sentence expressed the truth of the matter for Germany. Austria had been put outside the German pale, and Germany north of the Main had accepted unity under the hegemony of Prussia, but there still remained the four great States of South Germany to bring in. They had been the allies of Austria in 1866, and Prussia, had she willed it, might have incorporated them by conquest. But Bismarck saw that they must put themselves willingly under Prussia if the German Empire was to be a stable concern ; he therefore left them alone to think it over for a while. Sooner or later they would have to come in, since now that Austria had been excluded there remained only the choice between dependence on France and union with Prussia. Bismarck deliberately played upon South Germany's fear of France, and Napoleon III.'s restless foreign policy admirably seconded his efforts. But a war was necessary to bring matters to a head. The opportunity came in 1870, and Bismarck was able to make it appear a war not of his own choosing. The Southern States threw themselves into the arms of Prussia; France was crushed, and Alsace-Lorraine annexed; the German Empire was proclaimed, and modern Germany came into being. There had been no foreigner to expel from German soil, but Bismarck found that an attack upon France served his purpose equally well.

Germany was made by a war of aggression, resulting in territorial expansion at the expense of another nation; Italy by a war of liberation, driving the alien from her soil. And the subsequent history of the two nations is eloquent of this difference in their origins. Since 1860 Italy has in the main occupied herself with domestic reforms, with the working out of the " social idea " which had had to wait upon the realisation of the " national idea." She has had, it is true, her " adventures," more especially in Africa, and her Jingoism, which has taken the natural form of Irredentism or the demand for the recovery of Italian provinces still left in Austrian hands; but she has never threatened the peace of Europe, or sought power at the expense of other nationalities. Since 1870, on the other hand, Germany has had to sit armed to defend the booty taken from France. " We have earned in the late war respect, but hardly love," said General von Moltke soon after the conclusion of peace. " What we have gained by arms in six months we shall have to defend by arms for fifty years." At the beginning of 1914 more than forty out of the fifty years named by Moltke had passed by and the situation had undergone no material change. " The irreconcilability of France," writes the late Imperial Chancellor of Germany, " is a factor that we must reckon with in our political calculations. It seems to me weakness to entertain the hope of a real and sincere reconciliation with France, so long as we have no intention of giving up Alsace-Lorraine. And there is no such intention in Germany." [1] The annexation of two small provinces has thus made a permanent breach between two great nations, a breach which has poisoned the whole of European policy during the past half century, which has widened until it has split Europe into two huge armed camps, and which has at last involved the entire world in one of the most terrible calamities that mankind has ever known.

Why did Bismarck annex Alsace - Lorraine ? To strengthen, he said, the German frontier against France. But there was another reason. Fear of France had brought the Southern States into the Empire ; fear of France should keep them there. The permanent hostility of France was necessary to assure the continuance of Prussia's position as the supreme military power in Germany. And so the plundered provinces became the very corner-stone of the German imperial system. There is surely something very strange about all this. Why should it be necessary to retain the loyalty of nearly half Germany by what practically amounts to terrorisation ? The answer is that Germany is not a single national State but a number of *dynastic* States, federated together under the control of one predominant partner. In other words, the problem of Alsace-Lorraine has led us to the consideration of the second flaw in the development of the national idea in Germany.

The union of Italy meant a clean sweep of all the old dynastic frontiers and States which had strangled the country for so long ; the union of Germany, on the contrary, riveted these obsolete chains still more firmly than ever on the country's limbs. Bismarck claimed that this was necessary, inasmuch as the Germans, unlike all other nations, were more alive to dynastic than to national

[1] *Imperial Germany*, von Bülow, p. 69.

loyalty; that, in short, Germany was not really ready in 1870 for true unity.[1] The chief reason, however, for the retention of the old frontiers was that they suited the aims of Prussia. The reformers of 1848, as Professor Erich Marcks somewhat naïvely says, " had wanted to place Prussia at the head, but only as the servant of the nation ; Prussia was also to cease to be a State by itself, a power on its own account. She was to create the nation's ideal—complete unity—and then to merge herself in the nation. But Prussia would not and could not do this. She was far too great a power herself ; *she could very well rule Germany, but not serve.*" [2] Both Germany and Italy at first played with the idea of a Confederation, but each was eventually forced to look to one of its existing States to give it the unity it desired. There was only one possible choice for each : for Germany, Prussia ; for Italy, Piedmont ; but while Piedmont was content to serve, Prussia was too proud to do anything but rule. The dynastic State frontiers were therefore retained because Prussia refused to sacrifice her own State frontiers. The " unification of Germany," in short, was an episode in the gradual expansion of the Prussian dynastic State, which had begun far away back in the thirteenth century.[3] It assumed the air of a national movement, because Prussia cleverly availed herself of the prevailing nationalistic sentiment for her own ends. The German Empire is therefore something unique in the annals of the world ; it is at once a nation-State, like Italy, France, and Great Britain, and also a military Empire, like Rome under Augustus, Europe under Napoleon, Austria

[1] The chapter entitled " Dynasties and Stocks " in the *Reflections* should be carefully studied on this point. Bismarck was obviously uncomfortable about the old frontiers.

[2] *Lectures on the History of the Nineteenth Century*, p. 104.

[3] See Chap. III. p. 95.

under Joseph II., *i.e.* a State in which the territory that commands the army holds political sway over the rest of the country. It is not mere accident of geographical proximity, or even the kinship between Austrians and Germans, which has led to the long and unshakable alliance of Germany with the Hapsburg dominions. They are associated by common political interests and by similarity of political structure. Each stands for the supremacy of one dynastic State over a number of subordinate States or nationalities.

Her common nationality leads us to forget that the German Empire should more rightly be called the Prussian Empire.[1] Nor is there any reason at all why the Empire of Prussia should stop its process of expansion at the national boundaries ; it has indeed already stepped beyond them, into Poland in the east, into Denmark in the north, into France in the west. Why should not the process be carried farther still and Germany become in Europe, nay, in the world, what Prussia is in Germany ? By preserving her identity as a State, and by establishing her hegemony, Prussia, in the name of the national idea of Germany, has been able to spread her own ideals throughout the Empire, in other words to undertake that Prussianisation of Germany which is the most striking fact in her history since 1870. Piedmont was swallowed up in Italy, Germany has been swallowed up in Prussia ; she has become the sharer of her victories and the accomplice of her crimes. And so under the tutelage of the spirit of Bismarck the docile German people have adopted the Prussian faith ; and the policy of aggression and conquest once entered upon, there was no drawing back. Bismarck fed the youthful nation upon a diet of blood and iron, and its appetite has grown by what it fed

[1] German writers are fond of calling it " Prussia-Germany " (*Preussen-Deutschland*), a phrase of Treitschke's.

on. The success of 1870 turned the nation's head; the annexation of Alsace-Lorraine gave it the first taste of conquest. Germany began to imagine that German character and German culture possessed some magical and unique quality which would alone account for this success. Dreams of a European Empire, of infinite expansion, of world - power, floated before the national consciousness. The German people were no longer content, to use Mazzini's words, " to elaborate and express their idea, to contribute their stone also to the pyramid of history "; they now craved to impose their idea upon the world at large, and to place their stone on the top of the pyramid. Modern Germany is an example of nationalism " gone wrong," just as Napoleon was an example of democratic individualism " gone wrong." The Man of Destiny has been followed by the Nation of Destiny, the " super-man " by the " super-nation." Both have had to face a world in arms arrayed against them.

Thus the national idea in Germany has been cramped, contorted, and perverted by the Prussian system and the dynastic frontiers. Had the dreams of 1848 been realised, there might have been no Franco-German War, no Alsace-Lorraine question, no war of 1914. And what of our third test of nationhood? Do the people of Germany feel that their government adequately expresses their general will, that it is truly representative, by which is not necessarily meant that it is democratic in form?[1] There is no doubt that in 1848 the educated classes of Germany did actually desire a democratic form of polity. In that year Germany was as liberal as Italy; she also had risings in almost every State, not excluding Prussia itself, which were everywhere answered with promises of a " constitution." But when

[1] *E.g.* Russia has a representative government in this sense, though she is without "representative institutions " in the democratic sense.

reaction came in Germany, as in Italy, Prussia did not, like Piedmont, stand out for freedom and make itself the model State of Germany ; on the contrary she reverted to her old military absolutism at the first opportunity. And so the dreams of German liberty, like the dreams of complete German unity, disappeared before the stern necessity of accepting the supremacy of a politically reactionary State ; and the Prussianisation which followed did much to neutralise altogether the liberalising influences of the south. It is therefore possible to maintain that the political institutions of Germany have come to represent more and more the genius and will of the population. " The Germany of the twentieth century," maintains a recent writer, " is not two but one. The currents have mingled their waters, and the Prussian torrent now has the depth and volume of the whole main-stream of German thought." [1]

It may be so ; it may be that the Germany of Goethe, Schiller, and Beethoven has been absorbed by the Germany of Bismarck, Moltke, and Roon ; but it must not be forgotten at the same time that, since their day, yet another Germany has come into being, the Germany of Marx, Engels, and Bebel, a Germany which is represented by more than a third of the voters in the Empire. The old line of cleavage had barely closed up when a new and much more fundamental schism appeared in the State, that between imperialism and social democracy. The existence of this tremendous revolutionary force in Germany, determined to overthrow the militarist *régime* of Prussia and to re-establish the State on a democratic basis, is an unanswerable proof that the government of the Empire is not in any true sense representative. Prussia has in this direction also impeded the development of the national idea and given mechanical unity at the expense

[1] *Round Table*, Sept. 1914, p. 628.

of spiritual unity. It has created a vast political party of irreconcilables in the country, men who have been led to feel that they have neither part nor promise in the national life, and who therefore elect to stand outside it. " Our Social Democratic party," writes von Bülow, " lacks a national basis. It will have nothing to do with German patriotic memories which bear a monarchical and military character. It is not like the French and Italian parties, a precipitate of the process of national historical development, but since its beginning it has been in determined opposition to our past history as a nation. It has placed itself outside our national life." [1] And again : " In the German Empire, Prussia is the leading State. The Social Democratic party is the antithesis of the Prussian state." [2] Nevertheless, the Imperial Government, not finding it possible to suppress the social democrats, does its best to employ them for its own ends. It uses them in fact as it uses irreconcilable France, namely, for the purpose of terrorisation, since it has discovered that the spectre of socialism is as effective to keep the middle classes loyal as the spectre of French revenge is to keep the Southern States loyal. But it also hopes in time to eradicate socialism from the State. " A vigorous national policy " Prince von Bülow declares to be " the true remedy against the Social Democratic Movement " ; and though he makes no specific mention of war, it is obvious that a war like that in which Germany is at present engaged is the most vigorous form a national policy could possibly take. Was the outbreak of war last August in part occasioned by the desire on the side of the German Government to win over the workers of Germany ? If so, it had yet another spectre ready to its hand for the purpose—the spectre of Russia.

[1] *Imperial Germany*, p. 184.   [2] *Ibid.* p. 186.

In any case, with Germany in this condition, Europe could hardly have avoided a great war at some time or other; and 1914 follows naturally, almost inevitably, from 1870. The unification of 1870 was far from complete. The German national idea still awaits development in the direction of racial unity, political unity, and constitutional freedom. It is Prussia that bars the way in all these directions, Prussia, which, in itself not a nation but a military bureaucracy, a survival of the old territorial dynastic principle which the world has largely outgrown, has stamped its character and system upon the German people. " Prussia," says one of its apologists, " has put an iron girdle round the whole of German life." [1] But in the end life proves itself stronger than iron bands. Germany was bound to make another attempt to reach complete nationhood. She is doing so now. Prussia fights for conquest, for world-power, and makes docile Germany imagine that she is fighting for these also ; but what Germany is really fighting for, blindly and gropingly, is freedom and unity. She has indeed " to hack her way through." But it is not, as she supposes, hostile Europe which hems her in and keeps her from her " place in the sun " ; it is the Prussian girdle and the Prussian chains which hamper the free movements of her limbs and hold her close prisoner in the shadow of the Hohenzollern castle. The overthrow of Prussia means the release of Germany ; and France, who gave Germany greatness in 1870, may with the help of the Allies be able in the near future to give her an even greater gift, the gift of liberty.

§ 7. *The Map of Europe, 1814–1914.*—We have now watched the national idea at work in the three western countries of that Central European area which the Congress

[1] *Lectures on the History of the Nineteenth Century,* p. 106.

of Vienna left unsettled in 1814, and in a later chapter we shall see the same principle acting in the two great divisions of South-East Europe, Austria-Hungary and the Balkan Peninsula. Let us, then, use this opportunity to pause for a moment, take a general survey of the map, and consider in broad outline what has actually been accomplished during the past century and what still remains to do.

From 1814 to 1848, exhausted by the effort of the Revolutionary and Napoleonic Wars and disillusioned by reactionary statesmanship, the larger nations slumbered : but Belgium and Greece secured their present liberties, and outside Europe the national movement spread throughout the South American Continent. Then came 1848, the " wonderful year " of modern history. " There is no more remarkable example in history of the contagious quality of ideas than the sudden spread of revolutionary excitement through Europe in 1848. In the course of a few weeks the established order seemed everywhere to be crumbling to pieces. The Revolution began in Palermo, crossed the Straits of Messina, and passed in successive waves of convulsion through Central Italy to Paris, Vienna, Milan, and Berlin. It has often been remarked that the Latin races are of all the peoples of Europe most prone to revolution ; but this proposition did not hold good in 1848. The Czechs in Bohemia, the Magyars in Hungary, the Germans in Austria, rose against the paralysing encumbrance of the Hapsburg autocracy. The Southern Slavs dreamed of an Illyrian kingdom ; the Germans of a united Germany ; the Bohemians of a union of all the Slavonic peoples of Europe. The authority of the Austrian Empire, the pivot of the European autocracy, had never been so rudely challenged, and if the Crown succeeded in recovering its shattered authority it was due to the dumb and unintelligent loyalty of its Slavonic troops." [1]

Many of these risings were doomed to failure, but between 1848 and 1871 the alien governments in the Italian peninsula were abolished, making way for a unitary government, in the form of a constitutional monarchy, which embraces with small exceptions the whole of the Italian population of Europe. In 1871, after three successful wars in seven years against Denmark, Austria, and France, a Federal Government was established in Germany, with the kingdom of Prussia as its leading State and the King of Prussia as its monarch, with the title of German Emperor. This was a step forward, though the new Germany was neither a unitary nor a constitutional State. The Austrian territories have also come in for their share of the general ferment, and Francis Joseph came to the throne in 1848 amid the uprisings of his subject peoples; but these were successfully tided over, though the Hungarian portion of the Austrian dominion achieved national recognition and institutions in 1867.

After 1871 the national movement moved farther east. In 1878 Roumania and Serbia, both national States, were declared sovereign powers independent of Turkey; Bulgaria achieved its recognition as a principality; and Montenegro, a small mountain community, which had never submitted to the Turks, increased its territory and became a recognised European State. In 1908 and 1910 Bulgaria and Montenegro became kingdoms like their neighbours; and in 1913, after the two Balkan Wars, all the five Balkan States—Roumania, Serbia, Bulgaria, Greece, and Montenegro—obtained accession of territory, and the principality of Albania was constituted out of the Albanian

[1] H. A. L. Fisher, *The Republican Tradition in Europe*, p. 193.

portion of the old Turkish dominion. Finally, in quite
another region of Europe, Norway, which had been joined
in an anomalous union with Sweden since 1814, satisfied
her national aspirations unopposed by becoming an independent Constitutional Monarchy in 1905.

All this represents a considerable clearing up of the
Central European problem. Nevertheless, much still
remains to be done. Poland is as she was in 1814, a dismembered nation. The Czechs of Bohemia, the Roumanians
of Transylvania, and the Southern Slavs, not to mention
other and smaller subject races, continue to demand their
freedom from the joint tyranny of Vienna and Budapest.
Russia has not yet solved the problem of Finland, nor
England the problem of Ireland. The Turk still occupies
Constantinople. And finally, the Prussianised nationalism
of Germany has created new questions of nationality in
Alsace - Lorraine and Schleswig. All these problems
together were as so much tinder ready to take fire directly
the spark fell. They were the cause of the " armed peace "
of the past forty-three years ; they are the cause of the war
to-day. The conflagration of 1914 is a proof of a profound
dissatisfaction among civilised nations with the existing
political structure of the Continent. Alsatians, Poles,
Czechs, Finns, Serbo-Croats, Roumanians, and the rest
" still struggle for country and liberty ; for a word inscribed upon a banner, proclaiming to the world that they
also live, think, love, and labour for the benefit of all."
The framework of society does not fit the facts of nationality,
and so the framework has gone to pieces. " The map of
Europe has to be re-made. That is the key to the present
movement."

BOOKS

I. NATIONALITY

MAZZINI. *Essays.* The Scott Library. 1s.

MAZZINI. *Duties of Man*, etc. Everyman Library. 1s.

> Anything written by Mazzini, the prophet of the national idea, can be recommended.

LORD ACTON. *History of Freedom and other Essays.* 1907. 10s. net.

> Contains an acute historical analysis of nationality in the nineteenth century. The conclusion reached is that "the theory of nationality is more absurd and more criminal than the theory of socialism," but though the summing up is unfavourable, the whole essay is a masterly exposition of the national idea by one of the greatest of historical students. It forms a very useful foil to Mazzini.

HENRY SIDGWICK. *The Elements of Politics.* 1897. 14s. net.

> Chapter xiv., on "The Area of Government," contains useful paragraphs on the distinction between Nation, State, and Nationality; see esp. pp. 222-225.

SIR JOHN SEELEY. *The Expansion of England.* First published in 1883. 4s. net.

SIR JOHN SEELEY. *Introduction to Political Science.* 1896. 4s. net.

> Both these books, the first in particular, are important in this connection. There is no one chapter or section devoted exclusively to the consideration of nationality, but there are constant references to the subject. The point of view is, moreover, instructive. Seeley is, perhaps, the nearest English approach to Treitschke.

J. M. ROBERTSON. *Introduction to English Politics.* 1900. 10s. 6d. net.

> Critical from the Rationalistic as Acton is from the Catholic point of view. See esp. Part V., "The Fortunes of the Lesser European States," which after a preliminary essay on Nationality, which the author declares to be "essentially a metaphysical dream," while "the motive spirit in it partakes much of the nature of superstition," goes on to give a valuable account of the development of the "small nations," Holland, Switzerland, Portugal, etc., by way of showing their value to civilisation as a whole.

P. MILYOUKOV. *Russia and its Crisis.* 1905. 13s. 6d.

> Chap. ii. contains some interesting matter on Nationalism, especially of course as it has been developed in Russia.

J. S. MILL. *On Representative Government.* 2s.

> Chap. xvi., "Of Nationality as connected with Representative Government."

II. General Historical Works, etc.

Alison Phillips. *Modern Europe. 1815–1899.* 1903. 6s. net.

An excellent general history of Europe, 1815–1899.

Seignobos. *A Political History of Contemporary Europe since 1814.* 2 vols. 1901. 5s. net each.

One of the best general histories of this scope available. It is a translation from the French, with good bibliographies.

Lectures on the History of the Nineteenth Century. Cambridge. 1902. 4s. 6d. net.

A series of studies, by recognised authorities, of various aspects of modern European history. Chap. ii., on "The International History of Europe during the Nineteenth Century," by the late Professor Westlake, is suggestive on the topic of nationality; chaps. v. and vi., on Germany, by a German professor, are interesting as giving the German view of unification by Bismarck; and chaps. ix. and x., on "The Struggle for Italian Unity," and "Mazzini," by Mr. Bolton King, are especially valuable.

H. A. L. Fisher. *The Republican Tradition in Europe.* 1911. 6s. net.

Traces the development of the republican, as distinct from the nationalist tradition, in modern Europe, and therefore forms a useful complement to other writers. Chap. ix., on "Italy," and chap. x., on "The German Revolution," are excellent accounts of "1848" in those two countries.

H. A. L. Fisher. *The Value of Small States.* Oxford Pamphlets. 2d.

E. Levett. *Europe since Napoleon.* 1913. Blackie. 3s. 6d.

A useful little text-book.

The Cambridge Modern History. Vols. ix., x., xi., xii. 16s. net per vol.

Indispensable for knowledge of the facts of the period.

R. Nisbet Bain. *Slavonic Europe, 1447–1796.* 1908. 5s. 6d. net.

Chap. xviii. gives a good account of the partitions of Poland.

Bolton King. *A History of Italian Unity.* 2 vols. 1899. 24s. net.

Bolton King. *Mazzini.* 1903. Dent, Temple Biographies. 4s. 6d. net.

Bismarck. *Reflections and Reminiscences.* 2 vols. 1898. Smith Elder.

Out of print. To be bought second-hand.

Bülow. *Imperial Germany.* 1914. Cassell. 2s. net.

The last two are indispensable for a true understanding of the principles which underlie the German Empire.

T. J. Lawrence. *Principles of International Law.* 1910. 12s. 6d. net.

A useful text-book. See also *Cambridge Mod. Hist.* vol. xii. chap. xxii.

CHAPTER III

GERMANY

"The Germans are vigorously submissive. They employ philosophical reasonings to explain what is the least philosophic thing in the world, respect for force and the fear which transforms that respect into admiration."—MADAME DE STAEL (1810).

"Greatness and weakness are both inseparable from the race whose powerful and turbid thought rolls on—the largest stream of music and poetry at which Europe comes to drink."—ROMAIN ROLLAND (*Jean Christophe*).

§ 1. *The German State.*—The German Nation is one of the oldest in Europe : the German State is almost the youngest—of the great States quite the youngest.

Englishmen sometimes wonder why there are so many Royal princes in Germany—why it is that when a vacant throne has to be filled, or a husband to be found for a princess of royal standing, Germany seems to provide such an inexhaustible choice. The reason is that Germany consisted, until recently, not of one State but of a multitude of States, each of which had a court and a dynasty and sovereign prerogatives of its own. In 1789, at the outbreak of the French Revolution, there were 360 of these States of every sort and size and variety. Some were Kingdoms, like Prussia, some were Electorates, like Hanover (under our English George III.), some were Grand Duchies, some were Bishoprics, some were Free Cities, and some

75

were simply feudal estates in which, owing to the absence of a central authority, noble families had risen to the rank of independent powers. These families were the descendants of those " robber-barons " whose castles on the Rhine and all over South and West Germany the tourist finds so picturesque. Prince William of Wied, the first Prince of Albania, is a member of one of them, and is thus entitled to rank with the royalties of Europe : the father-in-law of ex-King Manoel of Portugal, the Prince of Hohenzollern-Sigmaringen, a branch of the Kaiser's own family, is another familiar recent instance. And every one remembers Prince Albert of Saxe-Coburg-Gotha, the husband of Queen Victoria.

In 1789 the possibility of a German National State was so remote that Germans had not even begun to dream of one. Each little Principality was jealously tenacious of its local rights, or, as we should say, of its vested interests, as against the common interests of Germany. Most of them were narrow and parochial in their outlook ; and the others, the more broad-minded, were not national but cosmopolitan in spirit. To the tradition of municipal thinking, which had lasted on uninterruptedly in the Free Cities of Germany from the Middle Ages, Germany owes the excellence of her municipal government to-day. To the broad and tolerant humanism of her more enlightened courts, such as Weimar and Brunswick, we owe the influences that shaped the work of Goethe and of Lessing, two of the greatest figures in European thought and letters.

Into these peaceful haunts of culture and parochialism Napoleon, with the armies and the ideas of Revolutionary France, swept like a whirlwind, breaking up the old settled comfortable life of the cities and countryside. One of the greatest of German writers, the Jew Heine, has described in a wonderful passage what the coming of Napoleon meant to the inhabitants of a little German Principality. It is worth transcribing at some length, for it gives the whole colour and atmosphere of the old local life in Western Germany, which has not even yet entirely passed away. The speaker is an old soldier giving reminiscences of his boyhood:

" Our Elector was a fine gentleman, a great lover of the arts, and himself very clever with his fingers. He founded the picture gallery at Düsseldorf, and in the Observatory in that city they still show a very artistic set of wooden boxes, one inside the other, made by himself in his leisure hours, of which he had twenty-four every day.

" In those days the Princes were not overworked mortals as they are to-day. Their crowns sat very firmly on their heads, and at night they just drew their nightcaps over them, and slept in peace, while peacefully at their feet slept their peoples; and when these woke up in the morning they said, ' Good morning, Father,' and the Princes replied, ' Good morning, dear children.'

" But suddenly there came a change. One morning when we woke up in Düsseldorf and wanted to say, ' Good morning, Father,' we found our Father gone, and a kind of stupefaction over the whole city. Everybody felt as though they were going to a funeral, and people crept silently to the market-place and read a long proclamation on the door of the City Hall. It was grey weather, and yet thin old tailor Kilian stood in his alpaca coat, which he kept for indoor use only, and his blue woollen stockings hung down so that his miserable little bare legs were visible above them and his thin lips were trembling, while he murmured the words of the proclamation. A veteran soldier at his side read somewhat louder, and at every few words a tear trickled down into his honest white beard. I stood by him and cried too, and asked him why we were crying. And then he told me : ' The Elector expresses you his gratitude '—then he went on reading, and at the words ' for your loyal and trusted obedience, and releases you from your duties,' his tears broke out afresh. . . . While we were reading, the Elector's arms were being taken down from the City Hall, the whole place became as terrifyingly quiet as though there were going to be an eclipse of the sun, and all the City Councillors went about hanging their heads as though no one had any more use for them. . . .

" When I woke up next morning, the sun was shining as usual, drums were beating in the streets, and when I came down to breakfast and said good-morning to my father I heard how the barber had whispered to him while he was shaving him that the new Grand Duke Joachim was to receive the homage of his subjects at the City Hall to-day, that he came of a very good family and had been given the Emperor Napoleon's sister in marriage, and had really a very good presence, and wore his fine black hair in curls, and would shortly enter the city in state and would certainly please all the ladies. Meanwhile, the drumming continued in the street, and I went and stood outside the door and watched the French troops marching in, those glorious happy Frenchmen, who marched through the world with songs and shining sabres, the gay firm-set faces of the Grenadiers, the bear-skins, the tricolour cockades, the gleaming bayonets, the merry skilful horsemen, and the huge great drum-major with his silver-embroidered uniform, who could throw his drum-stick with its gilt button up to the first floor, and his eyes up even to the girls in the second floor windows. I was pleased that we were to have soldiers billeted on us—my mother was not—and I hurried to the

market-place. There everything was quite different now.
The world looked as if it had had a new coat of paint. A
new coat-of-arms was hanging on the City Hall, the iron
railings on the balcony were covered with tapestry hangings,
French Grenadiers were standing sentry, the old City
Councillors had put on new faces, and were wearing Sunday
clothes, and looked at one another in French and said
' Bon jour,' ladies were looking out of all the windows,
curious bystanders and smart soldiers thronged the square,
and I and the other boys climbed on to the big horse of
the Elector's statue and looked down on the gay crowd." [1]

Napoleon and his French soldiers, " marching through
the world with songs and shining sabres," brought the
Germans more than this happy thrill of excitement and a
supply of new and more elegant princes. They brought
them that which gave strength to their own right arm—
the spirit of Nationality. " The soul of the German
people," says a recent German writer, " has always lain
very deep down, and has seldom come to the surface to
become the spirit of the time and to inspire the movements
of the world. Hardly ever except in times of the deepest
adversity has it come to the surface : but then it has
claimed its rights, or rather, discovered its duties." [2]
Napoleon, by humiliating her, laid bare the soul of Germany,
as Germany herself has laid bare the soul of Belgium to-day.
His arrogant pretensions roused the Germans as they had
never been roused since the days of the Reformation ;
while at the same time his attempts to secure the support
of the bigger German principalities by enlarging them at
the expense of the smaller, simplified the map and laid the

[1] Heine, *Collected Works*, i. 228 (Book *Le Grand*).
[2] Daab's Preface to Paul de Lagarde, *German Faith, German
Fatherland, German Culture*, p. vi. (Jena, 1913).

foundations of a United Germany. The thinkers and
dreamers of Germany, stung at last into a sense of political
reality, awoke from their dreams of cosmopolitanism and
devoted their powers to the needs of the German nation.

The years between 1806 and 1813, between the disastrous
battle of Jena and the overwhelming victory of Leipzig,
are the greatest years in German history. Shaking off
the torpor and the prejudices of centuries the German
nation arose and vanquished its oppressors.

But with the twilight of that glorious day the bats
returned. The defeat of Napoleon was not only the defeat
of French domination but the defeat of the French Revolution, and of the principles of Democracy and Nationality
which inspired it. The unity of spirit which the Germans
had achieved on the battlefield they were unable to transform after the victory into a unity of government or
institutions. The Congress of Vienna, which redrew the
map of Europe after the Revolutionary wars, did so, not
in accordance with the principle of nationality or the
wishes of the peoples of Europe but according to what was
called "legitimacy," that is to say, the interests of the
princes. There was only one idealist at the Conference,
the Russian Emperor Alexander, and he was put off with
empty phrases.

For Germany the result of the Conference was the re-
establishment, in smaller numbers and with larger units of
territory, of the old undemocratic principalities, and of a
Confederation embodying their dynastic interests. Several
of the larger States, such as Bavaria, Würtemberg, Saxony,
and Hanover, which Napoleon had raised to the status of
kingdoms, were confirmed in their new dignities, and the
kingdom of Prussia, the largest of them all, acquired, out
of the débris of the old Archbishopric of Cologne and other

GERMANY
1815
English Miles
0   50   100   150   200

——— Boundary of the German Confederation, 1815
———— Boundary of the North German Confederation, 1866.

ITAL —
Palatine
THUR. =
Thuringian States.
HOH. =
Hohenzollern.
OLD. =
Oldenburg.
S.L.=Schaumburg–Lippe.
ANH=Anhalt.
W=Waldeck.
BRUNS. =
Brunswick
SCHB. =
Schwarzburg-Sonderhausen & Schwarzburg-Rudolstadt.
L. = Lippe.
H.C. =
Hesse –Cassel.
H.N.=
Hesse-Nassau.

[PRUSSIA]
[AUSTRIA]

GERMANY IN 1815.

G

small ecclesiastical and temporal States, the important provinces of Westphalia and the Rhineland, which have made possible for her the industrial growth of the last half century. Cologne, Düsseldorf, Elberfeld, Essen, and other great industrial centres of Western Germany will next year be celebrating the centenary of their Prussian connection. But the chief State in the Confederation and its undisputed head was Austria, which had for centuries enjoyed the prestige of supremacy over the German States ; and it was the Austrian statesman Metternich who was mainly responsible for the Vienna settlement.

The German Confederation of 1815–1866 went far outside the boundaries of modern Germany. It included lands belonging to three non-German monarchs. The King of Holland was a member of it in virtue of the Dutch provinces of Limburg and Luxemburg ; the King of Denmark for the Duchies of Schleswig and Holstein ; and the Emperor of Austria (who, then as now, ruled over Hungary, Austrian Poland, and the Southern Slav provinces) for Bohemia, Moravia, and German-speaking Austria up to and beyond Vienna. The Confederation was in fact in no sense a national State, and was never intended to be so. It was a loosely knit assortment of principalities and free cities. Germany was still broken up and divided in a manner almost inconceivable to the inhabitants of an old-established unity like Great Britain or France. At least five different kinds of money, for instance, were in use in the different States of the Confederation, and, as stamp-collectors know, the postal system was bewildering in its complexity. More important was the deep gulf between different parts of the country due to religious divisions. The Reformation, which left England with a National Church, left Germany hopelessly divided ; and the division between the Protestants in the north and east, and the Catholics in the west and south, is still, half a century after the establishment of the United Empire, a source of difficulty.

Yet the Confederation has one undeniable achievement to its credit. It paved the way for German unity by facilitating the Zollverein, or Customs Union, which was extended between 1830 and 1844 to practically all the German States except those under Austrian rule. But the far-reaching importance of this development was not at that time appreciated. Western Europe was tired after the great Napoleonic struggle and was not in a mood for big designs. To all outward appearance Germany seemed to have relapsed, after the thrill and glamour of the Wars of Liberation, into the stuffy atmosphere of the old eighteenth century life. Only a very patient, a very docile, and a very philosophic and law-abiding people would have endured such an anti-climax ; and it is these qualities, together with a certain clumsiness and helplessness due to their complete inexperience of the responsibilities of a larger citizenship, which go far to explain the subsequent history of Germany.

But in the evil days after the Congress of Vienna the *idea* of German unity lived on, and formed a constant theme of discussion and speculation, like the idea of the unity of Poland and of the Southern Slavs in the present generation. The stirring memories of the Great Revolution were like a constant refrain at the back of men's minds all through that dreary time. In 1830, when the French established a Liberal Monarchy and the Belgians freed themselves from the unwelcome supremacy of Holland, there was much excitement throughout Germany. But nothing serious occurred until 1848, when the Liberal and Nationalist movement, which had been gathering force throughout the educated classes of Western Europe for a generation, at length came to a head. The whole of Germany was in a ferment, a strong Republican movement manifested itself, and in almost every one of the many capital cities there was a rising with a demand for a free constitution and parliamentary government, and for the consolidation of German national unity in accordance with the same democratic ideals. The princes had no alternative but to give way, and, as a result, local Constitutions were granted, and a national Parliament was summoned to meet at Frankfurt, to draw up a national German Constitution on democratic lines.

The task before the Frankfurt Parliament was similar to that which has confronted British statesmen several times during the last century, in framing the Dominion of Canada, the Commonwealth of Australia, and the Union of South Africa—the task of welding a number of separate State governments with the free consent of their populations into a homogeneous and democratic central authority. But in the case of an old and still largely feudal country like Germany the task was infinitely more difficult, for it could not be successful without a levelling-up of the political ideals of the backward States, such as Prussia, and the elimination of many ancient associations and dynastic interests. The Frankfurt Constitution did actually come into being, and it was nobly planned. It guaranteed to every German citizen the rights of civil liberty, equality before the law, and responsible parliamentary government, both central and local. But the mind of the German nation was not yet equal to its new responsibilities. The Frankfurt Parliament, like the first Russian Duma, was out of touch with realities ; it wasted precious time on the discussion of abstract questions of principle, and failed to meet the practical needs of the moment. While it sat and talked, the enthusiasm which had created it gradually evaporated.

Meanwhile the more reactionary States, and the princes whose prerogatives were endangered, became more and more openly hostile. All through 1849 the Parliament was losing members by defection, and by the end of the year its influence had sunk to vanishing point.

The movement which collapsed thus ignominiously was not a popular agitation in the English sense of the term : like other movements of its generation it sprang, not from the people but from the well-to-do, and its strength lay among the professional and educated classes. The Frankfurt Parliament was a predominantly middle-class assembly : lawyers and professors, always an important element in German national life, were strongly represented in it and largely responsible for its failure. Its collapse was a bitter disappointment, and drove many of its leaders into exile abroad, more particularly to the United States, where some of them, such as Carl Schurz, lived to play a noteworthy part under more democratic political institutions.

After the failure of the Frankfurt Constitution it slowly became clear to far-sighted Germans that there was only one way in which German unity could come about. If, unlike the separate provinces of Canada and South Africa, the German States would not voluntarily sink their identity in a larger whole, unity could only come through their acceptance of the supremacy of one of the existing States.

There were only two possible candidates for the supremacy, Austria and Prussia. Austria was still, at that time, as she had been for centuries, in a position of undisputed headship. But her German policy was always hampered because she had also to consider her non-German subjects. Prussia, a younger and more homogeneous State, with a better organised administration and a better disciplined people, was preparing to assert herself. In 1862, at a moment when liberalism was gathering strength in Prussia, Count Bismarck became chief Minister of the Prussian Crown and the dominating force in Prussian policy. Bismarck was a Conservative and a reactionary, wholly out of sympathy with the ideals of 1848. His immediate object was to secure the supremacy of Prussia among the German States. In the very first months of his leadership he made it clear, in a famous sentence, by what methods he hoped to achieve his end. "The great questions are to be settled," he told the Prussian Diet, with a scornful hit at the Confederation, "not by speeches and majority resolutions, but by blood and iron."

He was not long in translating words into action. In 1864 the King of Denmark died, and difficulties at once arose as to the succession to the Duchies of Schleswig and Holstein, which still belonged to the German Confederation. Austria and Prussia intervened jointly in the name of the Confederation, and, as a result, the Duchies were separated from Denmark, Schleswig being administered by Austria and Holstein by Prussia. The object of this rather clumsy plan, which originated with Bismarck, was to create difficulties which would enable him to pick a quarrel with Austria. In 1866 this manœuvre proved successful. Bismarck goaded Austria into war and succeeded, after a six weeks' campaign, in expelling her from the German State system, following this up by rounding off her own dominions with the annexation of a number of the smaller pro-Austrian States, amongst them the kingdom of Hanover. His victory also had the effect of completely checking the growing agitation for the establishment of responsible government in Prussia.[1]

[1] On this point see Bismarck's *Recollections*, and the good short account in Powicke's *Bismarck*.

Having made Prussia supreme in Germany, Bismarck was now in a position to solve the problem of German unity. He resolved to employ the same well-tried method. In 1870 the somewhat high-handed manner of Napoleon III. made it possible for him to bring about a war between the German States and France, in which Germany, under Prussian leadership, was completely victorious. In the flush of their success, after the capture of Paris in January 1871, the lesser States of Germany agreed to enter into a Federal Union under Prussian supremacy and to accept the King of Prussia as its head, with the title of Emperor.

Thus, at length, Germany became a National State, with a national constitution. The term Empire is misleading, for to English ears it suggests the government of dependencies. Germany is not an Empire in that sense : she is a Federation, like the United States and Switzerland, of independent States which have agreed to merge some of their prerogatives, notably the conduct of foreign affairs and of defence, in a central authority. Since some of these independent States were, and still are, monarchies, a higher title had to be provided for the Chief of the Federation. An ace, as it were, was needed to trump the kings. After much deliberation the title Emperor was agreed upon ; but it is noteworthy that the Kaiser is not " the Emperor of Germany " : he bears the more non-committal title of " German Emperor."

The German Imperial Constitution, devised by Bismarck in 1871, falls far short of the Frankfurt experiment of 1848. It does indeed provide for the creation of a Reichstag, or Imperial Parliament, elected by all male citizens over twenty-five. But the Reichstag can neither initiate legislation nor secure the appointment or dismissal of Ministers. In the absence of ministerial responsibility to Parliament, which is the mainspring of our English Constitutional system, the Reichstag might be described as little more than an advisory body armed with the power of veto. Like the English Parliament in the days of Charles I.'s ship-money, the Reichstag could in the last resort refuse supplies, and so bring the machinery of government to a standstill. But this situation has never yet arisen or seemed likely to arise. The Government has ridden the Reichstag with a strong hand, turning awkward corners by concessions to the various groups in turn, and the Reichstag has responded to this treatment. Bismarck " took his majorities where he could get them " ; and Prince Bülow's book contains some illuminating pages about the clever methods which that statesman adopted to " manage " his Parliaments.

Above the Reichstag is the Bundesrat or Federal Council, on which all the Federated States are represented, Prussia having seventeen members as against forty-two from the other States. The Bundesrat sits in secret ; its members are selected by the different State Governments and vote according to instructions received. All Bills originate in the Bundesrat before they are submitted to the Reichstag, and are re-submitted to the Bundesrat, to be passed or vetoed, after alteration in the Reichstag. The twenty-six members of the German Federation represented in the Bundesrat comprise four kingdoms (Prussia, Bavaria, Würtemberg, and Saxony), a number of Grand Duchies and smaller ducal States, three Free Cities (Hamburg, Lübeck, and Bremen), and the Imperial Territory of Alsace-Lorraine. All these (except the last named) preserve their own local Parliaments and institutions, and the second largest, Bavaria, even preserves in peace-time, like the British self-governing Dominions, her own military organisation and has also her own postal system. But Prussia in size, influence, and

military strength is by far the most important, and for
practical purposes her power preponderates over that of
all the other States combined. The real control of legislation naturally lies with the State which controls two-fifths
of the votes in the Bundesrat, where legislation is initiated
and can be vetoed; it is wielded by the Kaiser, as King
of Prussia, and by his Imperial Chancellor, President of the
Bundesrat and always a Prussian Minister. The Imperial
Chancellor, who is the only Imperial Minister, is chosen by
the Kaiser and is responsible to him alone : he countersigns
all the Kaiser's orders and edicts, and has the function,
it may be added, of explaining away his indiscretions.

It is inevitable, under these circumstances, that the policy
and legislation of the central government should largely
reflect Prussian views and ideals. On the other hand, the
temper of the rest of Germany must always be kept in mind.
As Prince Bülow, the late Imperial Chancellor, says : " If
the Empire is governed without reference to Prussia, ill-will
towards the Empire will grow in that country. If Prussia
is governed without reference to the Empire, then there is
the danger that mistrust and dislike of the leading State
will gain ground in non-Prussian Germany. . . . The art
of governing in our country will always have to be
directed chiefly towards maintaining the harmony between
Germany and Prussia, in the spirit as well as in the
letter." [1]

Why should the government of Germany be such an
" art " ? And why should there be any difficulty in maintaining a harmonious spirit between Prussia and non-
Prussian Germany ? To answer these questions we must
widen the scope of our inquiry. So far we have considered
only the growth and development of the German State.

[1] *Imperial Germany*, pp. 191-192.

It is now time to turn from the German State to the German people.

§ 2. *The Real Germany.*—The difficulty of establishing German Unity has lain in the fact that there have really always been two Germanies, different in history, in temper, in ideals, and in their stages of development in civilisation. There has been Prussia, or North-Eastern Germany; and there has been the real Germany, the Germany of the South and West. It is only since 1870, and especially within the reign of the present Kaiser, that, through education and common experience, the two have become fused into one; but even now, beneath the uniform surface of German life and public opinion, there is a great inner distinction.

Let us take what we have called the real Germany first. This Germany, the Germany of the Rhine country, of Frankfurt and Heidelberg and Cologne and Nüremberg, is the Germany which so many Englishmen know and admire. This Germany is an integral part of the civilisation of Western Europe, and is closely akin to ourselves. It has grown and developed alongside with France and the Netherlands and England, sharing in all the great spiritual and social movements of the West. It has passed, with them, through the Middle Ages, the Revival of Learning, the Reformation, and the long struggle against the domination of France. Its famous cities with their Cathedrals and Town Halls breathe the same proud, free, municipal spirit as those of their great neighbours in the Netherlands, Ghent, Antwerp, Louvain, Bruges, Ypres and the rest. Its scholars and teachers, poets, painters, and musicians, from Luther to Goethe, have made their special German contribution to the civilised life of the West—a contribution as great and as unique as that of Renaissance Italy or Elizabethan England.

Its people are very similar in character to their neighbours of kindred stock. As industrious as the Dutch, as persevering as the Scotch, as steady and good-hearted as the English, good workers, good citizens, devoted in their family relations, they have found it easy to live at peace and on a good understanding with their neighbours, and when they have migrated abroad, they have by common confession made the best of settlers, both in the United States and in the British Dominions.

Yet they have developed certain characteristic qualities in their social and political life, which distinguish them sharply from their western neighbours. History, which has deprived them, until recently, of a wider citizenship, has left them timid, docile, dreamy and unpractical in just that sphere of action where Englishmen have learnt for centuries to think and to act for themselves. Patriotism with Englishmen is an instinct. We do not much care to wave flags or make speeches or sing songs about it : we assume it as the permanent background of our national life and our national consciousness. With the Germans this is not so. In Germany, partly owing to German history, partly owing to the constitution of the German mind, patriotism is not an instinct but an *idea*. Now ideas do not grow up in men's minds by a natural process. They have to be implanted. The Germans have needed to be *taught* to be patriotic. The makers of German patriotism a century ago were teachers and philosophers. They did not simply appeal to their patriotic instincts, as Englishmen would have done : they argued the point and *proved* that Germany was worth fighting for : they founded a school of patriotic German philosophy. There are few more curious documents in history, or more instructive for the light they shed on future events, than the famous *Speeches to the German*

Nation addressed to his fellow-countrymen by the philosopher Fichte in 1808, when his country was under the heel
of Napoleon. They are not speeches at all, but philosophical
lucubrations, discussing in abstract terms the whole subject
of the nature of patriotism and of Germany's right to exist
as a nation. One argument, for instance, on which he lays
great stress, is that Germany is marked out to be a great
political power because of the peculiar excellence of the
German language, which he shows to his satisfaction to be
superior to French, Italian, and other Latin languages.
Again, he points out that there is no word in the German
language for "character" (*Karakter*), a word borrowed
from the Greek; the reason is, he explains, that there is no
need for one, because to have character and to be German
are the same thing—a curious foretaste of the German
arrogance of to-day. Yet these speeches, which, issued
in England at such a crisis, would have found no readers,
reverberated through Germany and helped to create the
self-confident spirit which freed her from the invader.
Then, as now, under the inspiration of ideas which they had
accepted from professors and philosophers, Germans fought
for the German language and for German culture. But
whereas in 1814 they fought to preserve them, in 1914 they
are fighting to impose them.

Just as patriotism in Germany is wholly different from
what it is in England, so also is democracy, and all those
elements in the national life which feed and sustain it.
British democracy does not depend upon our popular
franchise or on any legal rights or enactments. It depends
upon the free spirit and self-respect of the British people.
We have been accustomed for centuries to the unrestrained
discussion of public affairs; and we treat our governors
as being in fact, as they are in name, our " ministers " or

servants. There is a force called public opinion which, slow though it may be to assert itself, British statesmen have been taught by experience to respect. It is as true of British as it is of American democracy that "you can fool half the people all the time; and you can fool all the people half the time; but you cannot fool all the people all the time." But the German people, as a people, lacks this irreplaceable heritage of political self-respect. It has never yet dared to tread the path of democracy without leading strings. It has not yet learned to think for itself in politics, or formed the habit of free discussion and practical criticism of public affairs. This is the vital fact which must be borne in mind in all comparisons between German and British democracy. The Germans have a Parliament, elected by Universal Male Suffrage. But this Parliament is powerless to control policy, because the nation behind it does not give it sufficient support. It is because of the absence of the driving force of a public opinion in Germany that the German people submit complacently to the infringements on political liberty which form part of the normal *régime* of German life—the domineering arrogance of officers and officials, the restraints upon the Press and the shameless manufacture of news and inspiration of opinion from official sources, the control of the Universities, the schools, and the public services by the State in the interest of "orthodox" political opinions, and the ridiculous laws which have sent editors and cartoonists to prison in scores for criticising the behaviour and utterances of the Emperor or the Crown Prince. In England and in America underground attempts are sometimes made to injure the careers of men whose opinions are considered "dangerous" by those who employ them. In Germany such interference with freedom of political thought is not the exception : it

has become the rule.   No man can make a successful career
in the public service (and education is a public service)
unless he is considered politically " orthodox " (gesin-
nungstüchtig) ;   and orthodoxy does not simply mean
abstention from damaging criticism or dangerous opinions :
it means, in practice, deference to the opinions of those who
" know better," that is, to the clique of Prussian generals
and bureaucrats who, together with the Kaiser, control the
policy of the country.

British readers who do not know Germany may think
the foregoing indictment of German political incapacity
severe.   It is not so severe as Prince Bülow's.   The portion
of the late Imperial Chancellor's book which deals with
domestic policy opens with these crushing sentences :
" The history of our home policy, with the exception of a
few bright spots, is a history of political mistakes.   Despite
the abundance of merits and great qualities with which
the German nation is endowed, political talent has been
denied it. . . . We are not a political people."   A page or
two later he goes even further and quotes with approval
a dictum that the Germans are " political donkeys."   That
a modern statesman should think this of his fellow-countrymen is remarkable enough ;   that he should say it outright
is a still more remarkable proof of his unshakeable belief
in their submissiveness.   Therein lies the whole tragedy
of the present situation.   The German people, so kindly
and, alas ! so docile, is suffering, not for its sins, but for its
deficiencies ;   not for its own characteristic acts or natural
ambitions, but for what it has too tamely allowed others,
Prussian statesmen and soldiers, with alien ideals and an
alien temper, to foist upon it, until it has become an integral part of its natural life and consciousness.   Germany
has been indoctrinated and Prussianised not only into

acquiescence, but into sympathy with the policy of its rulers.

§ 3. *Prussia.*—This brings us to the consideration of the second and more powerful of the two Germanies—namely, Prussia. In order to understand Prussia and the Prussian spirit we must plunge ourselves into an atmosphere wholly different from that of the Germany that has just been described. The very names of the two countries mark the measure of the difference. Germany means the country of the Germans, as England means the country of the English. But the name Prussia commemorates the subjugation and extinction by German conquerors and crusaders from the west of the Prussians or Bo-Russians, a tribe akin to the Letts and Lithuanians. The old Duchy of Prussia, which now forms the provinces of East and West Prussia at the extreme North-East of the present German Empire, consisted of heathen lands colonised or conquered, between the thirteenth and sixteenth centuries, by a great religious and military organisation known as the " Knights of the Teutonic Order." While Southern and Western Germany was passing, with the rest of Western Europe, through the transition between mediaeval and modern Europe, what is now North-Eastern Germany was still in a wholly primitive stage of development, and the Knights of the Teutonic Order, with crusading fervour, were spreading Christianity and German " culture " by force of arms, converting or repelling the Slavonic population and settling German colonists in the territory thus reclaimed for civilisation. The great British admirer of Prussia, Thomas Carlyle, in the first volume of his *Frederick the Great,* gives a vivid account of their activities in their forts or " burgs " of wood and stone, and helps us to realise what memories lie behind the struggle between German and Slav to-day, and why the word " Petersburg " has become so odious to the Russians as the name of their capital. "The Teutsch Ritters build a Burg for headquarters, spread themselves this way and that, and begin their great task. The Prussians were a fierce fighting people, fanatically anti-Christian : the Teutsch Ritters had a perilous never-resting time of it. . . . They built and burnt innumerable stockades for and against : built wooden Forts which are now stone Towns. They fought much and prevalently, galloped desperately to and fro, ever on the alert. How many Burgs of wood and stone they built in different parts, what revolts, surprisals, furious fights in woody, boggy places they had, no man counted; their life, read in Dry-asdust's newest chaotic Books (which are of endless length, among other ill qualities) is like a dim nightmare of un-intelligible marching and fighting : one feels as if the mere amount of galloping they had would have carried the Order several times round the Globe. . . . But always some preaching, by zealous monks, accompanies the chivalrous fighting. And colonists come in from Germany ; trickling in, or at times streaming. Victorious Ritterdom offers terms to the beaten Heathen; terms not of tolerant nature, but which will be punctually kept by Ritterdom." Here we see the strange stern, medieval, crusading atmosphere which lies behind the unpleasant combinations, so familiar to us to-day in France and Belgium, of Uhlans and religion, of culture and violence, of " Germanisation " and devasta-tion. When we hear the German professors of to-day preaching of the spread of German culture by the German arms, and when we feel disgust at the exaggerated religious phraseology which pervades the Kaiser's oratory and seems to accord so ill with his policy and ambitions, we must remember the peculiar origins of the Prussian State and how comparatively recent those origins are. " I have once before had occasion," said the Kaiser at Marienburg in East Prussia on June 5, 1902, " to say in this place how Marienburg, this unique Eastern bulwark, the point of departure for the culture of the lands east of the Vistula, will always be a symbol for our German mission. There is work for us again to-day. Polish arrogance wishes to lay hands on Germanism, and I am constrained to call my people to the defence of its national possessions. Here in Marienburg I proclaim that I expect all the brothers of the Order of St. John to be at my service when I call upon them to protect German ways and German customs." The Kaiser's crusading appeals are not hypocritical or consciously insincere : they are simply many centuries out of date—a grotesque medley of medieval romanticism and royal megalomania. What was possible for the warrior knights in North-East Germany five or six centuries ago is a tragic absurdity and an outrageous crime to-day among a spirited and sensitive people like the Poles—still more so in a highly civilised national State such as Belgium or France. It is an absurdity that only a theatrical monarch could conceive and a crime that only a military autocracy could attempt to enforce.

In the sixteenth century the Reformation, spreading throughout the North of Europe, undermined the basis of the Teutonic Order. The Grand Master of the time transformed himself into a Lutheran Prince holding the hereditary Duchy of Prussia as a vassal of the King of the neighbouring Slavonic State of Poland. In 1611 the Duchy was amalgamated with the territory of Brandenburg farther west, and in 1647 the enlarged Prussian territories won their emancipation from Poland. Prussia now became a distinct State, essentially German in character (as opposed to the Poles and Lithuanians on its Eastern border), but still remaining for a time outside the community of the other German States.

The union between Prussia and Brandenburg had brought Prussia under the rule of the House of Hohenzollern, which, although originally a South German family, had borne rule in Brandenburg since 1415. Under the Hohenzollerns Prussia rapidly increased in territory and influence until in 1701 the ruler of the day, the grandfather of Frederick the Great, took on himself the title of King. Under Frederick the Great, Prussia's career of conquest and aggrandisement continued. Seizing a convenient opportunity, he invaded and annexed the Austrian province of Silesia, and later joined with Austria and Russia in promoting the shameful Partition of Poland. The old conquering and " civilising " policy of the Teutonic Knights was continued, but under new conditions and in a brutal and cynical spirit which rendered it impossible of success. " The surest means of giving this oppressed nation better ideas and morals," wrote Frederick the Great, in words quoted with approval by Prince Bülow, " will always be gradually to get them to intermarry with Germans, even if at first it is only two or three of them in every village." This spirit in Prussian policy may have extinguished the ancient Prussians, but it has not yet begun to Germanise the Poles, and has gone far to de-Germanise the Alsatians. But it explains the utterances and justifies the sincerity of those who believe that to-day, as in the early days of her history, Prussia is fighting on behalf of " culture."

Prussia remains to-day, what she has been for the last two centuries, an aggressive military monarchy. " Prussia attained her greatness," says Prince Bülow, " as a country of soldiers and officials, and as such she was able to accomplish the work of German union ; to this day she is still, in all essentials, a State of soldiers and officials." Power rests in the hands of the monarch and of a bureaucracy of military and civil officials, responsible to him alone, and traditionally and fanatically loyal to the monarch who is, before all things, their War Lord.

The Prussian outlook is so foreign to Western habits of thought that it is well that we should try to understand it at its best. Prussia proper has not been rich, like the rest of Germany, in poets and imaginative writers ; but she is fortunate to-day in possessing in the greatest living Greek scholar, Professor von Wilamowitz-Moellendorff, a man who by birth and breeding is able to put the highest inter- pretation upon the aims and spirit of the Prussian State. To Wilamowitz Prussia is not only nearer and dearer than Athens. She is better, and more advanced. At the close of a wonderful address on " the glory of the Athenian Empire," in which he has employed all the resources of his wide learning to paint a picture of Ancient Greece at her best, Wilamowitz breaks into this impassioned peroration : " But one element in life, the best of all, ye lacked, noble burghers of Athens. Your sages tell us of that highest love which, freed from all bodily entanglements, spends itself on institutions, on laws, on ideas. We Prussians, a rough, much-enduring tribe of Northerners, may be compacted of harder stuff ; but we believe that love is on a higher level when the fullest devotion to an institution and an idea is inseparably linked with an entirely personal devotion to a human being ; and at least we know how warm such a love can make a loyal heart. When our children have scarce learned to fold their hands before God, we set a picture before them, we teach them to recognise the noble features ; we tell them, ' This is our good King.' Our young men, when they are of age to bear arms, look with joy and pride

on the trim garb of war, and say, ' I go in the King's coat.'
And when the nation assembles to a common political
celebration, the occasion is no Feast of the Constitution,
no Day of the Bastille, no Panathenaic Festival. It is
then that we bow in reverence and loyalty before him who
has allowed us to see with our own eyes that for which our
Fathers dreamed and yearned, before him who ever extends
the bounds of the Kingdom in Freedom, Prosperity,
and Righteousness, before his Majesty the Emperor and
King." [1]

Here, far better expressed than in the Kaiser's speeches,
we see the spirit of the Prussian Junker at its best. It
is narrow, old-fashioned, and, to democratic ears, almost
grotesque. Yet, if it survives uncorrupted by the dangers
to which progress always exposes a military caste, it will
not be easy either to crush by defeat or to transform by
humiliation.

It is among the old Prussian nobility and the large
landed proprietors in the original Prussian provinces, who
have come to be known as the " Junkers," that this spirit
prevails. They stand for the old stern repressive military
discipline and unchanging Conservatism in its extremest
form, regarding with well-founded suspicion and misgiving
symptoms of development in any direction whatsoever.
No party in Germany acquiesced more unwillingly in the
changes necessitated by her commercial and industrial
development. Even their militarism stopped short at the
Army, and it required a substantial increase in the pro-
tective tariff safeguarding their agricultural interests to
purchase their reluctant adhesion to the Kaiser's policy

[1] *Speeches and Lectures*, 3rd edition, Berlin, 1913, p. 65. The
" good King " referred to is the old Emperor William, as the address
dates from 1877.

of naval expansion. Even now the German Navy, the
pride of the commercial and industrial classes throughout
the German Empire, is regarded by them with uneasy
suspicion as a parvenu service, in which the old Prussian
influences count for less in promotion than technical skill
and practical efficiency.

The institutions of the Prussian State represent the
spirit of its ruling caste. If the German Empire is not
democratic, Prussia lags far behind it. The electoral
system in use for the Prussian Lower House is too complicated to explain here. Its injustice may be gauged from
the fact that in 1900 the Social Democrats, who actually
polled a majority of the votes, secured seven seats out of
nearly 400. The whole spirit and practice of the Government is inimical to inborn British conceptions of civil
liberty and personal rights. There is one law and code
of conduct for officers and another for civilians, and woe
betide the civilian who resists the military pretensions.
The incidents at Zabern in Alsace in 1913 are still fresh in
public memory, reinforced by evidence of a similar spirit
in German military proclamations in France and Belgium.
But it is important to realise that these incidents are not
exceptional outbursts but common Prussian practice, upheld, as the sequel to the Zabern events proved, by the
highest authority.

Prussia, and through Prussia Germany, is in effect ruled
in accordance with the wishes of the official caste: and
short of a popular rising nothing but defeat can dethrone it.
"Any one who has any familiarity at all with our officers
and generals," says an authoritative German writer, in
words that we may hope will be prophetic, "knows that
it would take another Sedan, inflicted on us instead of
by us, before they would acquiesce in the control of the

Army by the German Parliament." [1] No clearer statement
could be given as to where the real power lies in Germany,
and how stern will be the task of displacing it.

The foreign policy of Prussia has reflected the same
domineering spirit. Its object has been the increase of its
power and territory by conquest or cunning : and by the
successful prosecution of this policy it has extended Prussian
authority and Prussian influence over a large part of
Western Germany. The best way of illustrating this will
be to quote a passage from the *Recollections of Prince
Bismarck*, who directed Prussian policy from 1862 to 1890.
In 1864 trouble arose as to the succession to the Duchies
of Schleswig and Holstein on the Danish border. Prussia
had no claim whatever to the Duchies ; but she coveted
Holstein because it would give her a Western sea-board,
with the results that we all know. Bismarck describes the
arguments which he used to persuade his Royal Master to
assert his claim. " I reminded him," he writes, " that each
of his immediate predecessors had won an addition to the
Monarchy " : he then went through the history of the six
previous reigns, and ended by encouraging King William
to be worthy of his ancestors. His advice, as we have seen,
was successfully adopted.

The conquest of France in 1870, by means of the military
power of Germany under Prussian leadership, made Prussia
supreme in Germany, and the German army supreme in
Central Europe. The Treaty of Frankfurt in May 1871,
by which the new French Republic ceded to the German
Empire the two French provinces of Alsace and Lorraine,
marked the opening of a new epoch in European history,

[1] Professor Delbrück (who succeeded to the chair of history in
Berlin held so long by Treitschke), in a book published early in 1914
(*Government and the Popular Will*, p. 136).

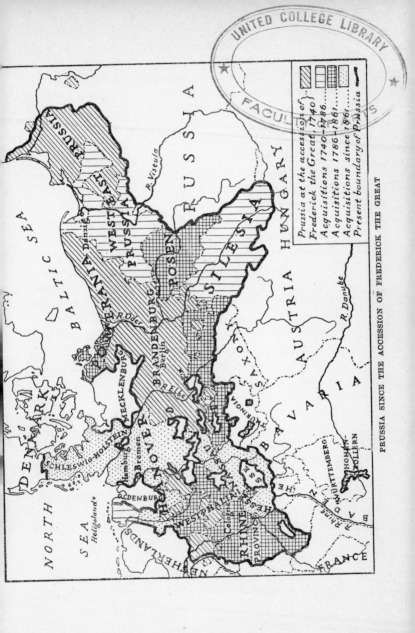

	Prussia at the accession of Frederick the Great, 1740
	Acquisitions 1740—1786
	Acquisitions 1786—1861
	Acquisitions since 1861
	Present boundary of Prussia

PRUSSIA SINCE THE ACCESSION OF FREDERICK THE GREAT

the period of the Armed Peace, which ended in 1914. It marked also the opening of a new epoch in Germany, some features of which we must now examine.

§ 4. *Germany since 1870.*—German history from 1871 to 1914 falls into two well-defined periods. During the first period, from 1871 to 1888, Germany was ruled by her Imperial Chancellor, Prince Bismarck. But the accession of the present Kaiser led to a change, not in the letter, but in the spirit of the new constitution, and since 1890, when William II. "dropped the pilot" and selected a more amenable successor, the real control of policy has lain with the Emperor.

The relations between Prince Bismarck and the old Emperor, who was over ninety when he died in 1888, form a touching passage in modern history. Although his grandson has publicly claimed for him a peculiar measure of divine inspiration, his strength lay in his implicit confidence in his great minister. Bismarck's attitude to him, as described in his *Memoirs*, is rather like that of an old family retainer who has earned by long and faithful service the right to assert his views and to pit his judgment against his master's. His one formidable antagonist was the Empress; and long experience, he tells us, enabled him to judge whether difficulties in persuading the old Kaiser to adopt a given line of policy were due to his own judgment or conceived "in the interests of domestic peace." The faithful servant had his own appropriate methods of winning his way in either case.

But with the new Kaiser the old minister's astuteness availed nothing, and the story of Bismarck's curt dismissal, after thirty-eight years of continuous service, from the post which he had created for himself, illustrates the danger of framing a constitution to meet a particular temporary situation. Bismarck, put out of action by his own machinery, retired growling to his country seat, and lived to see the reversal of his foreign policy and the exposure of Germany, through the Franco-Russian Alliance, to the one danger he always dreaded, an attack on both flanks.

Like Germany's present rulers, Bismarck was not a scrupulous man ; but unlike them he was shrewd and far-sighted, and understood the statesmen and the peoples with whom he had to deal. The main object of his foreign policy was to preserve the prestige of the German army as the chief instrument of power in Central Europe, and to allow the new Germany, after three wars in seven years, time to develop in peace and to consolidate her position as one of the Great Powers.

The situation was not an easy one ; for Germany's rapid rise to power, and the methods by which she had acquired it, had not made her popular. Bismarck's foreign policy was defensive throughout, and he pursued it along two lines. He sought to strengthen Germany by alliances, and to weaken her rivals by embroiling them with one another. The great fruit of his policy was the formation, completed in 1882, of the Triple Alliance between Germany, Austria-Hungary and Italy.

There was nothing sentimental about the Triple Alliance. The Italians hate the Austrians, whom they drove out of Venice as recently as 1866, while neither the German Austrians nor the other races in the Dual Monarchy have any love lost for the Prussians. But Bismarck decided that this combination was the safest in Germany's interest : so he set to work to play upon Austria's fear of Russia, and to embroil Italy with France in North Africa ; and his manœuvres were duly rewarded.

But this was not sufficient. Faced with the implacable

hostility of France, on account of the lost provinces, Bismarck saw danger of trouble from a French Coalition with the two remaining Great Powers, Britain and Russia. Bismarck never liked England ; but he never made his successors' mistake of despising her. He cultivated good relations, but he rejected the idea of an alliance, because, as he said, " the English constitution is not compatible with treaties of assured continuity." In other words, he fought shy of British democracy, which he felt to be an incalculable factor. This threw him back upon Russia.

The relations between the German and the Russian peoples have never been cordial. But between the reactionary bureaucracies of the Prussian and Russian governments there was a strong bond of mutual interest, which Bismarck exploited to the full. Both had popular movements to hold in check, both had stolen goods to guard in the shape of their Polish possessions, and both had an interest in the preservation of reactionary institutions. The influence of Prussia upon Russia, and of the efficient, highly-organised, relentless Prussian machine upon the arbitrary, tyrannical, but far less efficient and inhuman bureaucracy of Russia, has been wholly sinister,[1] both for Russia and for Europe. Bismarck's object, of course, was not so much to keep down the Russian revolutionaries as to check the aspirations of the Panslavists, whose designs for the liberation of the Slav nationalities, as we now see them unfolding, threaten the stability both of Prussia and of Austria-Hungary.

Throughout the 'eighties Bismarck succeeded in keeping on foot a secret understanding with Russia. How deeply he had implanted the necessity of this policy in the mind of William I. is brought home by the fact that it was the

[1] The same remark applies to the influence of Germany on Turkey.

thought uppermost in the old man's mind as he lay on his deathbed. " Never lose touch with the Tsar," whispered the old man to his grandson, when he was almost too weak to speak. " There is no cause for quarrel."

The old Emperor died in 1888. In 1890 the young Emperor " dropped the pilot." In the same year Russia refused to renew her secret treaty. In 1891 the first Franco-Russian Treaty was signed, and the diplomatic supremacy of Europe passed from the Triple Alliance to be shared between the two opposing groups with which we have been familiar in recent years.

The disappearance of Prince Bismarck marked the beginning of a new phase in German policy and in German life. The younger generation, which had come to maturity, like the Kaiser, since 1870, had never known the old divided Germany, or realised the difficulties of her statesmen. Every one wondered what use the young Kaiser would make of the great Army bequeathed to him. He was believed to be a firebrand. Few believed that, imbued with Prussian traditions, he would keep the peace for twenty-five years ; fewer still that, when he broke it, Germany would have the second Navy in the world.

But we are not now concerned with the baffling person-ality of the Kaiser himself. What is important for us here is the general attitude of mind among the German public of the Kaiser's generation, which has rendered possible the prosecution of the cherished ideas of their ruler.

The school of thought which has been steadily gaining force, under official encouragement, during the last twenty-five years is best summed up in the popular watchwords, " Germany's place in the sun " and " World - Policy " (*Weltpolitik*). These phrases embody, for Germans, who always tend to be abstract in their thinking, not only a practical policy, but a philosophy of human society and government.

This is not the place in which to analyse in detail the outlook upon life (*Weltanschauung*) of the man in the street in modern Germany. It is a confused and patchwork philosophy, drawn, consciously or unconsciously, from many quarters—from the old cosmopolitan tradition of German culture, dating from Goethe and Lessing ; from the brave and arrogant claims of Fichte and the prophets and poets of the Napoleonic era ; from the far-reaching influence of Hegel and his idealisation of the Prussian State ; from the reaction to " realism " in politics after 1848 ; from the prestige of Bismarck and the deep impression made by the apparent success of his methods and principles ; from the gifted Prussian historians, Treitschke and Sybel, who set their own interpretation upon Bismarck's work and imprinted it, by speech and pen, upon the mind of the German nation ; and from a hasty interpretation of the theories of writers like Nietzsche and Thomas Carlyle, with their exaltation of " heroes " and " supermen," their encouragements to " live dangerously," their admiration for willpower as against reason and feeling, and their tirades against legal shams, " ballot-box democracy," and flabby humanitarianism.

The practical object of the policy of *Weltpolitik* can be simply stated. It is to extend to the other continents, and to the world as a whole, the power and the prestige secured for Germany in Europe by the work of Bismarck. " When Germany had won a mighty position on a level with the older Great Powers," says Prince Bülow, " the path of international politics lay open to her. . . . In the Emperor William II. the nation found a clear-sighted, strong-willed guide who led them along the new road."

Some such expansion of German influence was inevitable from the facts of her economic development since 1871. The population of the Empire, which in 1871 was 41,000,000, has now risen to 65,000,000. The resources of the country, the neglect of which during the days of disunion had forced so many Germans to emigrate for a livelihood, have been rapidly and scientifically developed. Already in the 'eighties " Made in Germany " had become a familiar talisman, and, before the outbreak of the present war, Germany ranked with the United States as the second greatest commercial power in the world.

Simultaneously, of course, there has been a great change in the distribution of the population. In the year 1850 65 per cent, and in 1870 47 per cent of the working population were engaged in agriculture. By 1912 the proportion had sunk to 28·6 per cent.

It was inevitable also that Germany should share with the other Great Powers in the work of colonial government. The adjustment of the relations between the advanced and backward races of mankind is the greatest political task of our age ; it is a responsibility shared jointly between all the civilised States, and when in the 'eighties and 'nineties the vast regions of Africa were partitioned amongst them, Germany, late in the field, asserted her claims and received her share in the responsibility.

Rapid economic development and a colonial empire— what was there in these to cause hostility between Germany and Great Britain ? The United States have passed through a similar development and have accepted a similar extension of responsibility far outside their own continent. America is a great, a growing, and a self-respecting Power ; yet Americans see no ground for that inevitable conflict of interests between their country and Great Britain which

forms the theme of so many German books, from Prince
Bülow's candid self-revelations down to less responsible
writers like Bernhardi.

The explanation lies in the nature of German thought
and ambitions. When Germans speak of " a place in the
sun," they are not thinking of the spread of German trade,
the success of German adventure or enterprise, or of the
achievements of Germans in distant lands. They are
thinking of the extension of the German State. British
influence beyond the seas has been built up during the last
four centuries by the character and achievements of British
pioneers. Downing Street has seldom helped, often
hindered, and generally only ratified the accomplished
facts of British settlement and influence. That is not the
Prussian theory or the Prussian method. It is for the State
to win the territory, and then to set the people to work
there, on lines laid down from above. The individual
Englishman, when he goes out to colonise, carries England
with him, as a part of his personality. Not so the German,
at least on the Prussian theory. " The *rare case* super-
vened," says Prince Bülow,[1] of an instance typical of the
building up of the British Empire, " that the establishment
of State rule *followed and did not precede* the tasks of colonis-
ing and civilisation." The State itself, on this theory, has
a civilising mission of expansion towards which it directs
the activities of its citizens.

Under the influence of ideas such as these, Germany,
since the accession of William II., has built a Navy second
to that of Great Britain alone.

What was the purpose of the building of the German
Navy ? The German official answer is that its purpose
was the protection of German trade. " We are now

[1] *Imperial Germany*, 1st ed., p. 249.

vulnerable at sea," says Prince Bülow. " We have entrusted millions to the ocean, and with these millions, the weal and woe of many of our countrymen.   If we had not in good time provided protection for them . . . we should have been exposed to the danger of having one day to look on defence-lessly while we were deprived of them.   We should have been placed in the position of being unable to employ and support a considerable number of our millions of inhabitants at home.   The result would have been an economic crisis which might easily attain the proportions of a national catastrophe."

These words may yet prove prophetic.   But the cata-strophe will not be the result of Germany's lack of a Navy ; it will be the result of challenging the naval supremacy of Great Britain.

Prince Bülow's argument assumes, as a basis, the hostility of Great Britain.   This assumption, as we know, was un-justified ; and its persistence in the German mind can only be set down to an uneasy conscience.   The hard fact of the matter is that it is impossible for Germany or for any other Power successfully to defend her foreign trade in case of war with Great Britain.   No other Power thinks it necessary to attempt to do so, for no other Power has reason to desire or to foresee a naval conflict with Great Britain.

Ever since 1493, when the Pope divided the monopoly of traffic on the ocean between Spain and Portugal, and English mariners flouted his edict, Great Britain has stood for the policy of the Open Sea, and there is no likelihood of our abandoning it.   The German official theory of the purpose of their Navy, with its suspicious attitude towards British sea-power, was, in effect, a bid for supremacy, inspired by the same ideas which made the German army, under Bismarck, supreme in Central Europe. The Kaiser's speeches on naval matters, notably his famous declaration that " our future is on the water," provide an official confirmation, if one were needed, of the real nature of Germany's naval ambitions.

But what right, it may be asked, has Great Britain to this naval supremacy ? Why should we, more than any other Power, claim one of the elements for our own ? Has not Germany some reason to be jealous ? Why should we not allow her, together with ourselves, " a place on the Ocean " ?

The answer to this lies in the character of the British Empire. One quarter of the human race live under the Union Jack, scattered throughout the oceans and controlled from a small island in the Western seas. For Great Britain, alone among the States of the world, naval supremacy, and nothing less, is a daily and hourly necessity. India realised this truth recently in a flash when, after generations of silent protection by British sea-power, German shells fell one night at Madras. Any Power that challenges the naval supremacy of Great Britain is quarrelling, not with the British Government or the British people, but with the facts of history, of geography, and of the political evolution of the world. The British Empire has not been built up, like the German, by the work of statesmen and thinkers ; it is not the result, as Germans think, of far-seeing national policy or persistent ambition and " greed." It has slowly taken shape, during the last four centuries, since intercourse was opened up by sea between the different races of mankind, in accordance with the needs of the world as a whole. Its collapse, at the hands of Germany or any other Power, would not mean the substitution of a non-British Empire for a British. It would inaugurate a period of chaos in all five continents of the world.

The rulers and people of Germany, who counted on the " decadence " of Great Britain and the disintegration of her unorganised Empire, did not realise these simple facts. Their lack of perception was due partly to their political inexperience ; but a deeper reason for it lies in their wholly false estimate as to what " world-policy " and " world-empire " mean. Trained in the Prussian school, they thought of them, like soldiers, in terms of conquest, glory, and prestige. That way lies Napoleonism. None of the great Powers is wholly free from blame on this score. But until Germans realise, as the other Powers are slowly realising, that the true basis of Empire is not a love of glory but a sense of responsibility towards backward peoples, it will be hard to readmit them into the comity of the Great Powers. Only a sense of common purposes and ideals, and of joint responsibility for world-problems, can make the Concert of Europe a reality.

Such is the general attitude of mind among the German public of the younger generation. Let us now turn to the effect of this new outlook upon the political parties and groupings.

The chief result has been the extinction in Germany, as a political force, of the great liberal movement of the mid-nineteenth century which in England, France, and other Western countries has grown and developed during the last generation along lines corresponding to the needs of the new century. The younger generation of middle-class Germans, indoctrinated with " orthodox " and " national " opinions at school and on military service, eschew the ideals which attracted their fathers and grandfathers in 1848 ; and, although so-called " liberal," " free-thinking," and

I

Radical parties still exist, they have steadily been growing more militarist. Militarism in its new guise, bound up with ideas of industrial and commercial expansion, is far more attractive to them than in the form of the Prussian Army. The Emperor's Navy Bills were from the first more popular in commercial and industrial circles than with the old Prussian Conservatives. But as the years went on the Kaiser succeeded in converting both the Junkers to his Navy Bills and the middle classes to his Army Bills, so that by 1913, when he demanded the " great national sacrifice " of a levy of 50 million pounds by a tax, not on income, but on property, there as no difficulty whatever about " managing " the Reichstag. " The Army Bill of 1913," says Prince Bülow, " met with such a willing reception from all parties as had never been accorded to any requisition for armaments on land and sea. . . . So far as man can tell, every necessary and justifiable Army and Navy Bill will always be able to count on a safe Parliamentary majority." [1]

Prince Bülow's "safe Parliamentary majority" means, of course, a majority sufficient to outvote the Social Democrats, with whom every German Government has to reckon as a permanent opposition.

So far we have left the Social Democrats out of the picture. It was necessary to do this, in discussing German policy and the relation between the German Government and Reichstag opinion ; for the German Government itself habitually leaves them out of the picture. Hitherto in Germany, so far as opinion on political questions has mattered at all, it is upper- and middle-class opinion that has counted, as it counted in England up to fifty years ago. To the German Government and to the ordinary educated

[1] *Imperial Germany*, p. 169.

German the Social Democratic party, though it numbers
in its voting ranks over 4 million German workmen and
others, does not represent German opinion at all : it represents something un-German and anti-German—a public
enemy. Between the Social Democrats and the rest of
society a great gulf is fixed, across which no intercourse is
possible : as the pioneers who attempted to introduce the
Workers' Educational Association into Germany found,
such intercourse is forbidden from either direction. The
Social Democrats are the " Red Danger," " men who," in
the Kaiser's words, are " the enemies of Empire and Fatherland," and " unworthy " (except, of course, in war-time)
" to bear the name of Germans." We must go back a
hundred years in English history to realise the depth of the
animosity between the Social Democratic party and the
rest of German society. " The word Radical," says an
English historian, " conveyed a very different meaning in
1816 to what it does now. . . . The hands of the Radicals
were supposed to be against every man, and every man's
hand was against them. Scott, when he talks of rebels
in arms, always styles them Radicals. ' Radicalism is a
spirit,' wrote the Vicar of Harrow in 1820, ' of which the
first elements are a rejection of Scripture, and a contempt of all the institutions of your country, and of
which the results, unless averted by a merciful Providence, must be anarchy, atheism, and universal ruin.' " [1]
The Vicar of Harrow in 1820 very fairly sums up the
substance of innumerable German speeches, pamphlets,
and election addresses in 1912 on the subject of the Social
Democrats.

How is this extraordinary position maintained ? How
is it possible that in a modern, largely industrial com-

---

[1] Spencer Walpole, *History of England*, vol. i. p. 348.

munity, the representatives of working-class opinion should be regarded as public enemies ?

The chief reason lies, of course, in the fact that the German Empire is not a democracy and is not governed by ministers responsible to Parliament. The immense numbers and rapid growth of the Social Democrats have therefore not really been a menace to the Government. In fact, it has even been held in some quarters that it has been to the interest of the German Government, which is based on the Prussian military caste, to manœuvre the Social Democrats into an extreme position and then to hold them up as a terrible example of what democracy means. " This," they can tell the German people, " is the alternative to Prussian rule." A dangerous policy, it may be argued, for the Social Democrats may some day secure a majority in the Reichstag. The Prussian answer to this is that, without a redistribution of seats, this is barely conceivable ; and that, were it to take place, the Reichstag would promptly be dissolved for new elections on a narrower franchise. Bismarck himself contemplated this course, and his successors would not shrink from it.

Another reason why it has been possible for the Government to ignore the Social Democrats has been the absence of a practical alternative programme on the part of the Social Democrats themselves. " If I had to make out a school report for the Social Democratic Movement," said Prince Bülow in the Reichstag on one occasion, " I should say, ' Criticism, agitation, discipline, and self-sacrifice, I. a ; positive achievements, lucidity of programme, V. b.' " The taunt is not undeserved. The Socialist Movement in Germany has suffered, like so many German movements, through a rigid adherence to logical theories. Under the leadership of old revolutionary thinkers like Bebel it has failed to adapt itself to the facts of modern German life. The vague phrases of its republican programme, survivals from a past epoch of European thought, have attracted to it a large mass of inarticulate discontent which it has never been able to weld into a party of practical reformers. In the municipal sphere and in the field of Trade Unionism, under the education of responsibility, German Socialism can show great achievements ; but in national policy it has been as helpless as the rest of the German nation.

What effect, it will be asked, is the war of 1914 likely to have on the German working-class movement ?   In 1848 middle-class Germany made its stand for democracy.   May we hope for a similar and more successful movement, in the direction of Western ideals and methods of government, from working-class Germany as a result of 1914 ?

It is a tempting prophecy ; but the outlook is not propitious. Germany, Prussian and South German, noble, bourgeois, and working class, has rallied round the Emperor in this crisis of national history, as the brutal and cynical directors of German policy calculated that she would.   For the Social Democratic Movement the war comes with a peculiar appeal. It is a war against Russia, a country about which the German workman knows little and understands less, but which he considers to be the home of a reaction far blacker than that of his own country. A war of aggression against the Western Powers would have found the Social Democrats divided. By representing Russia as the aggressor and the Western Powers as the shameless allies of the " Mongol," German diplomacy, more successful within than without, made certain of enlisting Socialist support.

Moreover, the Socialists too have to pass through a natural reaction from their refusal to recognise the forces

of Nationality—from Utopian dreams of international
action by the peoples across the barriers of separate governments. For the first time in the history of the party,
German Socialism has been allowed to be patriotic. It is
an exhilarating and heartening experience, and it is certain
to leave an indelible mark upon the spirit of the movement.
The great party organisation, hitherto confined to the
sterile work of agitation, is being used to cope with the
many problems created by the war ; and this work, rather
than revolutionary agitation, is likely to occupy it for some
time to come.

A veil has fallen upon Germany : German books and
papers are stopped at our ports : we cannot know through
what thoughts the German nation is passing. But as we
look with the mind's eye across the North Sea, past de-
vastated Belgium to the populous towns of industrial
Germany, we see a people skilful, highly instructed, and
mechanically intelligent, yet equally devoid either of
personal initiative or of great and inspiring leadership.
Two generations of Prussian education have left German
public life practically empty of names of more than local
reputation. Great changes are needed—a change of
institutions and a change of spirit ; yet whence this will
come we cannot divine. Only, as democrats, we can say
with confidence that if the true spirit of the German people
is to be liberated from its long imprisonment, its freedom
must be won, not from without, but from within. Not
Europe but only the Germans can make Germany herself
again.

BOOKS

1. German History

Bryce. *Holy Roman Empire.* (Deals with mediaeval Germany, but also contains a most interesting final chapter on Germany in the Nineteenth Century, written in 1873.) 1904. (7s. 6d.)

Carlyle. *Frederick the Great,* vol. i. (Best account in English of the earlier history of Prussia.) (2s. 6d.)

H. A. L. Fisher. *Napoleonic Statesmanship : Germany.* 1903. (12s. 6d.) (Germany in the Napoleonic era.)

Seeley. *Life of Stein.* 1878. 3 vols. (30s.) (The standard work in English on reorganisation of Prussia after Napoleon.)

Bismarck. *Reflections and Reminiscences.* (The guiding mind in Germany, 1862–1888.) 2 vols. 1898. (Can only be bought second-hand.)

Headlam. *Life of Bismarck.* 1899. (6s.) (Heroes of the Nations.)

Holland. *Germany to the Present Day.* 1913. (2s. net.) A useful short history if supplemented by other books.

Powicke. *Bismarck.* 1914. (6d.) (People's Books.) (Excellent.)

The two great modern German historians are Treitschke and Sybel, for whom see Gooch's *History and Historians in the Nineteenth Century*, pp. 140-53. Treitschke's history is not available in English : Sybel's has been translated under the title, *The Founding of the German Empire by William I.* (5 vols., New York, 1890–1891).

2. Germany under William II.

Bülow. *Imperial Germany.* 1914. (2s. net.) (The mind of the German Government.)

Saunders. *The Last of the Huns.* 1914. (1s. net.) (In spite of its objectionable title this volume, by the late correspondent of the *Times* in Berlin, is written with fairness and lucidity, and contains much valuable information.)

Henri Lichtenberger. *Germany and its Evolution in Modern Times.* 1913. (10s. 6d. net.) (Translated from the French : suggestive, especially on economic questions and on the movements of German thought.)

W. H. Dawson. *The Evolution of Modern Germany.* 1908. (5s. net.) (The best general account of modern Germany in English.)

C. Tower. *Germany of To-day.* 1913. Home University Library. (1s.) (Good.)

C. Sarolea. *The Anglo-German Problem.* (2s.) (A useful popular account of German political conditions and German policy.)

Board of Education Special Reports, vols. iii. and ix. (3s. 3d. and 2s. 7d.) Articles by Dr. M. E. Sadler on German Education.

Memoirs of Prince Hohenlohe. (Imperial Chancellor, 1894–1900.) 2 vols. 1906. (24s. net.)

The Britannica War Books. *Germany.* (2s. 6d. net.) By W. Alison Phillips and J. W. Headlam. A somewhat carelessly abridged reprint from the standard article in the *Encyclopaedia Britannica.*)

3. GENERAL BOOKS

H. S. CHAMBERLAIN. *The Foundations of the Nineteenth Century.* English translation. 2 vols. 1910. (25s. net.) (This book had an immense vogue in Germany, and was particularly recommended by the Kaiser to his subjects. It is full of interesting, if ill-founded, generalisations tending to emphasise the importance of Race and to glorify the German race.)

THOMAS. *German Literature.* (6s.)

ROBERTSON. *German Literature.* 1914. Home University Library. (1s.)

HERFORD AND OTHERS. *Germany in the Nineteenth Century.* Manchester. 1912. (2s. 6d.) Essays on different aspects of German development.

BERNHARDI. *Germany and the Next War.* 1912. (2s. net.) (The philosophy and aims of German militarism worked out.)

CRAMB. *Germany and England.* 1914. (2s. 6d. net.) (An account of Treitschke and his school of thought : interesting for the light it throws on German misconceptions about Great Britain.)

TREITSCHKE. *Selections from his Lectures on Politics.* 1914. Translated by A. L. Gowans. (2s. net.)

The writings of the following German professors will be found interesting if procurable : Oncken, Meinecke (both contributors to the *Cambridge Modern History*), Delbrück, Sombart, Erich Marcks (see his lectures on Germany in *Lectures on the History of the Nineteenth Century,* edited by Kirkpatrick, Cambridge, 1900, 4s. 6d.), Schiemann, Lamprecht, Schmoller, and F. von Liszt.

Note.—Such considered German writings as have come to hand since the outbreak of the war show little tendency to cope with the real facts of the situation, or even to seek to understand them. They seem to indicate two developments in German opinion.

(1) A great consolidation of German national unity (except, of course, in Poland and Alsace-Lorraine).

(2) A tendency to forgo the consideration of the immediate issues and to hark back in thought to 1870 or even to the Wars of Liberation. It is difficult to judge of a nation in arms from the writings of its stay-at-homes ; but no one can read recent articles by the leaders of German thought without feeling that the Germans are still, before all things and incurably, " the people of poets and philosophers," and that, by a tragic irony, it is the best and most characteristic qualities of the race which are sustaining and will continue to sustain it in the conflict in which its dreams have involved it.

CHAPTER IV

AUSTRIA-HUNGARY AND THE SOUTHERN SLAVS

" For a century past attempts have been made to solve the Eastern Question. On the day when it appears to have been solved Europe will inevitably be confronted by the Austrian Question."—ALBERT SOREL (1902).

IN April 1909, a week after the international crisis evoked by Austria's annexation of Bosnia had come to an end, I paid my first visit to Cetinje, the tiny mountain-capital of Montenegro, and was assured by the Premier, Dr. Tomanović, that the conflict had merely been postponed, not averted—a fact which even then was obvious enough. " But remember," he said, " it is a question of *Aut aut* (either, or)—either Serbia and Montenegro or Austria-Hungary. One or other has got to go, and you may rest assured that in four, or at most five, years from now there will be a European war over this very question." At the time I merely regarded his prophecy as a proof of Serb megalomania, but it has been literally fulfilled.

In 1908–1909 Austria-Hungary, with the aid of her German ally, enforced her wishes in respect of Bosnia upon a reluctant Europe ; but instead of following up this success by a determined effort to solve the Southern Slav question on an Austrian basis, she allowed the confusion to grow yearly worse confounded, and gradually created an intolerable situation from which a peaceful exit was well-nigh impossible. The actual event which precipitated the struggle, the event from which the diplomatic contest of last July, and thus the great war, first proceeded, was the assassination of the Archduke Francis Ferdinand and his wife at Sarajevo on June 28 and the consequent acute friction between Austria-Hungary and Serbia. But the murder, as will be shown later, was merely made the pretext for Austria's declaration of war. The real causes lie far deeper, and can only be properly understood on the basis of an historical survey.

My apology for inflicting so many unfamiliar details upon the reader is that the key to the whole situation lies in Austria-Hungary, and that upon the fate of its provinces and races in this war depends to a very great extent the question whether the new Europe which is to issue from this fiery ordeal is to be better than the old Europe which is crumbling in ruins before our eyes. For the moment a thick fog of war obscures this point of view; but the time will assuredly come when it will emerge in its true perspective.

In recent years it had become a cheap journalistic commonplace to refer to the coming " inevitable " struggle between Teuton and Slav, and the present war is no doubt widely regarded as proving the correctness of this theory, despite the fact that the two chief groups of Teutons are ranged on opposite sides, and that the Slavs enjoy the active support of Celts and Latins also. That such a struggle has come, is in the last resort due to the false conceptions of Nationality which underly the policy of the two central Powers, Germany and Austria-Hungary. The freedom from foreign oppression which the Germans so nobly vindicated against Napoleon has not been extended to their own subject races, the Poles, Danes, and Lorrainers ; and recent years have seen the accentuation of a conflict the germs of which may be detected as far back as the fatal crime of the Polish Partition in the eighteenth century.   The policy of Germanisation in Austria has been gradually undermined by causes which it would take too long to enumerate, but its sting has survived in the maintenance of a foreign policy which treats 26,000,000 Slavs as a mere *annexe* of militant Germanism and as " gun-fodder " for the designs of Berlin ; while in Hungary the parallel policy of Magyarisation has increased in violence from year to year, poisoning the wells of public opinion, creating a gulf of hatred between the Magyars and their subject races (the Slovaks, Roumanians, Croats, Serbs, etc.), and rendering cordial relations with the neighbouring Balkan States impossible.   Nor is it a mere accident that official Germany and official Hungary should have pursued an actively Turcophil policy ; for the same tendencies have been noticeable in Turkey, though naturally in a somewhat cruder form than farther west.   Just as the Young Turk policy of Turkification rendered a war between Turkey and the Balkan States inevitable, so the policy of Magyarisation pursued by two generations of Hungarian statesmen sowed the seeds of war between Austria and the Southern Slavs.   In the former case it was possible to isolate the conflict, in the latter it has involved the greater part of Europe in a common disaster.

The struggle centres round the Austro-Serbian dispute. Let us then attempt a brief survey of the two countries.

§ 1. *Austria and the Habsburgs.* — Let us begin with Austria-Hungary.   In this country many misconceptions prevail regarding Austria-Hungary ; nor is this surprising, for it is unique among States, and whether we regard it

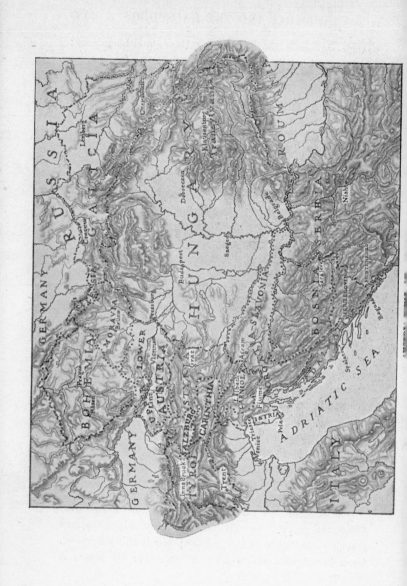

from a political, a constitutional, a racial, or a social point of view, the issues are equally complicated and difficult to sum up. With the aid of a good gazetteer it is easy enough to elicit the facts that the Austria-Hungary of to-day is a state of fifty-two million inhabitants, divided into three component parts : (a) the Empire of Austria, (b) the Kingdom of Hungary, each with subdivisions which will be referred to later, and (c) the annexed provinces of Bosnia-Herzegovina, jointly administered by the two Governments. But this bald fact is meaningless except in connection with the historical genesis of the Habsburg State.

Austria — Oesterreich — is the ancient Eastmark or frontier province, the outpost of Carlovingian power against the tribes of the east, then of the mediaeval German Empire against Slav and Magyar. Under the House of Habsburg, which first rose to greatness on the ruins of a Greater Bohemia, Austria grew steadily stronger as a distinct unit. Two famous mottoes sum up the policy of that dynasty in the earlier centuries of its existence. Austriae est Imperare Orbi Universo (Austria's it is to Rule the Universe) ran the device of that canny Frederick III., who, amid much adversity, laid the plans which prompted an equally striking epigram about his son and successor Maximilian, the " Last of the Knights "—Bella gerant alii, tu, felix Austria, nube (Let others wage war ; do thou marry, O fortunate Austria !). There were three great stages in Habsburg marriage policy. In 1479 Maximilian married the heiress of Charles the Bold, thus acquiring the priceless dowry of the Low Countries (what are now Belgium and Holland). In 1506 his son Philip added the crown of Spain and the Indies by his marriage with the heiress of Ferdinand and Isabella. In 1526, when the battle of Mohács placed Hungary at the mercy of the Turks, Maximilian's grandson

Ferdinand, in his wife's name, united Bohemia, Hungary, and Croatia with the Austrian duchies.

Henceforth for over two centuries Austria and Habsburg became the bulwark of Christendom against the Turks; though delayed by wars of religion and by the excesses of religious bigotry, they yet never lost sight of the final goal. Twice—at the beginning and at the end of this period, in 1527 and 1683—the Turks were before the very walls of Vienna, but the second of these occasions represents their final effort. In the closing years of the seventeenth and the first two decades of the eighteenth centuries the tide finally rolled back against them. Foremost among the victors stands out the great name of Prince Eugene, comrade-in-arms of our own Marlborough, whose song, " Prinz Eugen, der edle Ritter " (Prince Eugene, the noble Knight), has been sung in July and August 1914 on the streets of Vienna, just as " Marlbrook s'en va-t-en guerre " might be sung by our Belgian allies. The peace of 1718 represents Habsburg's farthest advance southwards; Belgrade and half of present-day Serbia owned allegiance to Vienna. Then came the check of 1739, when these conquests were restored to the Sultan. Due merely to incompetent generals, it need not have been permanent, had not Frederick the Great created a diversion from the north. By the time that the War of Austrian Succession and the Seven Years' War were over, that expansion southwards which had seemed so certain was irrevocably postponed. The organisation of fresh " Military Frontiers," the colonisation of waste lands in South Hungary —all was admirable so far as it went, but was already a defensive rather than an offensive measure. Meanwhile a formidable rival appeared in the shape of the Russian colossus, and the history of two centuries is dominated by

Austro-Russian rivalry in the Balkans. Here we are confronted by the first of those lost opportunities in which the history of modern Austria is unhappily so rich.

During the eighteenth century Austria became, as it were, the chief home of bureaucratic government, first under Maria Theresa, one of the greatest women-sovereigns, then under her son Joseph II. A series of " enlightened experiments " in government, typical of the age of Voltaire and of Frederick, and honestly conducted *for* the people, though never *by* the people, ended as such experiments are apt to end, in failure. The most that can be said is that the bureaucratic machine had become more firmly fixed in the groove which it was henceforth to occupy.

The failure of Joseph II. was above all due to his inability to recognise the meaning of Nationality, to his attempt to apply Germanisation as the one infallible remedy for all internal difficulties in his dominions. The idea of Nationality, already gaining strength, obtained a fresh impetus from the French Revolution. While in the west it sowed the seeds of United Italy and United Germany, which the nineteenth century was to bring to fruition, in the Balkans it stirred waters which had seemed dead for centuries, and led to the uprising of the Serbs and Greeks, then of the Roumanians, and finally a generation later of the Bulgarians. In the Habsburg dominions the same movement revealed itself in the revival of national feeling in Hungary, Bohemia, and Croatia, but nowhere more strongly than in Hungary, where it was accompanied by a remarkable literary revival and the appearance of a group of Magyar poets of real genius.

The Kingdom of Hungary, which from 1526 to 1687 had been partially under Turkish rule, led a vegetable existence during the eighteenth century. This lull was a necessary period of recuperation after exhausting wars. The ancient

Hungarian constitution, dating in its essentials from the thirteenth century, but fallen on evil days during the Turkish era, now came more and more out of abeyance. Its fundamental principles were reaffirmed by the famous laws of Leopold II. (1790–92), and after a further relapse due to the Napoleonic wars, a long series of constitutional and linguistic reforms were introduced by successive parliaments between 1825 and 1848.

Without entering into a discussion of the Hungarian constitution, it is well to point out one factor which lies at the root of all political and constitutional development in Hungary and explains the Magyar outlook for centuries past, even up to the present day. Till 1840 Latin was the official language of the country, and in that Latin the term for the political nation was *Populus*, which we would naturally translate as people. But populus contrasted in Hungarian law with plebs, the *misera plebs contribuens*, that phrase of ominous meaning to describe the mass of the oppressed and unenfranchised people, the populus being the nobles, a caste which was relatively very wide, but none the less a caste, and which enjoyed a monopoly of all political power. Till 1848 only the populus could vote, only the plebs could pay taxes—a delightful application of the principle, " Heads I win, tails you lose ! " In 1848 the distinction was broken down in theory, the franchise being extended beyond the privileged class by the initiative of that class itself. But in effect the distinction has survived to the present day in a veiled form. Political power, and, above all, the parliamentary franchise and the county elective bodies, continued to be a monopoly—henceforth a monopoly of the Magyar nobility, *plus* those classes whom they had assimilated and attached to their cause, *against* the other races, forming more than half the population of Hungary. This point of populus and plebs may seem at first sight somewhat pedantic and technical; but in reality it is the key which explains the whole social structure of Hungary, even its economic and agrarian problems.

The period from the death of Joseph II. to the great revolutionary movement of 1848 may be regarded, so far as eastern Europe is concerned, as a period when nationality is simmering everywhere. It is a period of preparation for the rise of national States—ushered in by the great crime of the Polish Partition, to which so many modern evils may be traced, and closed by a sudden explosion which shook Europe from Paris to Budapest, from Palermo to Berlin. The first stage was of course the long Napoleonic war, during which the seed was sown broadcast; the second, the era of reaction and political exhaustion (1815–1848), when all that was best in Europe concentrated in the Romantic movement in literature, art, and music.

For Austria this period was bound up with the name of Metternich, who personified the old hide-bound methods of the bureaucracy, the diplomacy of a past age, to which the nations were mere pawns on a chessboard. Under him the " Police-State " assumed its most perfect form, a form not even surpassed by Russia from 1881 to 1905.

Then came the year 1848, when the dams burst. The Hungarian constitution, restored in its entirety, became for a time the watchword and inspirer of the movement, while Austria for the first time received a serious constitution. Unhappily the issue between Reaction and Progress was not a clear one. The Magyars in Hungary unquestionably stood for historic development and constitutional rights, but they also stood for racial hegemony, for the forcible assimilation of all the other races, for a

K

unitary Magyar State instead of the old polyglot Hungary. They thus drove all the other races to coalesce with the dynasty and the forces of reaction. The result was a violent racial war, with all kinds of excesses. Slovaks, Croats, Serbs, Roumanians, Saxons, all fought against the Magyars, and finally the scale was turned by the Russian troops who poured across the Carpathians in the name of outraged autocracy.

There followed the inevitable reaction, which again can be best summed up in two phrases—that of Prince Felix Schwarzenberg, " Austria will astonish the world by her ingratitude," so strikingly fulfilled in the Crimean War, when Austria left Russia in the lurch ; and that of a Hungarian patriot, " The other races have received as reward what we Magyars receive as punishment." In short, the statesmen of Vienna, untaught by experience, reverted to the old bureaucratic and absolutist *régime*.

For ten years (1849–1859) this endured—Clericalism rampant, financial ruin, stagnation everywhere. Then Nationality burst its bonds once more. The war with Napoleon III. ended in Austria's loss of Lombardy and the creation of the Italian kingdom. Faced by the bankruptcy of the whole political and financial system, Francis Joseph launched into a period of constitutional experiment. Following the line of least resistance, as throughout his long reign, he inclined now to federalism, now to centralism, and he was still experimenting when the war of 1866 broke out. For Austria this war was decisive, for its results were her final expulsion both from Germany and from Italy, and the creation of that fatal Dual System which has distorted her whole subsequent development.

Under the Ausgleich or Compromise of 1867 the Dual Monarchy is composed of two equal and separate States, the Empire of Austria and the Kingdom of Hungary, each possessing a distinct parliament and cabinet of its own, but both sharing between them the three Joint Ministries of Foreign Affairs, War, and Finance. The chiefs of these three offices are equally responsible to both Delegations, which are committees of the two Parliaments, sitting alternately in Vienna and Budapest, but acting quite independently of each other.

This system really secured the political power in Austria and Hungary to two races —the Germans and the Magyars, and they, as the strongest in each country, bought off the two next strongest, the Poles and the Croats, by the grant of autonomy to Galicia and Croatia. The remaining eight were not considered at all At first this ingenious device seemed to offer fair prospects of success. But ere long— for reasons which would lead us too far—the German hegemony broke down in Austria, and the whole balance was disturbed. It gradually became clear that the system was only workable when one scale was high in the air. The history of the past forty-seven years is the history of the gradual decay of the Dual System. Austria has progressed in many ways ; her institutions have steadily grown freer, her political sense has developed, universal suffrage has been introduced, racial inequalities have been reduced though not abolished, industry, art, and general culture have advanced steadily. But she has been con- tinually hampered by Hungary, where racial monopoly has grown worse and worse. The Magyar Chauvinists attempted the impossible—the assimilation by seven million people of twelve million others. Yet in spite of every imaginable trick—a corrupt and oppressive adminis- tration, gross manipulation of the franchise, press persecu- tion, the suppression of schools and ruthless restriction of

every form of culture—the non-Magyar races are stronger
to-day than in 1867. And the result of the struggle has
been in Hungary a decay of political standards, a corruption
of public life, such as fills even the greatest optimists with
despair.

§ 2. *Hungary and Magyar Misrule.*—Such an assertion
may seem to run counter to the common idea of Hungary
as the home of liberty and the vanguard of popular uprisings
against despotism, and it is certainly incompatible with
the arrogant claim of Magyar Statesmen that " nowhere
in the world is there so much freedom as in Hungary." At
the risk of disturbing the proportion of this chapter, I pro-
pose to give a few classic illustrations of Magyar methods,
selected almost at random from an overwhelming mass of
damning evidence.

On paper Hungary possesses a most admirable and
enlightened law guaranteeing " the Equal Rights of Nationalities " (1868) ; in practice, it has remained almost from
the very first a dead letter. Let us take the field of education. Every effort, legal and illegal, has been made to
Magyarise the educational system, with the result that
in all the primary and secondary schools under State control
Magyar is the exclusive language of instruction, while the
number of denominational schools has been steadily
diminished and their sphere of action, as more favourable
to the non-Magyar races, materially restricted. Fifty
years ago the Slovaks, who even then numbered over
two millions, possessed three gymnasia (middle schools)
which they had founded and maintained by their own
exertions. In 1875 all three were arbitrarily closed by
orders of the Hungarian Government, and since that date
the unhappy Slovaks have not been allowed a single
secondary school in which their own language is taught,

while the number of their primary schools has been reduced
from 1821 in 1869 to 440 in 1911. The deliberate aim
is, of course, to prevent the growth of a Slovak middle
class. It is quite a common thing for schoolboys to be
persecuted or even dismissed for showing Slovak proclivities or even talking their mother-tongue " ostenta-
tiously " on the street. Only last year a brilliant young
Slovak student, known to me personally, was deprived by
the Magyar authorities of a scholarship in Oriental languages, for no other reason than that he was " untrust-
worthy in a national sense "![1] Such instances are even
more frequent among the Roumanians of Hungary. A
specially notorious case occurred in March 1912 at Gross-
wardein, when sixteen Roumanian theological students were
expelled from the Catholic seminary for the "demonstrative
use " of their language, which was regarded as offensive by
their fellow-students and professors !

Linguistic restrictions are carried to outrageous lengths.
There is not a single inscription in any language save Magyar
in any post office or railway station throughout Hungary.
Slovak medals and stamps, produced in America and
bearing such treasonable inscriptions as " For our Slovak
language " and " I am proud to be a Slovak," have been
confiscated in Hungary. Only Magyar inscriptions are
tolerated on the tombstones of the Budapest cemeteries.
The erection of monuments to Roumanian or Slovak
patriots has more than once been prohibited, and the funds
collected have been arbitrarily seized and applied to Magyar
purposes. National colours, other than the Magyar, are
strictly forbidden. Two years ago, at the funeral of a
Roumanian poet at Kronstadt (Transylvania) gendarmes
pressed up to the hearse and clipped off the colours from

---

[1] This document is in my possession.

a wreath which had been sent by the Society of Journalists
in Bucarest. About the same time a nurse was sent to
prison because a child of three was found wearing a
Roumanian tricolor bow, and its parents were reprimanded
and fined. Last July on the very eve of war, fifteen
theological students, returning to Bucarest from an excursion into Transylvania, were arrested at the frontier by
Hungarian gendarmes, hauled by main force out of the
train, sent back to Hermannstadt and kept for days in
gaol; their offence consisted in waving some Roumanian
tricolors from the train windows as they steamed out of
the last station in Hungary !

No law of association exists in Hungary, and the government uses its arbitrary powers to prohibit or suppress even
such harmless organisations as temperance societies, choral
unions, or women's leagues. Perhaps the most notorious
examples are the dissolution of the Slovak Academy in
1875 and of the Roumanian National Party's organisation
in 1894 ; but the treatment meted out to trades unions
and working-class organisations, both Magyar and non-
Magyar, for years past, has been equally scandalous. The
right of assembly is no less precarious in a country where
parliamentary candidates are arrested or expelled from their
constituencies, where deputies are prevented from addressing their constituents, where an electoral address is often
treated as a penal offence.

As for Hungary's electoral system, the less said the
better. Gerrymandering, a narrow and complicated
franchise, bribery and corruption on a gigantic scale, the
wholesale use of troops and gendarmes to prevent opposition
voters from reaching the polls, the cooking of electoral rolls,
illegal disqualifications, sham counts, official terrorism,
and in many cases actual bloodshed—such are but a few

of the methods which preserve a political monopoly in the
hands of a corrupt and increasingly inefficient racial
oligarchy, in a country where the absence of the ballot
places the peasant peculiarly at the mercy of the
authorities. Small wonder, then, if the non-Magyar races
of Hungary, who on a basis of population would have
had 198 deputies, never were allowed to elect more than 25,
and if even this scanty number was at the infamous elections
of 1910 reduced by terrorism and corruption to eight !

In judicial matters the situation is no less galling.
Petitions are not accepted in the courts, unless drawn up
in Magyar, and the whole proceedings are invariably
conducted in the same language. The non-Magyar " stands
like an ox " before the courts of his native land, and a
whole series of provisions exists for his repression, notably
the monstrous paragraphs dealing with " action hostile to
the State," with the " incitement of one nationality against
another " and with the " glorification of a criminal action "
—applied with rigorous severity to all political opponents
of Magyarisation but never to its advocates. Let me cite
one classic example of the latter. In 1898 a well-known
Slovak editor was sentenced to eight months' imprisonment
for two articles severely criticising the Magyarisation of
place-names in Hungary. On his return from prison he
was met at the railway station of the little county town by
a crowd of admirers : songs were sung, a short speech of
welcome was delivered and a bouquet of flowers was presented. The sequel of this perfectly orderly incident was
that no fewer than twenty-four persons, including Mr.
Hurban the leading Slovak poet, were sentenced to terms of
imprisonment varying from fourteen days to six months.
The three girls who had presented the flowers were let off
with a fine of £16.

Perhaps the reader will regard me as a very dangerous conspirator, when I tell him that in June 1910 an old lady of seventy-three, the widow of a high-school headmaster, was fined £4 because I had called at her house for twenty minutes on election day without its being notified to the police, and that in June 1914 an enquiry was instituted by the local authorities against some Slovak friends who had entertained me to luncheon! And yet I can honestly assert that I have never been guilty of any worse crime than Captain Grose, of whom Burns warned my countrymen a hundred years ago in the famous line:

A chiel's amang ye takin' notes!

The fabric of Magyar rule is far too rotten and corrupt to regard with equanimity any extensive note-taking on the part of the outer world.

Whole books might be written to illustrate the contention that in matters of education, administration, and justice, of association and assembly, of the franchise and the press, the non-Magyar nationalities of Hungary have long been the victims of a policy of repression which is without any parallel in civilised Europe. It is this Magyar system, from which I have lifted but a corner of the veil, that is one of the mainsprings of the present war, and if there is to be a new and healthy Europe in the future, this system must be swept away root, branch and stock. To such lengths has national fanaticism driven the Magyars that in 1906 it was possible for an ex-Premier of Hungary, speaking in open Parliament amid the applause of the majority, to lay down the following axiom: " The legal State is the aim: but with this question we can only concern ourselves when we have already assured the national State. . . . Hungary's interests demand its erection on the most extreme Chauvinist lines." Men who applaud such a sentiment are worthy allies of those so-called statesmen who regard international treaties as " a mere scrap of paper."

§ 3. *The Decay of the Dual System.*—The radical divergence of political development in Austria and in Hungary, its paralysing effect upon the foreign policy of the Monarchy as a whole, coupled with the growth of national feeling among the minor nationalities and their steady emancipation from the economic thraldom of the German and the Jew—all this has slowly but surely undermined the Dual System and rendered its final collapse inevitable. Indeed for some time past it has merely owed its survival to the old age of the Emperor, who has a natural reluctance to destroy his own creation. For some years it has been known that his heir, Francis Ferdinand, was the advocate of far-reaching changes, which would have taken the form of a compromise between a federalist and a centralist system. His abrupt removal from the scene was secretly welcomed by all those whose political and racial monopoly was bound up with the existing *régime.*

German dominance in Austria, it should be added, meant a close alliance with the German Empire ; and every fresh effort of the subject races to emancipate themselves from Germanising or Magyarising tendencies forged the chains of the alliance closer and increased the dependence of the Magyar oligarchy upon Berlin. As in mediaeval times, so in the twentieth century Habsburg policy is explained by two famous Latin mottoes—*Viribus unitis* (" Union is strength ") and *Divide et impera* (" Divide and rule "). Between these two watchwords Francis Joseph and his advisers have wavered for sixty-five years.

What then are the forces which have held Austria-

Hungary together under Francis Joseph ? First unquestionably comes the dynasty ; for it would be difficult
to over - estimate the power exercised by the dynastic
tradition on the many races under Habsburg sway. Next
comes the Joint Army ; for there is no finer body of men
in Europe than the Austrian officers' corps, poorly paid,
hard-worked, but inspired to the last man with unbounded
devotion to the Imperial house, and to a large extent
immune from that spirit of caste which is the most offensive
feature of the allied German army.[1] Hardly less important
are the Catholic Church, with its vast material resources
and its powerful influence on peasant, small tradesman and
court alike, and the bureaucracy, with its traditions of red
tape, small-mindedness, slowness of movement and genial
Gemütlichkeit (" easy-goingness "). It is only *after* these
forces that we can fairly count the parliaments and representative government. And yet there are no fewer than
twenty-three legislative bodies in the Monarchy—the two
central parliaments of Vienna and Budapest, entirely
distinct from each other ; the two Delegations ; the
provincial Diets, seventeen in Austria, one in Croatia ; and
the Diet of Bosnia, whose every legislative act requires the
ratification of the Joint Minister of Finance and of the
Austrian and Hungarian Governments.

Against all this there is one supremely disintegrating
force—the principle of Nationality. Only a map can make
clear the racial complications of the Dual Monarchy, and
even the largest scale map fails to show how inextricably
the various races are interwoven in many districts of
Hungary or Bohemia. The following table offers at least
a statistical survey :

---

[1] It is in no way a " preserve " of the aristocracy, being largely
recruited from the middle and even lower-middle class.

(1) Racial—	Austria.	Hungary.	Bosnia.
Germans . . .	9,950,266	2,037,435	..
Czechs . .	} 6,435,983	..	..
Slovaks . .		1,967,970	..
Poles	4,967,984	..	..
Ruthenes . .	3,518,854	472,587	..
Magyars (including 900,000 Jews) .	..	10,050,575	..
Croats . .	} 783,334	1,833,162	} 1,875,000
Serbs . .		1,106,471	
Slovenes . .	1,252,940	..	..
Roumanians . .	275,422	2,949,032	..
Italians . .	768,422	27,307	..
Others . .	..	374,105	..
(2) Religious—			
Roman Catholic .	22,530,000	10,888,138	451,686
Uniate Catholic .	3,417,000	2,025,508	..
Orthodox . .	660,000	2,987,163	856,158
Calvinist . .	} 589,000	2,621,329	..
Lutheran . .		1,340,143	..
Mohammedan . .	..	..	626,649
Jewish . .	1,314,000	932,458	..
Minor Sects . .	56,000	91,748	..
Total population .	28,324,940	20,886,487	1,898,044

§ 4. *The Genesis of the Southern Slavs.*—The foregoing
survey of tendencies in Austria - Hungary is utterly
incomplete and inadequate, but it may perhaps serve as a
basis for further study. Let us now consider her rival in
the dispute which has led to the great war—Serbia.

Here, at the outset, it cannot be emphasised too strongly
that those who regard the problem merely as a dispute
between the government of Vienna and the government of
Belgrade have not grasped even its elements. The Southern
Slav question goes far deeper and wider than that ; it must
be treated as a whole, and of it Serbia is only a part. In
any study of the Slavonic races the first fact which emerges
is that they fall naturally into two main groups—the
northern and the southern—divided by a solid wedge of

three non-Slavonic races, the German, the Magyar, and the Roumanian, stretching from the Kiel Canal to the Black Sea. It is with the southern group that we are concerned.

The Southern Slavs fall into four sections—the Slovenes, Croats, Serbs, and Bulgars, who between them occupy the whole country from southern Carinthia to central Thrace. The significance of the Bulgars will be dealt with elsewhere, and of the Slovenes it will suffice for our present purpose to say that they are a small and ancient race, of vigorous stock and clerical leanings, whose true importance lies in their geographical position and its latent possibilities for the future. The Croats and Serbs occupy the border-line between West and East, between Rome and Byzantium, between Catholicism and Orthodoxy. Broadly speaking, every Croat is a Catholic, every Serb an Orthodox. Broadly speaking again, the Croat language is Serb written with Latin characters, the Serb language Croat written in the Cyrilline alphabet.

Despite their common language, the two kindred races have never all been united under a single ruler. From the ninth to the end of the eleventh century the Duchy, then Kingdom, of Croatia was governed by native princes, upon whose extinction it was conquered by Hungary. For eight centuries Croatia has enjoyed an autonomous position under the Holy Crown of St. Stephen ; its scope has varied according to the political constellation, but till 1912 its constant tradition had remained unbroken. Meanwhile the Dalmatian coast towns remained a bone of contention between Venice and Hungary ; but the marble Lions on their battered walls are still the best proof of the triumph of Italian culture within them. Ragusa alone resisted both Venetians and Turks, and preserved herself inviolate as the home of commerce and the muses, until her tiny Republic was destroyed by Napoleon in 1808. The Kingdom of Serbia developed on more distinctively Slavonic lines. During its great days in the thirteenth and fourteenth centuries under the Nemanja dynasty it dominated the Balkan Peninsula, produced a code of law which is unique in mediaeval records, developed a prosperous commerce and mining industries, and seemed on the point of striking a new note in architecture. Her greatest Tsar, Stephen Dushan, died mysteriously of poison, when his hosts were already thundering at the gates of Constantinople (1356). But the greatness of his empire did not survive him, and only a generation later Serbian independence received its death-blow on the fatal field of Kosovo—the Flodden of the Balkans, but an event far direr in its consequences than Flodden was to Scotland. Bosnia and a fragment of Serbia lingered on under more or less independent rulers till the middle of the fifteenth century. Then the Turkish night replaced the Turkish twilight. From 1463 to 1804 the national life of the Serbs lay utterly crushed. In Serbia their nobility was literally wiped out, in Bosnia it accepted Islam in order to save its lands. The relations of conqueror and conquered are best characterised by the single fact that a Christian who failed to dismount from his horse on meeting a Turk was liable to be killed on the spot.

Throughout this period of utter gloom only two things served to keep alive the Serb tradition—their splendid popular ballads, unequalled in Europe for directness and imagination, save, perhaps, by the ballads of the Anglo-Scottish Border ; and the clergy of the Orthodox Church, poor ignorant despised peasants like their flock, yet bravely keeping the national flame burning. The one bright spot was the tiny mountain eyrie of Montenegro, which stub-

bornly maintained its freedom under a long succession of
warrior-priests.

The Serb Patriarchate, which had long had its seat in
Ipek, migrated to Austria in 1690, at the special invitation
of the Emperor Leopold I., and has ever since been established (though the title of patriarch lapsed for a time) at
Karlowitz on the Danube. Large settlements of refugee
Serbs from Turkey followed their spiritual chief to Croatia,
Slavonia and the southern plains of Hungary between 1690
and 1740. The special privileges granted to them by the
emperor were, however, gradually undermined and revoked
by the Hungarian Estates. Meanwhile the " Military
Frontiers " were extended on essentially democratic lines :
a land-tenure subject to military service bred a hereditary
race of soldiers and officers devoted to the Imperial idea, and
it has taken many long long years of bungling on the part of
Viennese and Magyar diplomacy to efface that devotion.

Thus the Habsburg dominions became the centre of
culture for the Serbs, whose literary revival came from
Neusatz, Karlowitz and even Buda. It was not only under
Prince Eugene that they looked to the Habsburgs for aid.
Kara George, who led their first serious rising in 1804 more
than once offered himself to Vienna.

In the Balkans the Serbs were the first to revolt, and won
their own freedom, with less help than Greeks, Roumanians
or Bulgarians, and under far less favourable circumstances.
Thus Serbia is essentially a self-made man among States,
built from the foundations upwards, and possessing no
aristocracy and hardly even a middle class. Her curse has
been the rivalry of two, or rather three native dynasties,
the Karageorgevitch, the Obrenovitch and the Petrovitch ;
and this rivalry has borne fruit in three dastardly political
crimes—the murder of the heroic Black George in 1817, by

order of his rival Milosh Obrenovitch; of Prince Michael,
Serbia's wisest ruler, by the adherents of George's son; and
finally of King Alexander and his wife in June 1903.   The
history of the Southern Slavs for the last century has been
a slow movement towards national unity, overshadowed,
sometimes hastened, sometimes paralysed, by the rivalry
of Austria and Russia for the hegemony of the Balkan
Peninsula.   Till 1875 the influence of the two Powers
alternated in Belgrade, and there was nothing definite to
suggest which influence would win, though of course Russia
may be said to have possessed an advantage in her position
as the foremost Orthodox power and as the greatest among
the Slavonic brotherhood of races.   That year, however,
brought a fresh rising of Bosnia and Herzegovina against
Turkish rule, and in defence of this purely Serbo-Croat
province public opinion in Serbia and Montenegro rose.
Side by side the two little principalities fought the Turks
and risked their all upon the issue.   The provinces were
to the last man friendly and welcomed their action.   Then,
when the battle seemed won, Austria-Hungary at the
Congress of Berlin stepped in and occupied Bosnia and
Herzegovina—with the active approval of Disraeli and
Salisbury.   The inhabitants resisted stoutly, but were overcome.   Thus was realised the first stage upon the road of the
Austrian advance towards Salonica.   Serbia received compensation at Niš, Pirot, and Vranja; Montenegro acquired
the open roadstead of Antivari and a scrap of barren coast-
line; but the hearts of both still clung to Bosnia.

Henceforth the friction between Vienna and Belgrade
has been permanent, though often latent.   It was accentuated by the fact that King Milan was little better than
an Austrian agent, the most notorious example of this being
the ill-considered and ill-managed war with Bulgaria into

which he plunged Serbia at the instigation of the Ballplatz [1] (1885). Afterwards, it is true, Vienna intervened to rob the Bulgarians of the fruits of victory and argued that Serbia was thus under her debt ; but this crass application of the principle of *divide et impera* could not deceive any one. Milan was a man of great ability, but vicious and corrupt. The ceaseless scandals of his private life, the frequent political *coups d'etat* in which he indulged, tended to confirm the dislike of his subjects for the Austrophilism with which he was identified. Alexander, his son and successor, was even worse ; indeed, it is not too much to say that he was the most " impossible " monarch whom Europe has known since the days of the Tsar Paul. His court was characterised by gross favouritism and arbitrary revisions of the constitution ; and his position became finally untenable when he committed the fatal error of marrying Draga Mashin, a woman of no position and notorious private character. Two incidents in her tragic story remind us of similar scandals in English history—the fond delusion of Mary Tudor and the legend of Mary of Modena's warming-pan. The last straw was the design, widely attributed to her and the infatuated king, for securing the succession to her brother, who had as little claim to the throne as any other Serbian subject. On June 10, 1903, Alexander and Draga were assassinated by a gang of Serbian officers, under circumstances of the utmost brutality such as nothing can excuse. In the light of recent events, however, it is important to note that both Austria and Russia knew of the plot at least ten days before the murder and did nothing to stop it. [2] On the day after the crime the *Fremdenblatt,*

---

[1] The Austro-Hungarian Foreign Office.

[2] In 1908 this was confirmed to me by a distinguished member of the then Austrian Cabinet, since dead, who was certainly in a position to know.

the organ of the Austro-Hungarian Foreign Office, published a leading article couched in terms of the utmost cynicism, and declaring that it mattered little to Austria-Hungary which dynasty reigned in Serbia. The Serbian Government might have been excused for enclosing a copy of this article in its reply to the Austrian Note of July 23, 1914 !

The Obrenovitch dynasty was thus at an end. Its rival, the Karageorgevitch dynasty, returned to power—naturally under a black cloud of European disgust and suspicion. King Peter is not, however, as black as he has sometimes been painted. He fought gallantly in 1870 as a French officer ; as a young man he translated Stuart Mill's *Essay on Liberty* into Serb, and for a generation he lived by pre- ference in democratic Geneva and in Paris. Under him Serbia has for the first time enjoyed real constitutional government. Quietly, as occasion arose, the regicides were removed to the background, the old methods of favouritism were steadily discouraged, and it is not too much to say that an entirely new atmosphere has been created in Belgrade since 1903. Among the younger politicians in Serbia, as in other Slavonic countries, the moral influence of Professor Masaryk, the great Czech philosopher and politician, has grown more and more marked.

The depth of Serb aspirations in Bosnia has two obvious grounds—on the one hand, pure national sentiment of the best kind ; on the other, the urgent economic need for a seaboard, Serbia being the only inland country in Europe save Switzerland, and not enjoying the latter's favoured position in the immediate vicinity of great world-markets. Austria-Hungary, on her part, set herself deliberately not merely to block this access to the sea, but also to keep Serbia in complete economic dependence. Under the new dynasty the little kingdom showed a keener desire to shake

L

off its vassalage and find new markets. The so-called "Pig War" — the breeding of swine is Serbia's staple industry, and the founders of her two rival dynasties were wealthy pig-breeders—proved an unexpected success, for new trade outlets were found in Egypt and elsewhere. But the initial strain hit every peasant in his pocket and thus greatly accentuated the feeling against Austria-Hungary. At this stage came the Young Turk revolution and its sequel, the annexation of Bosnia. To any impartial observer it had been obvious from the first that those who dreamt of Austria-Hungary's voluntary withdrawal from the two provinces were living in a fool's paradise. The formal act of annexation merely set a seal to thirty years of effective Austrian administration, during which the Sultan's rule had been confined to the official celebration of his birthday. Educational and agrarian problems had been neglected, popular discontent had smouldered, but at least great material progress had been made. Roads, railways, public buildings had been created out of nothing, capital had been sunk, a new machine of government had been constructed. Austria had come to stay, and Aehrenthal, in annexing the provinces, felt himself to be merely setting the seal to a document which had been signed a generation earlier. He had failed to reckon with the outcry which this technical breach of international law evoked : like Bethmann-Hollweg, he had no blind faith in " scraps of paper," and had no scruple in tearing up the Treaty of Berlin on which the whole Balkan settlement had rested. Nowhere was the outburst of feeling so violent as in Serbia and Montenegro, who had never ceased to dream of the lost Serb provinces. For some months the two little States challenged the accomplished fact, and seemed bent on staking their very existence upon war with the great

neighbouring Monarchy.   Aehrenthal remained unmoved
by their cries of impotent fury and settled down to a trial
of strength with his rival Izvolsky, the Russian Foreign
Minister, who encouraged the sister Slavonic States in their
resistance.   At length in March 1909 Germany stepped
forward in " shining armour " to support her Austrian ally,
and Russia, to avoid European war, gave way and abandoned
the Serbs to their fate.   Nothing was left but a humiliating
submission :   the Serbian Government was obliged to
address a Note to the Great Powers, declaring that the
annexation and internal condition of Bosnia did not in any
way concern her.[1]

§ 5. *The Renaissance of Serbia.*—From this diplomatic
defeat dates the renaissance of Serbia.   It restored her to
a sense of hard realities, and taught her to substitute hard
work for loud talk.   So rough a challenge put the national
spirit on its mettle.   The brief period between 1908 and
1912 worked a real transformation in Belgrade, which could
not fail to impress those who took the trouble to look
beneath the surface.   Nowhere was the change more marked
than in the Serbian army, from which the regicide elements
had been slowly but steadily eliminated.   The two Balkan
wars of 1912-1913 revealed Serbia to the outside world as
a military power, notable alike for the élan of its infantry,
the high efficiency of its artillery, the close camaraderie of
officers and men.   The first use made of her victories over
the Turks was the occupation of northern Albania, her only
possible outlet to the sea so long as Dalmatia remains in
Austrian hands.   Austria-Hungary, who had only remained
inactive because she had taken a Turkish victory for
granted, now intervened, and by the creation of an artificial

---

[1] This declaration was made the basis of the Austrian Note to
Serbia in July 1914.

Albanian State vetoed Serbia's expansion to the Adriatic.
The Austrian Foreign Minister, Count Berchtold, short-
sighted and indolent then as now, failed to realise that the
North Albanian harbours, for obvious reasons of physical
geography, could never be converted into naval bases, save
at a prohibitive cost, and that their possession by Serbia,
so far from being a menace to Austria, would involve the
policing of a mountainous tract of country, inhabited by
a turbulent and hostile population. It ought to have been
obvious to him that the moment had arrived for tempting
the Serbs into the Austrian sphere of influence by the bait
of generous commercial concessions through Bosnia and
Dalmatia. Several far-sighted politicians in Austria urged
this course upon him, and the Serbian Premier actually
approached Vienna with far-reaching proposals in this very
sense. Their contemptuous rejection by Berchtold and the
little clique of Foreign Office officials who controlled his
puppet figure, naturally strengthened still further the bonds
which united Belgrade and Petrograd. Serbia, shut out
from the Adriatic, had no alternative save to seek her
economic outlet down the valley of the Vardar towards the
Aegean, and in so doing she came into violent conflict with
Bulgarian aspirations in Macedonia. These facts alone
would justify the assertion that the war between the Balkan
allies was directly due to Austro-Hungarian initiative ;
but it has also transpired that the dissensions between Sofia
and Belgrade were actively encouraged from Vienna, that
Magyar influences were brought to bear upon King
Ferdinand, and that war material was sent down the Danube
from Hungary to Bulgaria. The outward and visible
sign of these intrigues was a speech of the Hungarian
Premier, Count Tisza, opposing the Tsar's intervention in
favour of peace and virtually inciting Bulgaria to fight it

out. The break-up of the Balkan League was the first condition to that Austrian advance on Salonica which has always remained the ideal of the advocates of a forward policy in Vienna and Budapest, and which lies at the root of Austria-Hungary's action in provoking the present war.

Serbia and Montenegro, however, are but one half of the problem. The issues involved are wider and deeper than the quarrels of Vienna and Budapest with Belgrade. Even if every man in Serbia were willingly prostrate before the Habsburg throne, there could be no real peace until the internal problem of Austria-Hungary's Southern Slav provinces is solved. What is at stake is the future of eleven million people, inhabiting the whole tract of country from sixty miles north of Trieste to the centre of Macedonia, from the southern plains of Hungary to the North Albanian frontier. Of these, roughly four millions are in the two independent kingdoms; the remaining seven millions are divided between Austria (the provinces of Dalmatia, Istria, and Carniola) and Hungary (the autonomous kingdom of Croatia-Slavonia), while Bosnia-Herzegovina are governed jointly by Austria and Hungary. The history of these provinces during the past generation is one of neglect and misgovernment. Croatia has been exploited economically by the Magyars, and the narrow interests of Budapest have prevented railway development and hampered local industries by skilful manipulation of tariffs and taxation. A further result is that even to-day Dalmatia (with the exception of Ragusa) has no railway connections with the rest of Europe, and those of Bosnia are artificially directed towards Budapest rather than towards Agram, Vienna, and Western Europe. It is not too much to say that the situation of those provinces had become less favourable (if compared with surrounding standards) than it was at earlier periods of their history ; for the old system of trade-routes had broken down there as elsewhere in Europe, but had not been replaced by modern communications.

§ 6. *Serbo-Croat Unity.*—Parallel with the new era instituted in Serbia since 1903, a strong movement in favour of national unity took root among her kinsmen across the Austro-Hungarian frontier. The disruptive tendencies which had hitherto been so marked in Croatian politics began to weaken. The so-called Serbo-Croat Coalition round which all the younger elements speedily rallied, put forward an ambitious programme of constructive democratic reform as the basis of joint political action on the part of both races, and held stubbornly together when the inevitable breach with the Magyar oligarchy occurred. The Magyar Government felt that every effort must be made to restore that discord between Croat and Serb which had been for a generation one of the main pillars of their racial hegemony. These designs happened to coincide with the aims of the Foreign Office in Vienna in connection with the annexation of Bosnia, and Budapest and Vienna combined in a systematic campaign of persecution against the Serbs of Croatia. " Wholesale arrests and charges of treason led up to the monster trial at Agram, which dragged on for seven months amid scandals worthy of the days of Judge Jeffreys. The Diet ceased to meet, the constitution of Croatia was in abeyance, the elections were characterised by corruption and violence such as eclipsed even the infamous Hungarian elections of 1910 ; the Press and the political leaders were singled out for special acts of persecution and intimidation." These tactics were revealed to the outside world in the notorious Friedjung Trial (December 1909), resulting out of a libel action brought by the Serbo-Croat Coalition leaders against Dr. Friedjung, the distinguished Austrian historian.

The documents, on the basis of which he had publicly accused them of being paid agents of the Serbian Government, had been supplied to him by the Austro-Hungarian Foreign Office, and the trial revealed them as impudent forgeries, concocted in the Austro-Hungarian Legation in Belgrade ! The moral responsibility for these forgeries was subsequently brought home to Count Forgách, the Minister in Belgrade, and indirectly, of course, to Count Aehrenthal himself as Foreign Minister. But Forgách, though publicly denounced as " Count Azev," [1] was not allowed to fall into disgrace ; on the contrary, he had become within two years of his exposure permanent Under-Secretary at the Ballplatz, and inspirer of new plots to discredit and ruin Serbia.

The scandals of the Friedjung Trial led to the fall of the Governor of Croatia, but there was no change of system. After a temporary truce the old conflict revived, and within eighteen months the friction between Magyars and Croats was as acute as ever. The Magyar Government employed every possible device of administrative pressure in order to create dissensions between the Croat and Serb parties— repeated elections, wholesale corruption and violence, persecution of the Press and of the political leaders. Yet so far from languishing under such a system, the movement for unity gained fresh strength and extended to the kindred Slovenes, striking root even among the extreme Clericals, who had hitherto regarded the Orthodox Serbs with distrust and suspicion.

In the spring of 1912 the conflict culminated in the abolition of the Croatian constitution by the arbitrary

---

[1] An allusion to the notorious Russian *agent provocateur* who was at one and the same time a member of the secret police and of the revolutionary organisation.

decree of the Hungarian Premier, in the appointment of a reactionary official as dictator, and a few months later in the suspension of the charter of the Serb Orthodox Church.

§ 7. *The Balkan Wars.*—Never in history had a more inopportune moment been chosen for such crying illegalities. For close upon the heels of the demonstrations and unrest which they evoked, came the dramatic events of the Balkan War, the crushing victories of the allies, the resurrection of the lost Serb Empire, the long-deferred revenge for the defeat of Kosovo. The whole Southern Slav provinces of Austria-Hungary were carried off their feet by a wave of enthusiasm for the allies, and an impossibly strained situation was reached when the Government of Vienna placed itself in violent conflict with Serbia, vetoed her expansion to the sea, insisted upon creating a phantom Albanian State, egged on Bulgaria against her allies, and finally mobilised in order to impose its will upon the Serbs. Every peasant in the Slavonic South naturally contrasted Magyar misrule in Croatia with the splendid achievements of his Serb kinsmen across the frontier. I know of poor villagers in the mountainous hinterland of Dalmatia who, having no money to give to the cause of the Balkan Red Cross, offered casks of country wine or even such clothes and shoes as they could spare from their scanty belongings. The total subscriptions raised among the Southern Slavs of the Monarchy in aid of the allies far exceeded any sums previously raised for charitable purposes among so poor a population. "In the Balkan sun," said a prominent Croat Clerical, "we see the dawn of our day."

The national rejoicings which "the avenging of Kosovo" evoked among the Croats, Serbs, and Slovenes of Austria-Hungary were accompanied by lively protests against the bare idea of an Austro-Serbian war, which, so far as the

Southern Slavs on both sides of the frontier were concerned, would have been a civil war in the most literal sense of the word (and this civil war, it must be remembered, is now actually being waged). The politicians, however, though well-nigh unanimous in their enthusiasm for the cause of the Balkan allies, could not at one breath throw off the habits of a lifetime. Petty jealousies still divided them and were skilfully played upon by the Magyar Government. The strain of five years of opposition and persecution had produced its effect upon the Coalition leaders and rendered them all too prone to further concessions. But the younger generation had been profoundly affected by the Croatian dictatorship and the Balkan wars ; at an age when our youth think of nothing but cricket and football, the students and even the school-boys of Croatia, Dalmatia, and Bosnia became engrossed in political speculation, brooded over the wrongs of their disunited race, and dreamt of Serbia as the new Piedmont of the Balkans. To all alike even the most advanced politician seemed no better than an old fogey, and it is no exaggeration to assert that the existing parties had lost all hold upon the overwhelming majority of those who in ten years' time will represent the manhood and the intellect of the race. The widespread nature of the movement may be illustrated by the school strike of the spring of 1912, during which every boy and girl above the age of fourteen in most of the primary and secondary schools of Croatia, Dalmatia, and Bosnia played truant as a protest against the misgovernment of Croatia. On that occasion a crowd of 5000 school children paraded the streets of Agram shouting " Down with Cuvaj " (the Ban or Governor of Croatia), and cheering the police when they tried to intervene !

As in all such movements, the views of individuals varied in intensity : some merely gave a theoretical adherence to the ideals of Mazzini or of Mill, others swallowed the Nihilist doctrine of Bakunin and dreamt of revolution, ushered in by terrorist propaganda. Out of this milieu came the two young assassins who murdered the Archduke Francis Ferdinand.

§ 8. *The Murder of the Archduke.*—By a hideous irony of fate Francis Ferdinand was the one man capable of restoring order to an already desperate internal situation. His very person was a programme and a watchword, and it had long been an open secret that his accession would be the signal for drastic reforms. It was his ambition to supersede the effete Dual system by a blend of centralism and federalism such as would reconcile the national sentiment of individual races with the consciousness of a common citizenship and would at the same time restore to foreign policy the possibility of initiative. This programme involved the emancipation of the non-Magyar races of Hungary from the intolerable racial tyranny of the Magyars, and at the same time a serious attempt to solve the Southern Slav question by unifying the race under Habsburg rule. As his Imperial uncle grew older and feebler, Francis Ferdinand is known to have elaborated his designs, and a regular staff of able lieutenants had grouped themselves round him. But on the very eve of action the strong man was removed, to the scarcely veiled relief of all those elements in the State whose political and racial monopoly was threatened by such far-reaching and beneficial changes.

The circumstances of the murder are still shrouded in mystery. It is known that no proper measures were taken for the protection of the Archduke and his wife in Bosnia, though it is still impossible to assign the responsibility for such criminal negligence. It is notorious that in a country like Bosnia, which has for years been infested with police spies and informers, and where every movement of every stranger is strictly under control, so elaborate and ramified a plot could hardly hope to escape the notice of the authorities. It has even been asserted that Princip and Čabrinović, the two assassins, were *agents provocateurs* in the pay of the police, and though no proof is as yet forthcoming, there is nothing inherently improbable in the idea.[1] Certain it is that the gravest suspicion rests upon those who connived at the disgraceful anti-Serb riots of which Sarajevo was the scene for nearly forty-eight hours after the murder.

The murder provided an admirable pretext for aggression against Serbia, and at the same time tended to revive all the latent prejudice with which the country of the regicides was still regarded in the West. Yet those who seek to establish a connection between the crime of Sarajevo and the Serbian Government are on an utterly false scent. I have tried to describe the atmosphere of universal and growing discontent which produced the explosion. Those who know the Slavonic South are well aware that Bosnia, Dalmatia, and Croatia are a seething pot which needs no stirring from the outside, and that the assassins are but the natural successors of the wild young students who during the last five years fired upon the Governors of Croatia and Bosnia.[2] But quite apart from this, the complicity of official Belgrade is rendered incredible by urgent considerations of internal Serbian politics. After a long and delicate negotiation the Concordat with the Vatican had just been

[1] The fact that they have only been sentenced to terms of imprisonment, while some of their accomplices have been condemned to death, has a much simpler explanation. Both men are under the age of twenty, and therefore by Austrian law immune from the death penalty.

[2] June 1910, June and November 1912, June 1913.

concluded : the Orient railway question had reached the critical stage : above all, a customs and military union between Serbia and Montenegro was on the point of being concluded. But, of course, quite apart from such considerations, Serbia was suffering from the extreme exhaustion consequent upon waging two wars within a year, and her statesmen, despite the rebuffs administered by Count Berchtold, were genuinely anxious for a *modus vivendi* with the neighbouring Monarchy, as an essential condition to a period of quiet internal consolidation. But this was the very thing which the controllers of Austrian foreign policy—the phantom Minister Berchtold, the sinister clique in the Foreign Office, and the Magyar oligarchy, led by that masterful reactionary, Count Tisza, the Hungarian Premier—were anxious to avoid. They had never reconciled themselves to the new situation in the Balkans ; and having twice backed the wrong horse (Turkey in the first war, Bulgaria in the second) still continued to plot against the Bucarest settlement of August 1913. Salonica still remained the secret Austrian objective, and Serbia the main obstacle to the realisation of this dream. Not for the first time, the interests of Vienna and Constantinople coincided, and the occult interests which link Budapest with Salonica played their part in the game.

The crime of Sarajevo removed the chief restraining force in the councils of the Monarchy and placed the fate of Europe at the mercy of a group of gamblers in Vienna, Budapest, and Berlin. The military party under Konrad von Hoetzendorf, chief of the Austrian General Staff (who a year ago was seriously speculating as to the collapse of Austria-Hungary), joined hands with the Magyar extremists, whose political monopoly was threatened by the advancing Slavonic tide, and with the inner ring of Prussian diplomacy, which believed the psychological moment to have arrived for measuring swords with Russia. The murder served as an admirable pretext to veil grossly aggressive tactics. It was hoped that Russia might be manœuvred into a position where autocracy would rather abandon the Slav cause than seem to condone assassination ; and it was confidently believed that Britain would hold aloof from a quarrel whose origin was so questionable. Stripped of all outward seeming, the true issues of the conflict were very different. Just as the policy of violent Turkification adopted by the Young Turks inevitably provoked the Balkan War, so the policy of Magyarisation, which has dominated Hungarian affairs for forty-five years and poisoned the relations of Austria-Hungary with her southern neighbours, has led directly to the present conflagration.

§ 9. *The Future of the Southern Slavs.*—There have always been two fatal obstacles to an Austrian solution of the Southern Slav problem,—Magyar hegemony and the Dual System, to which alone that hegemony owed its survival ; and it is these two worn-out and reactionary ideas (if they can be described as " ideas ") that are at present fighting their death-struggle. It was the ambition of Francis Ferdinand to achieve Serbo-Croat unity within the Monarchy, and thus simultaneously to counteract the attractions of Pan-Serb propaganda and to remove the most fertile source of friction between Austria-Hungary and Serbia. His death destroyed the last chance of such a solution ; for the statesmen of Vienna and Budapest were not merely incapable but openly hostile. An appeal was to be made to the arbitrament of the sword.

Long before war broke out it had become a commonplace of political theory that the Southern Slav question could be solved in one of two ways—either inside the

Habsburg Monarchy or outside it—either with its help and under its aegis, or against it and despite its resistance. With the outbreak of war the problem assumed a new form; the alternatives are the absorption of the two independent Serb States in the neighbouring Monarchy—in other words, the union of the entire Southern Slav race under Habsburg rule—or the liberation of her kinsmen in the Monarchy by Serbia as the Southern Slav Piedmont. This latter ideal, it has always been obvious, could only be achieved through the medium of a general European war, and it is in this manner that it is actually in process of achievement.

The Austrian Note to Serbia was deliberately framed in such a manner as to be unacceptable by any State which valued its self-respect or prestige. The military leaders desired war, while the Foreign Office, already committed for years to a violently Serbophobe policy, was working hand in glove with the German Ambassador Tschirschky, and with the very highest quarters in Berlin. The German Government in its official case admits having given Austria "a free hand against Serbia," while there are good grounds for believing that the text of the Note was submitted to the German Emperor and that the latter fully approved of (if he did not actually suggest) the fatal time-limit of forty-eight hours, which rendered all efforts towards peace hopeless from the outset.

The Austrian case against Serbia, as embodied in this Note, rested upon a secret investigation in the prison of Sarajevo. The persistent rumours that the assassins are *agents - provocateurs*, and that pressure of a somewhat drastic kind was brought to bear upon them after their arrest, cannot of course be accepted as proved. But the essential point to bear in mind is the fact that the details

of the Austrian " case," as embodied in the notorious Note
of July 23, originated in the same quarter as the previous
attempts to slander and discredit Serbia. Count Forgách,
the arch-forger of the Austrian Legation in Belgrade, was
permanent Under-secretary in the Foreign Office, and as
Count Berchtold's right hand and prompter in Balkan
affairs, was directly responsible for the pronounced anti-
Serb tendencies which have dominated the foreign policy
of the Dual Monarchy since the rise of the Balkan League.
As a Magyar nobleman with intimate Jewish connections,
Forgách was an invaluable link between Magyar extremist
policy and Berlin on the one hand and Salonica and Constantinople on the other. In view of his record as the
inspirer of the Vasić forgeries, we are amply justified in
declining to accept any " evidence " prepared by him and
his subordinates, and insisting upon a full and open trial
of the murderers as the only conceivable foundation for
charges of complicity.

When all is said and done, however, the murder of the
Archduke, though an event of world-importance so far as
the internal development and future of the Dual Monarchy
is concerned, is none the less a side-issue in the Southern
Slav question. This seeming paradox will not surprise
those who consider the currents of national life among the
Southern Slavs. The diplomatic conflict between Belgrade
and Vienna or Budapest is but the outcome of a far deeper
and wider movement. We are witnessing the birth-throes
of a new nation, the rise of a new national consciousness,
the triumph of the idea of National Unity among the three
Southern Slav sisters—the Croats, Serbs, and Slovenes.
Fate has assigned to Britain and to France an important
share in the solution of the problem, and it is our duty to insist that this solution shall be radical and permanent, based

upon the principle of Nationality and the wishes of the
Southern Slav race. Only by treating the problem as an
organic whole, by avoiding patchwork remedies and by
building for a distant future, can we hope to remove one of
the chief danger-centres in Europe.

BOOKS

Unfortunately some of the indispensable books are in German or
French, but the following list offers a very considerable choice :—

(A) Austria-Hungary

Austria-Hungary and Poland, by H. W. Steed, W. Alison Phillips,
and D. Hannay. (Britannica War Books.) 2s. 6d. net. Un-
critical reprint of very valuable articles from the *Encyclopaedia
Britannica*.

Louis Leger. *History of Austria-Hungary.* 1889 (from French)
(out of print).

Geoffrey Drage. *Austria-Hungary.* 21s. net. 1909. A mine of
economic facts.

H. W. Steed. *The Habsburg Monarchy.* 1914. (3rd ed.) 7s. 6d.
net. Far the best summary of tendencies, on the lines of
Bodley's *France* and Bryce's *American Commonwealth*.

R. W. Seton-Watson (Scotus Viator). *Racial Problems in
Hungary.* 1908. 16s. net.

R. W. Seton-Watson. *Corruption and Reform in Hungary.* 1911.
4s. 6d. net.

Hon. C. N. Knatchbull-Hugesson. *The Political Development of
the Hungarian Nation.* 1910. 2 vols. 14s. net. A good ex-
position of the extreme Magyar Chauvinist point of view.

R. Mahaffy. *The Emperor Francis Joseph.* 1910. 2s. 6d. A
useful character-sketch.

C. E. Maurice. *Bohemia.* (Story of the Nations.) 1896. 5s.
An admirable text-book.

C. E. Maurice. *The Revolutionary Movement of* 1848–49. 1887.
16s. The best epitome in English.

Count Francis Lutzow. *Bohemia.* 1896. (Everyman Library.) 1s.

Emily G. Balch. *Our Slavic Fellow Citizens.* New York. 1910.
The best book on emigration. 10s. 6d. net.

(B) Serbia and the Southern Slavs

W. Miller. *The Balkans.* 1896. (Story of the Nations.) The best
general text-book. 5s.

W. MILLER. *The Ottoman Empire, 1801-1913.* 1913. (Cambridge
    Historical Series.)   An excellent book, with a misleading title;
    it is really a history of the Balkan Christians, with special
    reference to the Greeks. Turkish history is only introduced
    incidentally. 7s. 6d. net.

EMILE DE LAVELEYE. *The Balkan Peninsula.* 1887. (Out of
    print.) By a distinguished Belgian professor, who was in his
    day recognised as an authority on Balkan questions.

LEOPOLD VON RANKE. *History of Servia.* 3s. 6d. (Bohn's Library.)
    This brilliant and sympathetic study by the greatest of German
    historians is of permanent value.

SIR ARTHUR J. EVANS. *Through Bosnia on Foot.* 1877. (Out
    of print.) The distinguished archaeologist took part, as a young
    man, in the Bosnian rising against the Turks.

R. W. SETON-WATSON. *The Southern Slav Question and the Habsburg
    Monarchy.* 1911. 12s. 6d. net. (Greatly modified and ex-
    tended in a German edition published in 1913.)

R. W. SETON-WATSON. *Absolutism in Croatia.* 1912. 2s. net.

ČEDO MIJATOVIĆ. *Servia of the Servians.* 1911. 16s. net.

ELODIE MIJATOVIĆ. *Serbian Folklore.* 1874.

(C) THREE OTHER BOOKS DEALING WITH THE BALKANS ARE STRONGLY RECOMMENDED

SIR CHARLES ELIOT (ODYSSEUS). *Turkey in Europe.* 2nd ed.
    7s. 6d. net.

H. N. BRAILSFORD. *Macedonia.* 1906. 12s. 6d. net.

LUIGI VILLARI AND OTHERS. *The Balkan Question.* 1905. 10s. 6d.
    net.

CHAPTER V

RUSSIA

"God will save Russia as He has saved her many times. Salvation will come from the people, from their faith and their meekness. Fathers and teachers, watch over the people's faith, and this will not be a dream. I have been amazed all my life in our great people by their dignity, their true and seemly dignity. I have seen it myself, I can testify to it; I have seen it and marvelled at it; I have seen it in spite of the degraded sins and poverty-stricken appearance of our peasantry. They are not servile; and, even after two centuries of serfdom, they are free in manner and bearing,—yet without insolence, and not revengeful and not envious. 'You are rich and noble, you are clever and talented, well be so, God bless you. I respect you, but I know that I too am a man. By the very fact that I respect you without envy I prove my dignity as a man. . . .'

"God will save His people, for Russia is great in her humility. I dream of seeing, and seem to see clearly already, our future. It will come to pass that even the most corrupt of our rich will end by being ashamed of his riches before the poor; and the poor, seeing his humility, will understand and give way before him, will respond joyfully and kindly to his honourable shame. Believe me that it will end in that; things are moving to that. Equality is to be found only in the spiritual dignity of man, and that will only be understood among us. If we were brothers, there would be fraternity; but before that they will never agree about the division of wealth. We preserve the image of Christ, and it will shine forth like a precious diamond to the whole world. So be it, so be it!"—DOSTOIEFFSKY, *The Brothers Karamazov.*

"THE French are a decent civilised lot of people; but I wish we were not allies of Russia." This, or something very like it, is the spoken or unspoken thought of a very large number of persons, especially among the working-classes in England at the present time. English suspicion of Russia is no new thing, though there is no doubt that the suppression of the revolution during the years 1906–1909 made it more general than ever before. It was responsible, for example, for the Crimean War, and the " crafty Russian" has become a catch-word almost as widely accepted in England as the phrase " perfidious Albion " is upon the Continent. I have seen Russia at her worst : I saw the revolution stamped out cruelly and relentlessly ; I have lived three years in Finland, and know the weariness of spirit and aching bitterness of heart that comes to a fine and cultured race in its perpetual struggle for liberty against an alien Government to whom the word liberty means nothing but rebellion. And yet I am firmly persuaded of the innate soundness of the Russian people, and of the tremendous future which lies before it in the history of the world. I believe too that the English are suspicious of Russia, not because Russia is crafty or evil or barbaric, but because English people find it very difficult to understand a race which is so extraordinarily different from themselves. We fear the unknown ; we suspect what is unlike ourselves ; yet we shall do well, in the present crisis, whether we are thinking of our enemy Germany or our ally Russia, to remember the axiom laid down by Edmund Burke, the greatest of English political thinkers : " It is impossible to bring an indictment against a whole nation."

In any case, for good or ill, Russia is our ally, and if Germany is beaten, Russia seems likely to play as great a part in the settlement as she did in 1815. It therefore behoves us, in our own self-interest if for no higher motive, to try and understand the spirit and ideals of a great people, who, as they did a century ago at the time of Napoleon, are once again coming forward to assist Europe in ridding herself of a military despotism.

§ 1. *The Russian State.*—Many of us do not realise the most obvious facts about Russia. For example, our atlases, which give us Europe on one page and Asia on another, prevent us from grasping the most elementary fact of all—her vastness. Mr. Kipling has told us that "East is East and West is West, and never the twain shall meet." But Russia confounds both Mr. Kipling and the map-makers by stretching from the Baltic to the Pacific. For her there is not Europe and Asia but one continent, and she is the whole *inside* of it. All Europe between the four inland seas, and all Asia north of lat. 50° (and a good deal south of it too)—that is Russia, a total area of $8\frac{1}{4}$ million square miles! This enormous country, which comprises one-sixth of the land-surface of the globe, is at present thinly populated; it has roughly 20 persons to the square mile as against 618 to the square mile in England and Wales. Yet for all that it contains the largest white population of any single state on earth, numbering in all 171 million souls. Moreover, this population is increasing rapidly; it has quadrupled itself during the last century, and with the advent of industrialism the increase is likely to be still more rapid. Many among us alive to-day may see Russia's population reach and perhaps pass that of teeming China. As yet, however, industrialism is only at its beginning in Russia; more than 85 per cent of the inhabitants live in the country, as tillers of the soil.

It will be at once evident that this fact gives her an immense advantage over industrial nations in time of war. She has, on the one hand, an almost inexhaustible supply of men to draw upon, while, on the other hand, her simple economic structure is hardly at all affected. A great

European war may mean for a Western country dislocation of trade, hundreds of mills and pits standing idle, vast masses of unemployed, leading to distress, poverty and in the end starvation ; for Russia it means little more than that the peasants grow fat on the corn and food-stuffs which in normal times they would have exported to the West. Furthermore, her geographical and economic circumstances render Russia ultimately invincible from the military point of view, as Napoleon found to his cost in 1812. She has no vital parts, such as France has in Paris or Germany has in Silesia or Westphalia, upon which the life of the whole State organism depends ; she is like some vast multicellular invertebrate animal which it is possible to wound but not to destroy. Russia has much to gain from a great European war and hardly anything to lose.

At first sight, therefore, there seems to be a great deal in favour of the theory, somewhat widely held at the moment, that to crush Germany and Austria will be to lay Europe at the feet of Russia, and that when Germany has been driven out of France and Belgium, the Allies in the West might have to patch up a peace with her in order to drive the Russians out of Germany. Behind this theory lies the assumption that Russia is an aggressive military state, inspired by the same ideals as have led Germany to deluge the world with blood. This is an assumption which is, I believe, absolutely unwarranted by anything in the history or character of the nation.

Historically speaking, the Russian Empire is an extension of the old Roman Empire ; it is the direct heir of the Eastern Roman Empire, which had its capital at Constantinople, as the mediaeval " Holy Roman Empire," founded by Charlemagne in A.D. 800, was the heir of the Western Roman Empire, which had its capital at Rome itself. But the Eastern Empire survived its Western twin by a thousand years; the Goths deposed the last Roman emperor in 476, the Turks took Constantinople in 1453. The Russian Empire, therefore, which did not begin its political development until after the fall of Constantinople, entered the field some six and a half centuries later than the mediaeval empire of Charlemagne, which was indeed already falling to pieces in the end of the fifteenth century. Thus Russia presents the strange spectacle of a mediaeval State existing in the twentieth century, and she is still in some particulars what Western Europe was in the Middle Ages. She has, however, attained a unity, a strength and a centralisation which the Holy Roman Empire never succeeded in acquiring. There is nothing corresponding to the feudal system, with all the disruptive tendencies which that system carried with it, in modern Russia; partly owing to the constant danger of Mongolian invasion which threatened Russia for so many centuries, partly as a result of Ivan the Terrible's destruction of the *boyars,* who were analogous to the mediaeval barons, and of Peter the Great's substitution of a nobility of service for that of rank, Russia is politically more centralised than any mediaeval, and socially more democratic than any modern, country. Russia has also solved that other great problem which perpetually agitated the mediaeval world—the conflict between the secular and the spiritual power. She is the most religious nation in the world, but she has no Papacy; Peter the Great subordinated the Church to the State by placing the Holy Synod, which controls the former, under the authority of a layman, a minister appointed by the Tsar. Yet, while she appears united and centralised when we think of her nebulous prototype, the Holy Roman Empire, we have only to compare her with her Western neighbours, and especially with that triumph of State-organisation, Germany, to see how amorphous, how inefficient, how loose, how mediaeval is the structure of this enormous State.

Peter the Great, who was more than any other man the creator of modern Russia, saw clearly that the only way of holding this inchoate State-mass together was to call into existence a huge administrative machine, and he saw equally clearly that, if such a machine was not itself to become a disruptive force through the personal ambition and self-aggrandisement of its members, it must be framed on democratic and not aristocratic principles. As Mr. Maurice Baring puts it, "Peter the Great introduced the democratic idea that service was everything, rank nothing. He had it proclaimed to the whole gentry that any gentleman, in any circumstances whatsoever and to whatever family he belonged, should salute and yield place to any officer. The gentleman served as a private soldier and became an officer, but a private soldier who did not belong to the nobility, and who attained the rank of a commissioned officer, became, *ipso facto*, a member of the hereditary nobility. . . . In the civil service he introduced the same democratic system. He divided it into three sections : military, civil, and court. Every section was divided into fourteen ranks, or *Chins* ; the attainment of the eighth class conferred the privilege of hereditary nobility, even though those who received it might have been|of the humblest origin. He hereby replaced the aristocratic hierarchy of pedigree by a democratic hierachy of service. Promotion was made solely according to service ; lineage counted for nothing. There was no social difference, however wide, which could not be levelled by means of State service." This is partly what was meant when it was stated in the last paragraph that Russia was socially the most democratic of modern countries. The system established by Peter the Great exists to-day. Russia is governed, not by a feudal nobility like that which ground the faces of the poor in France before the revolution of 1789, nor by a number of capitalists who live by exploiting the workers ; for neither feudal nobility nor capitalism (as yet) has any real power in Russia. She is governed by a civil service, and by a civil service more democratic than our own, where the higher posts are as a rule only open to members of the upper and middle classes, less exclusive than that of India, where the higher officials are nearly all recruited from the members of an alien race—a civil service, in short, whose only close parallel is the hierarchy of the Roman Catholic Church. Imagine the Roman Church as a secular institution, with a monarch at its head ruling by hereditary right instead of an elected president like the Pope, and you get a very fair idea of the Russian Government machine. All that we associate with the word aristocracy in the West, the hereditary principle, primogeniture, the accumulation of the land and capital of the country in the hands of a small class, the spirit of caste, the traditions of nobility handed down with the title-deeds from father to son, are either non-existent or of comparative unimportance in Russian society.

There is also none of the keen sensitiveness to minute social distinctions and to the social proprieties which mark them that is so striking a feature of the life in " democratic " England and to which we have given the name " snobbery." There are of course social strata in Russia, but they are broadly marked and there is no sense of competition between them. A peasant is not ashamed of being a peasant, and when he meets a nobleman he meets him on terms of spiritual equality while acknowledging his superior position

in the social scale. A twin-brother of English " snobbery "
is English " hypocrisy." This, as has been well said, is a
kind of " social cement," for it is a tribute to a standard of
social conduct set up by the dominant class in a nation.
And since there exists no dominant class in Russia, but only
a dominant hierarchy drawn from all classes, hypocrisy is
absent from the Russian character. Mr. Stephen Graham,
who was, I believe, at one time a clerk in a London office,
found our civilisation so intolerable that one day he flung
it off and escaped to Russia, where he has lived as a peasant
tramp for many years. To revolutionaries who met him
and expressed their astonishment that an Englishman
should choose Russia of all places to live in, he replied,
" I came to Russia because it is the only free country left
in the world." There is, in truth, much to be said for this
startling remark. In no country on earth is there such
unaffected good-will, such open hospitality, such an instinctive respect for personal liberty—liberty of thought
and of manners—such tolerance for the frailties of human
nature, such an abundance of what the great Russian
novelist Dostoieffsky called " all-humanness " and St.
Paul called " charity," as in Russia. All this, of course,
did not come about as a result of the bureaucratic system ;
it springs like that system itself from the fundamentally
democratic spirit of the Russian people.

§ 2. *Religion.*—The last paragraph will read strangely
to those people whose only ideas about Russia are gleaned
from newspaper accounts of the revolution of 1905. We
shall come back to the revolution and its significance
later ; but meanwhile we must notice another very
striking fact about Russian life—its all-pervading religious
atmosphere. Russia is a land of peasants. In England
and Wales 78 per cent of the population live in towns and

the remaining 22 per cent in the country ; in Russia something like 87 per cent live in the country as against 13 per
cent in the towns. These figures are enough to show where
the real centre of gravity of the Russian nation lies. The
peasant, or *moujik*, is a primitive and generally an entirely
illiterate person, but he possesses qualities which his more
sophisticated brothers in the West may well envy and
admire, a profound common-sense, a grand simplicity of life
and outlook, and an unshakable faith in the unseen world.

The interior of Russia is almost wholly unknown in
the West; until a few years back it was as much of a
terra incognita as Central Africa. But the revolution led
English writers and journalists to explore it, and when the
dust and smoke of that upheaval, which had obscured the
truth from the eyes of Europe, passed away, an astonished
world perceived the real Russia for the first time. " Russia,"
writes Mr. Stephen Graham, who has done more than any
other man to bring the truth home to us, " is not a land of
bomb-throwers, is not a land of intolerable tyranny and
unhappiness, of a languishing and decayed peasantry, of a
corrupt and ugly church ; the Russians are an agricultural
nation, bred to the soil, illiterate as the savages, and having
as yet no ambition to live in the towns ; they are as strong
as giants, simple as children, mystically superstitious by
reason of their unexplained mystery." Russia is in fact
145 million peasants—ploughing and praying. And here
once again one is reminded of the Middle Ages. Cross
the Russian frontier and you enter the mediaeval world.
Miracles are believed in, holy men are revered as saints,
thousands of pilgrims journey on foot every year to Jerusalem, which is to every true believer the centre of the
universe and therefore becomes at Easter almost a Russian
city. Russia is the most Christian country in the world,

and her people are the most Christ-like. The turbulence and violence, so contrary to the Christian spirit, which was an inseparable feature of mediaeval feudalism is absent from Russia ; and the gospel of non-resistance, of brotherly love, of patience under affliction, of pity and mercy, which Tolstoi preached so eloquently to the world at large, he learnt from two teachers—the peasant of modern Russia and the Peasant of ancient Palestine, who was crucified upon the Cross.

Yet it is a mistake to talk, as some do, of the power of the Russian Church, or of " priestcraft." The Church has little political power or social prestige. It is the power of religion, not that of ecclesiastical institutions, which is the arresting fact about modern Russia. It is not so much that Russia has a church, as that she *is* a church. In England we have narrowed religion down to one day of the week and shut it up in special buildings which we call churches ; in Russia it is impossible to avoid religion. As you pass out of the gangway of the ticket-office at the railway station, you find yourself in front of a sacred picture with a lamp burning continually before it, and you are expected to utter a prayer before beginning your journey. Every room in Russia has its *eikon*—is in fact a chapel, every enterprise is sanctified by prayer and ceremony. All English travellers in Russia have acknowledged this profound national sense of religion, and contrasted it with the religious formalism of the West. " Italy," wrote Mr. H. G. Wells, on his recent visit to Russia, " abounds in noble churches because the Italians are artists and architects, and a church is an essential part of the old English social system, but Moscow glitters with two thousand crosses because the people are organically Christian. I feel in Russia that for the first time in my life I am in a country where Christianity is alive. The people

I saw crossing themselves whenever they passed a church, the bearded men who kissed the relics in the Church of the Assumption, the unkempt grave-eyed pilgrim, with his ragged bundle on his back and his little tea-kettle slung in front of him, who was standing quite still beside a pillar in the same church, have no parallels in England." Mr. Rothay Reynolds, in his interesting and sympathetic book *My Russian Year*, writes in much the same strain : " In Russia God and His Mother, saints and angels, seem near ; men rejoice or stand ashamed beneath their gaze. The people of the land have made it a vast sanctuary, perfumed with prayer and filled with the memories of heroes of the faith. Saints and sinners, believers and infidels, are affected by its atmosphere ; and so it has come about that Russia is the land of lofty ideals." And Mr. Stephen Graham, again, in his *Undiscovered Russia*, speaks with glowing admiration of the Russian Church. " The Holy Church," he says, " is wonderful. It is the only fervid living church in Europe. It lives by virtue of the people who compose it. If the priests were wood, it would still be great. The worshippers are always there with one accord. There are always strangers in the churches, always pilgrims. God is the Word that writes all men brothers in Russia and all women sisters. The fact behind that word is the fountain of hospitality and friendship."

The religious aspect of Russian life has been dwelt upon at some length, because it is the key to everything in Russia and has a direct bearing upon the present war. " Religion in Russia," writes Mr. Maurice Baring, " is a part of patriotism. The Russian considers that a man who is not Orthodox is not a Russian. He divides humanity, roughly, into two categories—the Orthodox and the heathen—just as the Greeks divided humanity into Greeks and Barbarians.

Not only is the Church of Russia a national church, owing to the large part which the State, the Emperor, and the civil authority play in it, but in Russia religion itself becomes a question of nationality, nationalism, and patriotism." Russian Christianity, like Russian Tsardom, is derived from the old Roman empire of Constantinople. The Russian Church is a branch, and far the most important branch, of the Greek Orthodox Church, which drifted apart from the Catholic Church, which had its centre at Rome, and finally separated from it in the eleventh century. As the greatest Orthodox Christian power in the world, Russia naturally regards herself as the rightful protector of all Orthodox Christians. Her mortal enemy, with whom so long as he remains in Europe any lasting peace is impossible, is the Turk; and her eyes are ever directed towards Constantinople, as the ancient capital of her faith. The spirit of the Crusades is far from dead in the Russian people; the Crimean War, for example, was fought in that spirit.

It will be at once apparent that Russia takes and must continue to take a profound interest in the Christian peoples of the Balkans. Greeks, Roumanians, Servians, Bulgarians and Montenegrins all belong to the Orthodox Church; all have been engaged throughout the nineteenth century in a struggle for existence against the common foe, Islam. Moreover, all except the two first-mentioned peoples are allied to Russia by ties of race as well as by religion, since they are members of the Slavonic stock. To the average Russian, therefore, the bulk of the Balkan peninsula is as much Russia Irredenta, as the north-east coast of the Adriatic is Italia Irredenta to the average Italian; and as a matter of fact there is a good deal more to be said for Russia's case than for Italy's. There is, however, another great power which possesses interests in the Balkans and which is viewed by Russia with a suspicion and dislike hardly inferior to that entertained towards Turkey—I mean the empire of Austria-Hungary. A Catholic state, controlled by Germans and Magyars, Austria-Hungary contains in its southern portion a population of over seven million Slavs, some three millions of whom are of the Orthodox faith. The Dual Monarchy has constantly outraged national and religious feeling in Russia by her treatment of this Slavonic population, and her annexation in 1908 of Bosnia and Herzegovina, both of them Slavonic countries, was regarded as an open challenge to Russia.

It is not therefore surprising that the Tsar has intervened in the present crisis. Had it refused to come to the assist-ance of Servia when Austria attacked her, the Russian Government would have been unable to face public opinion. Even those who know Russia best are amazed at the com-plete unanimity of the country in the matter of this war; and proof that it is not merely a war of aggression inspired by Pan-Slavist sentiment may be found in the fact that all political parties, revolutionaries, constitutionalists and reactionaries, have enthusiastically approved it. How far Germany misunderstood (or affected to misunderstand) the real state of feeling in Russia may be seen in the des-patch of July 26 by the British Ambassador in Vienna, who, in talking the crisis over with the German Ambassador and asking " whether the Russian Government might not be compelled by public opinion to intervene on behalf of a kindred nationality," was told that " everything depended on the personality of the Russian Minister for Foreign Affairs, who could resist easily, if he chose, *the pressure of a few newspapers.*" England drew her sword in this struggle on behalf of Belgium and in the name of civilisa-tion and treaty rights; Russia has done the same on behalf of Serbia and in the name of common blood and a common altar. I, for one, firmly believe that her hands are as clean as ours.

§ 3. *The Revolutionary Movement and its Significance.*— It is now time to say something of the revolutionary movement of 1905 and of its ruthless suppression which gave Russia so evil a reputation in the eyes of Western Europe. It was my good fortune to be a resident in the dominions of the Tsar during the critical years of 1906–9, to be present at a session of the first Duma and to mingle with the members of that historic assembly in the lobby of the Parliament House, to catch something of the extraordinary belief in the coming of the millennium which was prevalent among all classes in Petrograd in the first charmed months of 1906, and finally to have been acquainted with active revolutionaries and their friends throughout the whole of my period of residence. I can therefore speak with a certain amount of inner knowledge of the revolution; and though I do not wish to claim any particular authority for the opinions stated below, which are after all nothing but the opinions of a single individual who has lived for three years in a corner of the Russian Empire, yet they have at least this advantage over those entertained on the subject by the average Englishmen, viz. that they are based not on newspaper reports but on actual experience, and that they were arrived at gradually and—it may be added— with considerable reluctance, since they had, as it were, to win their way through a number of my own personal sympathies and political prejudices. There is, of course, no room here for any detailed treatment of a movement upon which a big book might be written, and I shall therefore have to limit myself to a few rather bald generalisations which I must ask the reader to accept not as the truth, but as what one man of limited experience and vision conceives to be the truth about the Russian revolution.

The main reason why English people get mistaken ideas about Russia is that they imagine Russians to be nothing but Englishmen picturesquely disguised in furs and top-boots, and because they interpret the political situation in Russia in terms of English history and politics. As I have already tried to show, Russians are built differently from English people, *from the soul outwards,* while the political and social condition of the Russian Empire is totally unlike anything that has ever existed in this country. If therefore the real causes of the movement of 1905 and of its failure are to be rightly understood, we must put away from our minds the desire to find analogies in the English revolutions of 1642 and 1688, or the French Revolution of 1789, or the social revolution of which Karl Marx dreamed ; Russia can only be interpreted in terms of Russian history and Russian conditions. In one thing, however, the Russian revolution was like all revolutions which have ever been or are ever likely to be, viz. that it was concerned with two distinct issues, one a narrow question of political and constitutional reform, and the other a far wider question involving an attempt to reconstruct not merely the institutions of society but also to transform the ideals and conceptions upon which society rested.

Let us first of all consider the narrower political issue. This was simple enough ; the outbreak of 1905 had as its primary object the setting up of some form of representa-tive government which would control the bureaucratic machine. It has been already pointed out that the constitution of modern Russia was largely due to the genius of Peter the Great. During the nineteenth century, however, it became apparent to thinking Russians that the constitution, for the sake both of stability and efficiency, needed development in the direction of popular representation. The plea of efficiency was really far the stronger of the two. Had Peter the Great been eternal, he might possibly have continued to exercise an effective control over the administrative system which he created ; for he was a man of superhuman energy and will-power. But most Tsars, who are men of ordinary capacity, found it impossible to do so. The consequence was that the bureaucracy acquired what amounted in practice to absolute irresponsibility. Now irresponsibility is demoralising to any administration, however democratic be the principles upon which its officials are selected. A bureaucracy, ruling without proper external control, becomes a prey to the demons of red tape, routine, officialdom and place-hunting ; it tends to stifle individual initiative and the sense of moral responsibility, since it forgets the real object of its existence—the good government of the country—in its passion for self-preservation and its desire to secure the smooth-working of the machine ; it becomes inhuman, intensely conservative and corrupt. Above all it develops a hyper-sensitiveness to lay criticism, which compels it to do all in its power—and in Russia that power is unlimited—to crush freedom of speech and freedom of the press. The problem, however, of devising some popular check upon its action was an extremely difficult one for the simple reason that the mass of the Russian people never have taken, and even to-day do not take, any interest in political questions. Nevertheless the Tsar, Alexander II., who was one of the most enlightened monarchs that ever sat upon the Russian throne, determined to attempt a solution. Unfortunately on March 1, 1881, the very day when Alexander had given his approval to a scheme of constitutional reform, involving the establishment of representative institutions, he was assassinated by revolutionaries. This fatal act put back the clock for twenty-five years, the court and the nation were thrown into the arms of the bureaucracy as their only protector against terrorism, and reaction reigned supreme. Meanwhile the bureaucracy grew more corrupt, more tyrannical, more inefficient every day, while on the other hand the party of reform, thrust as it were underground and hunted like rats, became more and more bitter in spirit and more and more extreme in theory.

It is important to bear in mind that the struggle has never from beginning to end been one which divided the nation as a whole into two hostile camps. Public opinion, when it has not been indifferent, has swayed now to one side and now to the other, according as it was stirred by some flagrant act of oppression on the part of the bureaucracy or some outrageous act of terrorism on the part of the revolutionaries. The truth is that the civil war in Russia—for it was nothing less—was confined to quite a narrow section of society. It has been said that there are practically speaking no class distinctions in the English sense of the word, in Russia; there is, however, a very real distinction between the *intelligentsia* and the peasants. The *intelligentsia* are the few million educated Russians who control, or seek to control, the destinies of the 145 million uneducated tillers of the soil. There is nothing quite like them in this country, though the expression "the professional class" describes them in part. Broadly speaking, they are people who have passed through school and university, and can therefore lay claim to a certain amount of culture; their birth is a matter of no moment, they may be the children of peasants or of noblemen. It is from this

" class," if we can call it so, that both the bureaucracy and the revolutionary movement draw their recruits. The real tragedy of Russia is that neither the party of reform nor the party of reaction shares, or even understands, the outlook and ideals of the people. Russian culture is still so comparatively recent that it has not yet passed out of the imitative stage ; and, in spite of the work of Pushkin, Gogol, and Dostoieffsky, the books that are read and studied in Russia are for the most part translations from foreign authors. The result is that the political and social ideas of the *intelligentsia* are almost wholly derived from countries whose structure is totally different from their own. We shall presently see that this fact had an important bearing on the development of the outbreak of 1905. It is sufficient here to notice that the struggle was one between two sections of the *intelligentsia*, political idealism against political stagnation, the Red Flag *versus* Red Tape.

After twenty years of bureaucratic government the country as a whole began to grow once again restless. In this period a proletariate had come into being. It was a mere drop in the bucket of 145 millions of peasants, but its voice was heard in the towns, and it was steeped in the Marxian doctrines of Social Democracy. Moreover the peasants themselves had their grievances. They cared nothing and understood less of the political theories which the revolutionaries assiduously preached among them, but they pricked up their ears when the agitators began to talk about land and taxation. Up to 1861 the peasants had been serfs, the property, with the land on which they lived, of the landowner. At their emancipation it was necessary to provide them with land of their own ; the State, therefore, bought what was considered sufficient for the purpose from

the landowners, handed it over to the peasants, and re-
couped itself by imposing a land-tax on the peasants to
expire after a period of forty-nine years. This tax was
felt to be exceedingly onerous, and in addition to this by
the beginning of the twentieth century it became clear that
the land acquired in 1861 was not nearly enough to support
a growing population. These factors, together with the
disastrous Russo-Japanese war, which revealed an appalling state of corruption and incompetency in the government of the country, furnished the revolutionaries with
an opportunity which was not to be missed. A rapid
series of military and naval mutinies, agrarian disorders,
assassinations of obnoxious officials, socialist risings in the
towns, during the year 1905, culminating in the universal
strike of October, brought the Government to its knees,
and on the 17th of the same month the Tsar issued his manifesto granting freedom of speech, freedom of the press, and
a representative assembly. The revolution had, apparently,
won on the constitutional issue.

Yet what looked like the end of bureaucratic absolutism
proved to be the destruction of the revolutionary party.
Had the reformers of 1905 concentrated their energies
upon the task of turning the new legislature into an adequate check upon the bureaucratic system, there is little
doubt they would have succeeded. As it was their success
in this direction was only partial. It is true that a Duma
still sits at the Taurida Palace at Petrograd, but it is
elected on a narrow property franchise, and its relations with
the bureaucracy are as yet not properly defined; it criti-
cises but it possesses no real control. This failure of the
revolution was almost wholly due to the revolutionaries
themselves, who, instead of confining their attacks to the
Government machine, sought to undermine the entire

structure of society and to overthrow the moral and religious ideals of the nation. Moreover, their attitude was entirely negative, and they possessed little or no constructive ability of any kind. Even the first Duma, which contained the ablest politicians among the reformers, did not succeed in passing acts of parliament, affirming the most elementary principles of civil liberty ; and it damaged itself irreparably in the eyes of the country by refusing to condemn " terrorism " while demanding an amnesty for all political offenders. The unique opportunity which the first Duma afforded was frittered away in futile bickerings and wordy attacks upon the Government.

Meanwhile, though a temporary truce was observed during the Duma's sessions, its dissolution on July 21, 1906, two and a half months after opening, was the signal for a fresh outburst of outrages on both sides. The country was fast drifting into anarchy ; agrarian risings, indiscriminate bomb-throwing, *pogroms*, highway robberies carried out in the name of the " social revolution " and euphemistically entitled expropriation, outbreaks of a horrible kind of blood-lust which delighted in motiveless murder for the sake of murder, were the order of the day. The revolution was strong enough neither to crush the reactionaries nor to control the revolutionaries themselves. The foundations of the social structure seemed to be dissolving in a welter of blood and crime, and public opinion, which in its hatred of bureaucracy had hitherto sided with the revolution, suddenly drew back in horror from the abyss which opened out in front of it. Stolypin, the Strafford of modern Russia, who condemned the extremists of both sides, was called to the helm of the State ; his watchword, " Order first, reform afterwards," was backed by the force of public opinion ; and, as he stamped out the revolution with a heel of iron, the country shuddered but approved. The peasants were pacified by the remission of the hated tax, and by measures for providing them with more land ; and Russia sank once more into her normal condition.

But political incompetency is not a reason sufficiently weighty in itself to account for the remarkable revulsion of public feeling against the revolutionary party. Behind the narrow political issue lay the larger philosophical and moral one ; and it was the discovery by the country of the real character and ultimate aims of the party which for a few months in 1906 seized the reins of power that will alone provide a sufficient explanation of one of the most astonishing political debacles of modern history. The revolution was nothing less than an attempt by a small minority of theorists and moral anarchists to force Western civilisation upon Russia, and not Western civilisation as it actually is but a sort of abstract " Westernism " derived from books. For the revolutionaries were far more Western than the Westerns. They had not merely swallowed wholesale the latest and most extreme political and social fads, picked up from the literature of England, France, and Germany, but they possessed a courage of their convictions and a will to carry them out to the logical conclusion which many " advanced thinkers " of the West lack. They were not modernists or new theologians but atheists, not Fabians or social reformers but revolutionary socialists armed with bombs, not radicals but republicans, not divorce - law - reformers but " free lovers." A remarkable book was published in 1910 called *Landmarks*. It was written by a number of disillusioned revolutionaries, and gives a vivid picture of the effect which the foregoing principles had upon the lives of those who upheld them. Here is one extract :

"In general, the whole manner of life of the *intelligentsia* was terrible ; a long abomination of desolation, without any kind or sort of discipline, without the slightest consecutiveness, even on the surface. The day passes in doing nobody knows what, to-day in one manner, and to-morrow, as a result of a sudden inspiration, entirely contrariwise —everyone lives his life in idleness, slovenliness, and a measureless disorder—chaos and squalor reign in his matrimonial and sexual relations—a naïve absence of conscientiousness distinguishes his work ; in public affairs he shows an irrepressible inclination towards despotism, and an utter absence of consideration towards his fellow-creatures ; and his attitude towards the authorities of the State is marked at times by a proud defiance, and at others (individually and not collectively) by compliance."

As a set-off to this picture of moral chaos, it should be remembered that these people when called upon to die for their revolutionary faith did so with the greatest heroism. Nor is the picture true of all revolutionaries ; some of the noblest men it has ever been my good fortune to meet were Russian revolutionaries. But these were the product of an earlier and sterner school, the puritanical " Nihilism " of the 'eighties ; and it is impossible to deny the substantial truth of the above description as far as the rank and file of the modern revolutionary school are concerned.[1] Such people were divided by a whole universe from the peasants to whom they offered themselves as leaders and saviours ; and the schemes of regeneration which they preached were not merely useless, because purely negative, but were exotic

[1] It is confirmed by all impartial observers, see *e.g.* Professor Pares' *Russia and Reform*, chap. ix., entitled " Lives of the Intelligents."

plants which could never flourish on Russian soil. Thus the revolution triumphed for about twelve months as a purely destructive force, but when the necessity for construction arose its adherents found that they were entirely ignorant of the elements of the problem before them. This problem was the peasant, and the revolutionaries, though they had worshipped the People (with a capital P) for years and had done their best to convert them, had never made any attempt to understand them. And when the peasant discovered what the revolutionary was like, he loathed and detested him. " They hate us," a writer in *Landmarks* confesses, " because they fail to recognise that we are men. We are, in their eyes, monsters in human shape, men without God in their soul ; and they are right."

There is a characteristic story told by Mr. Maurice Baring about a certain revolutionary who one day arrived at a village to convert the inhabitants to socialism. " He thought he would begin by disproving the existence of God, because if he proved that there was no God, it would naturally follow that there should be no Emperor and no policeman. So he took a holy picture and said, ' There is no God, and I will prove it immediately. I will spit upon this *eikon* and break it in pieces, and if there is a God He will send fire from heaven and kill me, and if there is no God nothing will happen to me at all.' Then he took the *eikon* and spat upon it and broke it to bits, and he said to the peasants, ' You see, God has not killed me.' ' No,' said the peasants, ' God has not killed you, but we will ' ; and they killed him."

This story, whether true or not, is a parable, in which one may read the whole meaning of the failure of the Russian revolution. It shows how an attack upon what they hold sacred may rouse to acts of fury a people who are admitted by all who know them to be the most tolerant, most tender-

hearted, and most humane in Europe. The notion that
Russia is a humane country may sound strange in English
ears. Yet capital punishment, which is still part of our
legal system, was abolished in Russia as long ago as 1753,
except for cases of high treason. From 1855 to 1876 only
one man was executed in the whole of that vast empire; and
from 1876 to 1903 only 114. On the other hand between
the years 1905 and 1908 the total of executions reached the
appalling figure of 3629. This is but to translate into
criminal statistics the story just quoted; for the years
1905–8 were the years when martial law reigned in Russia,
the years of revolution. The Tsar, it is true, wore the
black cap, and the hangman's rope was manipulated by
the bureaucracy, but the jury who brought in the verdict
was a jury of 145 million peasants.

Such, in broad outline, is the history of the revolutionary
movement which is still so greatly misunderstood in England. It was not the uprising of an oppressed nation, which
successful for a brief while was finally crushed by the brute
force of reaction; it was a civil war between two sections
of a small educated class, in which the sympathies of the
nation after fluctuating for a time eventually came down
heavily against the revolutionaries. There is in truth every
excuse for misunderstanding amongst English people,
especially if they belong to the party of progress in English
politics; for the obvious things about Russia are so decep-
tive. All that one saw on the surface were, on the one
hand, an irresponsible bureaucracy using the knout, the
secret agent, the *pogrom*, and Siberia for the suppression of
anything suspected of threatening existing conditions; and,
on the other, a band of devoted reformers and revolutionaries
risking all in the cause of political liberty, and dying, the
" Marseillaise " on their lips, with the fortitude of Christian

martyrs. But, beneath all this, something immensely bigger was in progress, which can only be described as a conflict of two philosophies of life diametrically opposed or, if you like, a life-and-death struggle between two civilisations, so different that they can hardly understand each other's language ; it is a renewal of the Titanic contest, which was decided in the West by the Renaissance and the Reformation, the contest between the mediaeval and the modern world. To the modern mind no period is so difficult to grasp as the Middle Ages ; our dreams are of progress which is another word for process, of success which implies perpetual change, in either case of " getting on " somewhere, somehow, we know not where or how ; our very universe, from which we have carefully excluded the supernatural, has become a development machine, a huge spinning-mill, and our religion, if we have one, a matter of " progressive revelation." We look before and after, forwards to some dim utopia, backwards to some ape-like ancestor who links us with the animal world. Our outlook is horizontal, the mediaeval outlook perpendicular. The mediaeval man looked upward and downward, to heaven and hell, when he thought of the future, to sun and cloud, land and crops, when he thought of the present. He lived in the presence of perpetual miracle, the daily miracle of sunrise, sunset, and shower ; and in the constant faith in resurrection, whether of the corn which he sowed in the furrow or of his body which his friends would reverently sow in that deeper furrow, the grave. And his life was as simple and static as his universe ; the seasons determined his labours, the Church his holidays. Books did not disturb his faith in the unseen world, for he was illiterate ; nor the lust of gold his contentment with his existence, for commerce was still confined to a few towns. Russia to-day is in spirit

what Europe was in the Middle Ages.[1] The revolutionaries
offered her Western civilisation and Western philosophy,
and she rejected the gift with horror.

Will she continue to maintain this attitude ? " The
Russian peasant," says Mr. Maurice Baring, " as long as he
tills the ground will never abandon his religion or the observance of it. . . . Because the religion of the peasant is
the working hypothesis taught him by life ; and by his
observance of it he follows what he conceives to be the
dictates of common sense consecrated by immemorial
custom." The crucial point of this passage is the condi-
tional clause : " as long as he tills the ground." Of course,
Russia, the granary of Europe, must always be predominantly
an agricultural country ; yet she is at the present moment
threatened in many parts with an Industrial Revolution,
the ultimate effects of which may prove far more subversive
than the attempted revolution of 1905. For beneath her
soil lie explosive materials more deadly than any dynamite
manufactured by *intelligentsia*. Her mineral wealth, at
present almost untouched, is incalculable in quantity and
amazing in variety. When her mines are opened up
Russia will become, according to the judgment of Dr.
Kennard, editor of *The Russian Year-Book*, " without a
doubt the richest Empire the world has ever seen." Attracted by her vast mining possibilities, by her enormous
virgin forests, by her practically unlimited capacity for
grain-production, the capital of Europe is knocking at the
doors of Russia. Factories are rising, mines being started
all over the country. Russia is about to be exploited by

[1] This, of course, by no means implies that she is *behind* the West,
or that she is of necessity bound to pass through the same process
of development. The problem of modern Russia is not to imitate the
West but to discover some way of coming to terms with Western
ideals without surrendering her own.

European business enterprise, just as America and Africa have been. The world has need of her raw materials, and is only interested in her people as potential cheap labour. Thus within the last few years something analogous to the proletariat and the bourgeoisie of Europe has come into existence in Russia. We may catch a glimpse of what these new classes are like from a recent book by Mr. Stephen Graham, called *Changing Russia*. He writes:

" The Russian bourgeois is of this sort; he wants to know the price of everything. Of things which are independent of price he knows nothing, or, if he knows of them, he sneers at them and hates them. Talk to him of religion, and show that you believe the mystery of Christ; talk to him of life, and show that you believe in love and happiness; talk to him of woman, and show that you understand anything about her unsexually; talk to him of work, and show that though you are poor you have no regard for money— and the bourgeois is uneasy. . . . Instead of opera, the gramophone; instead of the theatre, the kinematograph; instead of national literature, the cheap translation; instead of national life, a miserable imitation of modern English life. . . . It may be thought that there is little harm in the commercialisation of the Russian, the secularising of his life; and that after all the bourgeois population of England, France, and Germany is not so bad as not to be on the way to something better. But that would be a mistake; if once the Russian nation becomes thoroughly perverted, it will be the most treacherous, most vile, most dangerous in Europe. For the perverted Russian all is possible; it is indeed his favourite maxim, borrowed, he thinks, from Nietzsche, that ' all is permitted,' and by ' all ' he means all abomination, all fearful and unheard-of bestiality, all cruelty, all falsity, all debauch. . . . Selfish as it is possible to be, crass, heavy, ugly, unfaithful in marriage, unclean, impure, incapable apparently of understanding the good and the true in their neighbours and in life—such is the Russian bourgeois."

Mr. Graham's picture of the new proletariat in the Ural mines is an equally horrible one :

" Gold mining is a sort of rape and incest, a crime by which earth and man are made viler. If I had doubted of its influence on man I needed but to go to the Ural goldfields. A more drunken, murderous, brother-hating population than that of this district I have not seen in all Russia. It was a great sorrow to see such a delightful peasantry all in debauchery. . . . The miner has no culture, no taste, not even a taste for property and squiredom, so that when at a stroke he gains a hundred or a thousand pounds, it is rather difficult to know how to spend it. His ideal of happiness has been vodka, and all the bliss that money can obtain for him lies in that. . . . Mias is a gold-mining village of twenty-five thousand inhabitants. It has two churches, four electric theatres, fifteen vodka shops, a score of beer-houses, and many dens where cards are played and women bought and sold to the strains of the gramophone. It is situated in a most lovely hollow among the hills, and, seen from the distance, it is one of the most beautiful villages of North Russia ; but seen from within, it is a veritable inferno."

Mr. Graham writes as a poet rather than as an economist or a sociologist, but there is no doubt a grave danger to Russia in a sudden adoption of industrial life.

Intelligentsia, bourgeoisie, and proletariate are all products of the same forces, all belong to the same family; they are westernised Russians; they have passed from the fourteenth to the twentieth century at one stride, and the violent transition has cut them completely adrift from tradition and from all moral and religious standards; books, commerce, and industry, the three boasted instruments of our civilisation, have not civilised such Russians, they have *de-civilised* them. But, as yet, Russians of this character form only a tiny fraction of the nation; and there are happily signs that the dangers of an exotic culture are being realised even by the *intelligentsia* themselves. Since the failure of the revolution there has been a remarkable revival of interest among Russian thinkers in the native institutions, habits, and even the religion of the country; and it may be that in time there will emerge from this chaos of ideals a culture and a civilisation which will " make the best of both worlds " by adopting Western methods without surrendering an inch of the nation's spiritual territory, above which floats the standard of religion, simplicity, and brotherly love. The present war, terrible as it is, may do something towards bringing this about, for the Russian people, faced by a common danger and united in a common purpose, are now of one mind and one heart, in a way that they have not been since a century ago Napoleon was thundering at the gates of Moscow.

And let this be said: if Russia should ever cease to be Russia, if she ever loses those grand national characteristics which make her so different from the West, and therefore so difficult for us Westerns to understand, the world as a whole will be infinitely the poorer for that loss. We need Russia even more than Russia needs us; for, while we have grasped the trappings, she possesses the real spirit of democracy. Of the three democratic ideals, proclaimed by France in

1789, the mystical trinity : Liberty, Fraternity, Equality, how much has yet been realised by the peoples of the West ? And Russia is in the way of realising them all ! Fraternity and equality are, as we have seen, the distinctive features of her national spirit and social structure, and, if her liberty is as yet imperfect on the political side, it is far more complete than ours on the side of moral tolerance and respect for the sanctity of human personality. After all, the reason why Russia has not got complete political freedom is because, as a nation, she has hitherto taken no interest in politics ; for the first time in 1905 she discovered the use of political action, and she got out of it a solution of the agrarian distress and a representative assembly ; when she *wants* more liberty in this direction, she will have no difficulty in securing it.

§ 4. *The Subject Nationalities.*—It may fairly be objected at this point that while Russia may possess these excellent qualities, she has consistently refused to allow liberty to other peoples, to the Jews, for example, the Poles, and the Finns. It is necessary therefore to say something on the matter of Russia's subject nationalities before bringing these remarks to a conclusion.

Out of the six or seven million Jews in the world, over five million live within the boundaries of the Russian Empire. Russia is therefore the motherland of the Children of Israel ; though, perhaps, the phrase step-motherland would express more truly the actual relationship, both in its origin and its character. Russia has inherited her tremendous responsibilities towards the Hebrew race from Poland, and her vexed " Jewish question " is in part a just punishment for her complicity in the wicked partitions of that country in the eighteenth century The matter, however, goes back much farther than the eighteenth century. In the Middle Ages Poland was a more powerful state than Russia, and comprised territory stretching from the Gulf of Riga to the Black Sea and from the Oder to the Dnieper. She was also the one country in Europe which offered to the Jews security from persecution and an opportunity of developing the commercial instincts of the race without interference. The result was that Jews settled in large numbers all over the King of Poland's possessions, and the presence of Jews in any part of modern Russia is almost a sure sign that that particular town or province has been Polish territory in former times. The Russian Government has never, except for a short period, allowed the Jews to live in Russia proper, and it is very rare to find Jews in north or central Russia. Even in large cities like Petrograd and Moscow their numbers are small, while it is interesting to note that the Finns have copied the rest of Russia in this respect at least that they have always resolutely refused to admit the Hebrew. Where Russia found Jews among the new subjects which she acquired by her gradual encroachments upon Poland, she had of course to let them remain, but she has confined them strictly to these districts. The existence of this Jewish pale is one of the grievances of the Jews of Russia, but it is not the heaviest. The liberal-minded Alexander II. had shown himself lenient to them ; but his assassination in 1881 at the hands of terrorists and the accession of the reactionary Alexander III. began a period of persecution which has continued until the present day.

Alexander III. was much influenced by his tutor, Pobiedonostsev, who for the next thirty years was the most prominent exponent of the philosophy of Slavophilism. This, which in its modern form may be traced back to 1835, was in fact nothing else than a perverted glorification of the Russian national characteristics which have been dwelt upon above. The Slavophils declared not only that the Russians were a great and admirable nation, which few who really know them will be disposed to deny, but that their institutions—and in particular, of course, autocracy and bureaucracy—were a perfect expression of the national genius which could hardly be improved upon. Furthermore, it was maintained that, since all other countries but Russia had taken a wrong turn and fallen into decadence and libertinism, it was Russia's mission to bring the world back into the paths of rectitude and virtue by extending the influence of her peculiar culture—and in particular again, of course, its special manifestations, autocracy and bureaucracy—as widely as possible. A variant of Slavophilism is Pan-slavism, which works for the day when all members of one great Slav race will be united in one nation, presumably under the Russian crown. Both these movements are examples of that nationalism run mad to which reference has been made in the second chapter.[1] But the Slavophils, who are of course ardent supporters of the Orthodox Church, were faced at the outset with a great difficulty ; the western provinces of Russia, from the Arctic to the Black Sea, contained masses of population which were neither Russian nor Orthodox. The Finns in the north were Lutherans; the Poles in the centre, though Slavs, were Roman Catholic in religion and anti-Russian in sentiment; and the Jews in the centre and south were—Jews. The first step, therefore, towards the Slavophil goal was the " Russification " of the subject peoples of Russia. In theory " Russification " means conferring the benefits of Russian customs, speech, and culture upon those who do not already possess them ; in practice it amounts to the suppression of local liberties and traditions.

[1] See p. 57.

O

It is obvious that it is no easier to make a Jew into a Russian by force than to change the skin of the proverbial Ethiopian ; nor is it likely that the Russian Government ever entertained the idea of making such an attempt. If it had any definite plan at all, it was to render things so uncomfortable to the unfortunate Hebrews that they would gradually leave the country. Real persecution began at the accession of Alexander III. in 1881, when it spread into Russia, significantly enough, from Germany, where a violent anti-Semite agitation had sprung up at the beginning of the year. Riots directed against the Jews, and winked at if not encouraged by the authorities, broke out in the towns of Southern Russia. Edicts followed which excluded the Jews from all direct share in local government, refused to allow more than a small percentage of Jews to attend the schools and universities, forbade them to acquire property outside the towns, laid special taxes upon their backs, and so on. This attitude of the Government encouraged the populace of the towns to believe that they might attack the Jews with impunity. The Jews are regarded in modern Russia in much the same light as they were regarded by our forefathers in the Middle Ages. They are hated, that is to say, on two counts : as unbelievers and as usurers. The condition of affairs in a township where the population is half-Jewish, half-Christian, and where the Christians are financially and commercially in the hands of the Jews, and the Jews are politically and administratively in the hands of the Christians, is obviously an extremely dangerous one. Add to this the presence of a large hooligan section which is found in almost every Russian town of any size, the open disfavour shown towards the Jews by the Government, and the secret intrigues and incitement of the police, and you get a train of circumstances which lead

inevitably to those violent anti-Semitic explosions, known
as *pogroms*, which have stained the pages of modern Russian
history. The revolutionary movement has complicated
matters still further ; for Jews are naturally to be found
in the revolutionary ranks, and the bureaucracy and its
hooligan supporters have tended to identify the Jewish
race with the Revolutionary Party. Nothing can excuse
the treatment of the Jews in Russia during the last thirty-
five years, and the guilt lies almost entirely upon the Government, which, instead of leading the people and educating them
by initiating an enlightened policy towards the Jews, a policy
which might in fact have done more than anything else to
" Russify " the latter, has persistently aided and abetted the
worst elements of the population in their acts of violence.
It has reaped its reward in the rise of one of the most formidable of the revolutionary parties in modern Russia, the
so-called Jewish " Bund."   The Governor of Vilna, in a confidential report written in 1903, declared that " this political
movement is undoubtedly a result of the abnormal position
of the Jews, legal and economic, which has been created
by our legislation. A revision of the laws concerning the
Jews is absolutely urgent, and every postponement of it is
pregnant with the most dangerous consequences."

Yet when we condemn Russia for her *pogroms* and
her Jew-baitings, we must not forget two facts : first,
that these occurrences are the work, not of the real Russian
people, the peasantry which has been described above,
but of the dregs of the population which are to be
found at the base of the social structure in the towns
of Russia as in towns nearer home; second, that Russia
is not the only country in the world that has these racial
problems to face.   I once heard a Russian and an American
discussing the comparative demerits of their respective

lands, and I am bound to say that the former held his own very well. When, for example, the American said, " What about the Jews ? " the other answered, " Well, what about the negroes ? " and he parried the further question, " What about *pogroms* ? " with another of his own, " What about lynching ? " The problems are not, of course, quite on all fours, nor do two wrongs make a right, but a reminder that similar problems exist in other parts of the world will perhaps be enough to show that the Jewish question in Russia is neither unique nor at all easy to solve. Let us, instead of visiting the sins of a few townships upon the heads of the entire Russian nation, be thankful that we have no such problems in our own islands. Recent riots outside the shops of German pork-butchers in different parts of the country do not, it must be confessed, lead one to hope that our people would behave much more calmly and discreetly than the Whites of the Southern States or the Christians of South-West Russia, were they placed in the same circumstances.

The Polish question is at once simpler and its story less damaging to the Russian Government than that of the Jews. The partitions, an account of which has already been given,[1] were of course iniquitous, but, as we have seen, Prussia must bear the chief blame for them. In any case, the Tsar Alexander I. did his utmost for Poland at the Congress of Vienna in 1815. He pleaded eloquently for a reunited Poland, and he almost won over Prussia by making arrangements to compensate her for her Polish territory at the expense of Saxony. But France, England, and Austria opposed his project, and he was obliged to yield to the combined pressure of these powers. Russia is, therefore, not more but less guilty of the present dismembered state of Poland than her

[1] Pp. 24-27.

Western neighbours, among whom we must not forget ourselves ; [1] and she is to-day only attempting to carry out the promise which she made, but was not allowed to fulfil, a century ago. Disappointed as he was, Alexander I. made the best of a bad job by granting a liberal constitution to that part of Poland which the Congress assigned to Russia. Indeed he did everything possible, short of a grant of absolute independence, which at that time would have been absurd, to conciliate public opinion in the Grand-Duchy of Warsaw. Unfortunately the experiment proved a complete failure, largely owing to the factious and self-seeking Polish nobility who have always been the worst enemy of their country. Alexander after a time lost patience, and in 1820 he felt compelled to withdraw some of the liberties which he had conferred in 1815. After this the breach between the Russian Government and the Polish people began to widen, partly owing to stupid and clumsy actions on the side of Russia, partly to the incurable lack of political common-sense on the side of the upper classes in Poland, partly to the fact that the country could never be anything but restless and unsatisfied while it remained divided. The history of Russian Poland since the time of Alexander is the history of two great failures to throw off the Russian yoke, the failure of 1830 and of 1863. These risings were marked by heroism, disunion, and incapacity on the one side, and by relentless repression on the other. The upshot was that Poland was deprived of her constitutional rights one by one, until finally she became nothing more than so many provinces of Russia itself. To some extent, however, the failure of 1863 proved a blessing in disguise. The

---

[1] As a matter of fact our representative, Lord Castlereagh, was Alexander's chief opponent at the Congress in the question of Poland. See *Camb. Mod. Hist.* vol. x. p. 445.

rising had been almost entirely confined to the nobility; Russia therefore turned to the peasants of Poland, released them from all obligations to work upon the estates of the large landowners, and handed over to them at least half the land of the country as freehold property. The result of this measure, and of the removal of the customs barrier between the two countries in 1877, was twofold : the power of the factious nobility was shattered for ever, and a marvellous development of industry took place in Poland which has united her to Russia "with chains of self-interest likely to prove a serious obstacle to the realisation of Polish hopes of independence." [1] It is indeed doubtful whether at this date the Poles cherish any such hopes. What they desire is national unity and self-government rather than sovereign independence, and they know that they are at least as likely to receive these from Russia as from Prussia.

While of late years the relations between Russia and Poland have steadily improved, those between Russia and Finland, on the contrary, have grown rapidly worse. Until 1809 Finland was a Grand-Duchy under the Swedish crown, but in that year, owing to a war which had broken out between Russia and Sweden, she passed into the control of the nearer and more powerful State, after putting up a stubborn resistance to annexation which will always figure as the most glorious episode in the annals of the country. Alexander I., who was at that time Tsar, adopted the same policy towards Finland as he did towards Poland. He refused to incorporate the new province into the Russian State-system, he took the title of Grand-Duke of Finland (thereby implying that she lay outside the Empire), and he confirmed the ancient liberties of the Finns. Later on they even secured greater liberty than they had possessed under

[1] *Camb. Mod. Hist.* vol. xi. p. 629.

Sweden by the grant of a Finnish Diet, on the lines of the Swedish Diet in Stockholm, which should have full control of all internal Finnish affairs. Finland, therefore, gained much from the transfer; she possessed for the first time in her history complete internal autonomy. This state of things lasted for practically ninety years, during which period Finland made wonderful progress both economic and intellectual, so that by the end of the nineteenth century she was one of the happiest, most enlightened, and most prosperous countries in Northern Europe. " As regards the condition of Finland," Alexander I. had declared, " my intention has been to give this people a political existence, so that they may not feel themselves conquered by Russia, but united to her for their own clear advantage ; therefore, not only their civil but their political laws have been maintained." This liberal policy was continued by the various Tsars throughout the century, the reformer Alexander II. taking particular interest in the development of the Grand-Duchy, which he evidently regarded as a place where experiments in political liberty were being worked out that might later be applied to the rest of Russia. The weakness of Finland's position lay in the fact that her liberties really depended upon the personal whim of the Grand-Duke : in theory her constitutional laws were only alterable by the joint sanction of monarch and people ; in practice the small but courageous nation had no means of redress should the Tsar, swayed by bureaucratic reaction, choose to go back upon the policy of his ancestors. And in 1894 a Tsar mounted the throne, Nicholas II., who did so choose.

The word went forth for the " Russification " of Finland. After picking a quarrel with the Diet on the military question, the Tsar on February 18, 1899, issued a manifesto

suspending the Finnish Constitution and abolishing the
Diet. Finland became with a stroke of the pen a department of the Russian Empire. A rigorous Press censorship
was established, the hated governor-general Bobrikoff
filled the country with gendarmes and spies, native officials
were dismissed or driven to resign, an attempt was made to
introduce the Russian language into the schools, and, though
the Finns could only oppose a campaign of passive resistance to these wicked and short-sighted measures, at the
end of seven years the nation which had for almost a century
been the most contented portion of the Tsar's dominions
was seething with ill-feeling and disloyalty. The inevitable
outcome was the assassination of General Bobrikoff by a
young student in June 1904; and when the Russian universal
strike took place in October 1905, the entire Finnish nation
joined in as one man. Finland regained her liberties for a
time, and immediately set to work putting her house in
order by substituting for her old mediaeval constitution a
brand new one, based on universal suffrage, male and
female, and employing such up-to-date devices as propor-
tional representation. The only result of seven years'
" Russification " was the creation of a united democracy,
with a strong socialistic leaven, in place of a nation governed
by an antiquated aristocratic Diet, and divided into two
hostile political camps on the question whether Swedish or
Finnish should be the language of the national culture.
But the fortunes of Finland were accidentally but inextricably bound up with those of the party of reform in Russia,
and when the bureaucracy, after the downfall of the
revolutionaries, found itself once more firmly seated in the
saddle, it returned to the attack on the Finnish Constitution, not indeed with the open and brutal methods of
Bobrikoff, but by gradual and insidious means no less

effective. And it must be admitted that the Russian Duma, as " reformed " by Stolypin, so far from being of any help to Finland in the struggle, has been made the instrument of the destruction of her liberties.

Finland is in a very unfortunate position. Geographically she is bound to form part of the Russian Empire; even the extremest Russophobes in the country have long ago given up hopes of re-union with Sweden; and yet the frontier between Finland and Russia is one which divides two worlds, as all who have made the journey from Helsingfors to Petrograd must have noticed. In literature, art, education, politics, commerce, industry, and social reform Finland is as much alive as any of the Scandinavian States from whom she first derived her culture. In many ways indeed she is the most progressive country in Europe, and it is her proud boast that she is "Framtidsland," the land of the future. Lutheran in religion, non-Slavonic in race, without army, court, or aristocracy, and consequently without the traditions which these institutions carry with them, she presents the greatest imaginable contrast to the Empire with which she is irrevocably linked. Finland is Western of the Westerns, and keenly conscious of the fact just because of this irrevocable link; Russia is—Russia! And yet, as part of the Russian system, she must come to terms sooner or later with the Empire; she cannot receive the protection of the Russian military forces, a protection to the value of which, if reports be true, she is at the present moment very much alive, and yet retain her claims to be what is virtually an independent State. That these claims have been pitched on a high note is no doubt largely the fault of the blundering and cruel policy of the Russian bureaucracy. But it must be admitted that Finland has never tried in the very least to understand her mighty neighbour; she has always sat, as it were, with her back to Russia, looking westwards, and her statesmen have not even taken the trouble to learn the Russian language. There has, in fact, been something a little "priggish" in her superior attitude, in her perpetually drawn comparison between Russian "barbarism" and Finnish "culture." Though her capital, Helsingfors, is but twelve hours by rail from Petrograd, Finland knows as little of the interior of Russia as people do in England.

The policy of the Russian Government, on the other hand, has been marked by that inconsistency, political blindness, and arbitrariness which one expects from an irresponsible bureaucracy. For ninety years Finland was left alone to work out her own salvation, entirely apart from that of the rest of the Empire; and then suddenly it was discovered that her coasts were of the highest strategical importance, and that she was developing a commercial and industrial system in dangerous competition with the tender plant of commerce and industry in Russia itself. The Slavophils raised an outcry, and the decree went out that the Russian whale should swallow this active and prosperous little Jonah. The former policy was really as stupid, though less cruel, than the latter. Had there been anything like that steady political tradition and wide political experience in Russia which we can draw upon in England, the Imperial Government would have from the first endeavoured to draw Finland closer to the Empire, not by bands of steel and iron but by the more delicate and more permanent ties of considerateness, affection, and self-interest. It is political stupidity, based upon ignorance and inexperience, and not inhumanity, which is the real explanation of Russia's unfortunate relations with her subject peoples during the past century. Moreover, the political machinery which has hitherto served her own internal needs is the worst possible instrument for dealing with provinces which possess a full measure of Western political consciousness together with the traditions of political liberty. Russia, therefore, requires representative institutions not merely for the political education of her own people and as a check upon bureaucratic tyranny and incompetency, but also in order that she may adopt some fair and *consistent* policy towards her subject nationalities.

It may be optimistic, but I cannot help feeling that the present war will do much for Russia, much for Finland, much for Poland. Russia is fighting to defend a small nation against oppression, she is fighting a life-and-death struggle with the military bureaucracy which we call " Germany " for the moment, she is fighting on behalf of " liberty " and of the " scraps of paper " upon which the freedom of States and individuals depends. All this will leave a profound effect upon the national consciousness, and may even bring home for the first time to the people at large the meaning of political freedom. Russia is so vast, so loose in structure, so undeveloped in those means of intercommunication such as roads, railways, newspapers, etc., which make England like a small village-community in comparison, that it takes the shock of a great war to draw the whole people together. That it has done so, no one who has read the papers during the last two months can doubt. War, as a historical fact, has always been beneficial to Russia ; the Crimean War led to the emancipation of the serfs, the Japanese War led to the establishment of a Duma, and the present war has already led to surprising results. The consumption of alcohol has been abolished, concessions have been promised to a reunited Poland, and, except against the unhappy Jews in the Polish war-area, there has been a sub-sidence throughout the Empire of racial antagonism. It is the hope of all who love Russia, and no one who really knows her can help loving her, that these beginnings may be crowned not only with victory over Germany in the field of battle but with victory over the German spirit in the world of ideas, a victory of which the first-fruits would be the firm establishment of representative government, a cleansing of the bureaucratic Augean stables, and a settlement of the problem of subject nationalities upon lines of justice and moderation.

But whatever the outcome may be, let us in England be fair to Russia. The road to fairness lies through understanding; and we have grossly misunderstood Russia because we have not taken the trouble to acquaint ourselves with the facts, the real facts as distinct from the newspaper facts, of her situation. When those facts are realised, is it for us to cast the first stone? Russia needs political reform, the tremendous task of Peter the Great needs completing, the bureaucracy must be crowned with representative institutions; but is Russia's need in the sphere of political reform greater than ours in the sphere of social reform?

Look at our vast miserable slums, our sprawling, ugly, aimless industrial centres, inhabited by millions who have just enough education to be able to buy their thinking ready-made through the halfpenny Press and just enough leisure for a weekly attendance at the local football match and an annual excursion to Blackpool or Ramsgate; who seldom, if ever, see the glorious face of Nature and, when they do, gaze into it with blank unrecognising eyes; whose whole life is one long round of monotony—monotonous toil, monotonous amusements, monotonous clothes, monotonous bricks and mortar;—until the very heaven itself, with its trailing cloud-armadas and its eternal stars, is forgotten, and the whole universe becomes a cowl of hodden grey, " whereunder crawling cooped they live and die." And then look at those other millions—the millions of Russia—look at the grand simple life they lead in the fields, a life of toil indeed, but of toil sweet and infinitely varied ; Russia is their country, not merely because they live there but because they—the peasants—now actually possess by far the greater part of the arable land ; God is their God, not because they have heard of Him as some remote Being in the Sunday School, but because He is very near to them— in their homes, in their sacraments, and in their hearts ; and so contentment of mind and soul is theirs, not because they have climbed higher than their fellows, whether by the accumulation of knowledge or wealth, but because they have discovered the secret of existence, which is to want little, to live in close communion with nature, and to die in close communion with God.

BOOKS

MAURICE BARING. *The Mainsprings of Russia.* 1914. Nelson. 2s. net.

This is an excellent introduction to the subject, recording as it does the general impressions of an acute and sympathetic observer ; it does not, of course, pretend to be comprehensive, and says nothing, for example, of the Jews, Poles, Finns, etc.

BERNARD PARES. *Russia and Reform.* 1907. 10s. 6d. net

MILYOUKOV. *Russia and its Crisis.* 1905. 13s. 6d. net.

MAURICE BARING. *The Russian People.* 1911. 15s. net.

These three books may be consulted for the Revolution of 1905 and the events which led up to it. Professor Milyoukov's book was actually published before the Revolution, but its author was leader of the Cadet party in the First Duma, and it is therefore something in the nature of a liberal manifesto. Professor Pares' book, which is perhaps the most penetrating and well-balanced of all and contains most valuable chapters on the *Intelligentsia*, does not, unfortunately, deal with the years of reaction which followed the dissolution of the First Duma. Mr. Baring's book may be recommended especially for the later chapters which deal with the causes of the failure of the Revolution. All three contain a good deal of sound historical matter.

H. W. WILLIAMS. *Russia of the Russians.* 1914. 6s. net.

ROTHAY REYNOLDS. *My Russian Year.* 1913. 10s. 6d. net.

Two good books dealing with life in contemporary Russia. The first is the best and most comprehensive treatment of the new Russia which has emerged from the revolutionary period, and gives one not merely the political but also the social and artistic aspect. The other book is lightly and entertainingly written.

STEPHEN GRAHAM. *Undiscovered Russia.* 1911. 12s. 6d. net.

STEPHEN GRAHAM. *Changing Russia.* 1913. 7s. 6d. net.

STEPHEN GRAHAM. *With the Russian Pilgrims to Jerusalem.* 1913. 7s. 6d. net.

Mr. Stephen Graham may be said to have discovered the Russian peasant for English people, and his books give an extraordinarily vivid and sympathetic picture of Russian peasant-life by one who knows it from the inside. They afford also the best account of religion in Russia as a living force, while those who wish to know more of the Orthodox Church as an institution may be referred to chaps. xxvi. and xxvii. of Mr. Baring's *Russian People*; chap. viii. of the same writer's *Mainsprings of Russia*; and chap. vi. of Sir C. Eliot's (Odysseus) *Turkey in Europe* (7s. 6d. net). The second of Mr. Graham's books deals with the threatening industrial changes in Russia. The third is a fine piece of literature as well as being the only account in any language of one of the most characteristic figures in modern Russian life—the peasant-pilgrim.

SIR D. M. WALLACE. *Russia.* 2 vols. 1905. 24s. net.

Russia and the Balkan States. Reprinted from the *Encyclopædia Britannica.* 2s. 6d. net.

Both these accounts, though written many years ago, have now been brought up to date in view of present events.

R. NISBET BAIN. *Slavonic Europe, 1447–1796.* 1908. 5s. 6d. net.

F. H. SKRINE. *The Expansion of Russia, 1815–1900.* 1903. 4s. 6d. net.

W. R. MORFILL. *Russia.* 1890. 5s.

W. R. MORFILL. *Poland.* 1893. 5s.

Are all useful for the history of Russia, and of her relations with Poland and Finland. Readers may also be referred to the *Cambridge Modern History* (vol. ix. chap. xvi.; vol. x. chaps. xiii., xiv.; vol. xi. chaps. ix., xxii.; vol. xii. chaps. xii., xiii.).

V. O. KLUCHEFFSKY. *A History of Russia.* 3 vols. 1913. Dent. 7s. 6d. net each.

The standard economic and social history of Russia up to the reign of Peter the Great.

H. P. KENNARD. *The Russian Year-Book.* Eyre and Spottiswoode. 10s. 6d. net.

Excellent for facts and figures.

E. SÉMÉNOFF. *The Russian Government and the Massacres.* 1907. 2s. 6d. net.

An account of the *pogroms* in Russia from the Jewish point of view.

J. R. FISHER. *Finland and the Tsars, 1809–1899.* 1899. 12s. 6d.

The best account in English of the history of Finland's relations with Russia up to the beginning of the reactionary period.

K. P. POBIEDONOSTSEV. *Reflections of a Russian Statesman.* 1898. 6s. For Slavophilism.

P. KROPOTKIN. *Memoirs of a Revolutionist.* 1907. 6s.

MAURICE BARING. *Russian Literature.* (Home University Library.) 1s.

A. BRÜCKNER. *A Literary History of Russia.* 1908. 12s. 6d. net.

MAURICE BARING. *Landmarks in Russian Literature.* 1910. 6s. net.

The last-named are the best available books in English on Russian literature. The works of the great Russian novelists are now accessible to English readers. Nothing helps one to understand Russia so well as reading the works of Tourgeniev, Tolstoi, and Dostoieffsky. The best translations are those of Mrs. Garnett. The following are recommended to those who are beginning the study of Russian literature and who are desirous of reading novels which throw light on the springs of Russian life and thought :—

TOURGENIEV. *Fathers and Children.* Heinemann. 2s. net.

A study of Russian Nihilism in the 'eighties, which may be read and compared with Kropotkin's *Memoirs.*

TOLSTOI. *War and Peace.* Heinemann. 3s. 6d. net. *Anna Karenin.* Heinemann. 3s. 6d. net.

The first of these is perhaps the finest treatment of war in modern literature, the subject being the Russian campaign of Napoleon in 1812. No other book gives one a better idea of the way the Russians make war and of the essential greatness of the Russian national spirit.

DOSTOIEFFSKY. *The Brothers Karamazov.* Heinemann. 3s. 6d. net.

This, which is one of the greatest novels ever written, depicts, at once relentlessly and with infinite tenderness, the spiritual conflict which has agitated Russian society for at least fifty years past.

JOSEPH CONRAD. *Under Western Eyes.* 6s.

A powerful study of modern revolutionary types. Conrad, of course, is not a Russian novelist, but he is of Polish origin.

GOGOL. *The Inspector-General.* Walter Scott. 1s. net.

A comedy first produced in Petrograd in 1836. Gogol is one of Russia's classics. This play is a humorous treatment of bureaucratic corruption and inefficiency.

CHAPTER VI

FOREIGN POLICY

THE present war has raised in the minds of many men a question which we as a people will soon be called upon to answer. Was this war necessary ? Or was it caused by the ambitions and foolishness of statesmen ? Might it not have been averted if the peoples of Europe had had more control over the way in which foreign policy was carried on ?

Out of these questions has arisen a demand for the " democratisation of foreign policy " ; that is, for greater popular control over diplomatic negotiations. In view of this, it becomes necessary for every British citizen to gain some idea of what foreign policy is and by what principles it should be governed.

It is the purpose of this chapter to give, first, some account of the actual meaning of the words " foreign policy," and then, secondly, to consider how foreign policy may best be controlled in the interests of the whole population of the British Empire, and in the interests of the world at large.

A. THE MEANING OF FOREIGN POLICY

§ 1. *The Foreign Office.*—To the ordinary man foreign policy is an affair of mystery, and it not unnaturally rouses his suspicions. He does not realise, what is nevertheless the simple truth, that he himself is both the material and the object of all foreign policy.

The business of the Government of a country is to maintain and further the interests of the individual citizen. That is the starting-point of all political institutions. The business of the Foreign Office is a part of this work of Government, and consists in the protection of the interests of the individual citizen where those interests depend upon the goodwill of a foreign Government.

But just as in domestic politics the individual citizen is inclined to suspect—too often with truth—that the Government does not give impartial attention to the interests of all the citizens, but is preoccupied in protecting the interests of powerful and privileged persons or groups, so in foreign policy the individual citizen is particularly prone to believe that the time of the Foreign Office is taken up in furthering the interests of rich bondholders or powerful capitalists. Moreover, the charge is sometimes heard that some of the most powerful of these capitalists are engaged in the manufacture of armaments, and that the Foreign Office aims at securing orders from foreign Governments for these firms, thus encouraging the nations of the world to provide themselves with means of destruction.

Now, just as no sensible man will say that Governments do not often oppress the people under their care, so no sensible man will contend that Foreign Offices do not sometimes sin in the same way. But let us try to give an accurate picture of the work on which the British Foreign Office spends its time.

The organisation of the Foreign Office consists of :

(1) An office, situated in Downing Street, manned by a number of clerks, under the direction of the Secretary of State for Foreign Affairs.

P

(2) The Diplomatic Service—that is to say, from three to eight officials residing in the capital of each foreign country. In the more important countries these officials are called an Embassy, and are under the direction of an Ambassador ; in the smaller countries they are called a Legation, and are under the direction of a Minister. These Ambassadors and Ministers receive instructions from and report to the Secretary of State for Foreign Affairs, and are the mouthpiece of the British Government in all business which Great Britain transacts with foreign countries.

(3) The Consular Service—that is to say, a large number of officials, called Consuls, distributed over all the towns of the world where British subjects have important trade connections or where there are a considerable number of British subjects. These Consuls are under the direction of the Foreign Office and of the Embassy or Legation in the country where they reside, and their business is to assist British trade and protect British subjects.

§ 2. *The Work of the Foreign Office.*—The work of this whole organisation may be divided into four classes :

(1) The protection of individual British subjects. This protection often extends to the most petty matters. Through the offices of a Consul and of an Embassy or Legation flows day by day a continual stream of British subjects who are in small difficulties or have small grievances against the officials of the country. One old lady has lost her luggage ; a working man is stranded without work and wants to get back to England ; a commercial traveller has got into trouble with the customs officials and asks for redress. But the protection thus given is often concerned with very important matters, and is constantly employed on behalf of the poorest and the most helpless. For instance, our officials in the United States are constantly

occupied, in assisting British immigrant working men and women who are suffering hardships under the stringent provisions of the United States immigration laws.

(2) The furthering of British trade. It is the duty of the whole Foreign Office organisation, but especially of the Consuls, to give advice to the representatives of commercial firms, to report openings for the sale of British goods abroad, and generally to give assistance to British trade in its competition with foreign trade. Enquiries will, for instance, be received by a Consul at a Chinese port from a manufacturer of pottery or harness or tin-tacks, asking what type of goods will be likely to find a market in that locality. The Consul will then enquire and give such information as his local knowledge enables him to supply. Or again, a foreign country will sometimes make regulations which hinder the importation of English products. English oats may, for instance, be affected with a blight which Italy fears may infect her crops if she allows their importation. It may then become the duty of the British Embassy at Rome to make arrangements with the Italian Government in order that English farmers may not suffer by losing the market for their produce. But one important point must be remembered, because it is too often forgotten by those who criticise the Foreign Office. There is one general restriction on the activities of the Foreign Office in assisting British trade : no British official is allowed to invite, or try to persuade, any foreign Government to give orders to British firms, whether for war material or for any other article.

What we have already said applies to the relations between civilised countries. But the relations between civilised countries on the one hand, and uncivilised or semi-civilised countries on the other hand, are very much more difficult in many ways. Difficulties especially arise with regard to commerce. Many of the less-developed countries of the world, such as some South American countries and China, cannot, like their richer neighbours, undertake the development of their own resources. They lack money, scientific training, business ability, and so on. They therefore give what are called " concessions " to foreign companies or capitalists ; that is, the Government of the country leases some industry for a term of years to the foreign company. The Mexican Government, for instance, has leased its oil-wells to English, American, and Dutch companies, and the Chinese Government has largely confided the construction and management of its railroads to English, French, and German companies.

Now, in many countries where this happens, the Government is not strong enough or permanent enough to guarantee proper security of tenure to the foreign company to which it grants a concession ; very likely some official is bribed to grant the concession to one company and then bribed by another company to cancel it, or the Government is overthrown by a revolution and its successor cancels the concessions it has granted. By this means, British workmen may be thrown out of work and their employment may pass to workmen in the United States or Germany. Consequently, foreign Governments—the Governments of civilised countries—gradually begin to intervene and give protection to their subjects who have concessions in such countries, provided that they have obtained their concessions in a respectable and proper manner. Competition between the different foreign companies then grows up ; their Governments gradually begin to support them against each other in this competition, until at last it becomes necessary for the different Governments, if bad feeling is to be avoided, to try to arrive at some arrangement among themselves, fixing the way in which the concessions granted by this or that semi-civilised country shall be distributed among the subjects of the Great Powers. Something like this has been recently happening in China.

To a certain extent this line of action seems to be necessary in dealing with backward countries, and it may be made mutually beneficial both to those countries themselves and to the commerce of the Great Powers, but, on the other hand, the whole policy is obviously liable to great abuse. Consequently, every self-respecting Government knows that all matters relating to concessions must be treated with the greatest caution and forbearance, and that the interests of all concerned will be best served in the long run by gradually helping backward countries along the path of civilisation and strengthening their Governments so that they may be able to assume complete control of their own finance and commercial enterprises.

We have now described roughly the personal and the commercial work of the Foreign Office. This work covers all the immediate interests of individual British citizens in regard to foreign countries. If each British subject is protected when abroad, and if the trade and industry of the country on which the welfare and livelihood of every individual citizen ultimately depends is fostered and safeguarded, then the primary duties of the British Government in relation to other Governments have been discharged.

But this is not enough. If the interests of the individual citizen of Great Britain are to be permanently secured in relation to foreign countries, we must be assured that the policy of foreign Governments is civilised and generally friendly to British subjects. There must be a general rule of law throughout the world on which British subjects can count with assurance of safety. And so the Foreign Office has a third and even more important class of work :

(3) The maintenance of permanent good relations with foreign countries. These good relations are secured, not only by continually friendly communication with foreign Governments over innumerable questions of policy, but also by the conclusion of a network of treaties, some of them designed to establish international co-operation in particular social or economic questions such, for instance, as the existing treaty between Great Britain and France providing for the mutual payment of compensation under the Workmen's Compensation Laws of the two countries, and others concluded with the object of defining the mutual policy of different countries in general matters such as the regulation of trade. The newest and most important class of treaties are those which, like the Hague Conventions and the treaties guaranteeing the neutrality of Belgium and Luxemburg, attempt to lay down general rules of law which all countries agree to observe. In other words, the office of diplomacy is to secure *certainty* in the government of the world, so that every man may know what to expect in dealing with his fellow-man of a different nationality.

It is difficult to describe adequately the complexity of this diplomatic work. The economic and social systems of the world have become so involved and intertwined that there is hardly anything one country can do which does not react in some way on the interests of the subjects of another country.

In every European country, and in the United States, the Government is being more and more called upon to regulate the delicate economic and social machinery on which modern life depends. Each Government adopts

an attitude towards such problems which is determined
partly by the thought and the beliefs of its public men, and
partly by the course of historical development through
which each country has passed. There thus arises gradually
in each country a more or less definite policy with which
the country becomes identified. Formerly the policy of
most European countries was mainly confined to questions
arising in Europe itself, but in these days of industrial
expansion the real aims of their policy generally lie
outside Europe.

There are vast regions of the world where civilised
government does not exist, or is only beginning to exist,
but where the citizens of civilised countries travel and carry
on trade. No civilised country can prevent its traders
going where they please—indeed, the prosperity of every
great country now depends to some extent at least upon
its traders finding new markets for the sale of their goods
—but if these traders go to an uncivilised country like
Central Africa or the interior of China or the South Sea
Islands the civilised country not only feels obliged to
protect them there, but it must also, by every claim of
justice and humanity, prevent them from ill-using the uncivilised and helpless natives.

The horrors which accompany the unregulated activity
of foreign traders in a savage country may be seen from the
Life of John G. Paton, a missionary in the New Hebrides
Islands of the Southern Pacific. These islands, before they
came under the government of any civilised Power, were
visited by European and American traders, especially
traders in sandalwood. " The sandalwood traders,"
wrote Paton, " are as a class the most godless of men. . . .
By them the poor defenceless natives are oppressed and
robbed on every hand ; and if they offer the slightest

resistance they are ruthlessly silenced by the musket or revolver. . . . The sale of intoxicants, opium, fire-arms, and ammunition by the traders among the New Hebrideans, had become a terrible and intolerable evil." It became necessary for the civilised Powers to prohibit, by international regulation, the sale of fire-arms and intoxicants in the islands. Such international regulations are always very difficult to enforce, and finally the administration of the islands was taken over by Great Britain and France, who now govern them jointly.

Hence the civilised countries of the world have gradually been led to assume jurisdiction in uncivilised regions, and have converted many of them into colonies or " protectorates " or " spheres of influence." By this process the interests of the nations of Europe reach out into all the far corners of the earth, and constant care and arrangement is needed to prevent those interests clashing. Where the interests of the different Powers do clash in an uncivilised or semi-civilised part of the world a general international agreement is often necessary to put things straight ; for instance, during recent years the interests of Germany, France, and Spain—and to a less degree those of many other countries—were continually clashing in Morocco, till it became necessary in 1906 to conclude a general international treaty called the Algeciras Act, whereby the relations of all the Powers with regard to Morocco were defined in great detail.

§ 3. *The Balance of Power.*—It is this continual attempt to arrange matters and to keep the different Powers clear of each other in order that their interests may not clash, which is the real underlying cause to-day of what is known as the " Balance of Power." The doctrine of the " Balance of Power " grew up at the end of the seventeenth and

beginning of the eighteenth century when Europe was
threatened by the policy of aggression and conquest under-
taken by Louis XIV. of France. From that day onward,
European statesmen have sought to establish a definite
European system and to limit the growth of the European
States in such a way as to ensure that no State should be
so strong as to threaten its neighbours.

The history of this attempt has been somewhat as
follows. A coalition of the States of Europe was formed
against the aggressions of Louis XIV. After a series of
wars a peace was signed at Utrecht in 1713 defining the
boundaries of the European States in such a way as to
establish equality and a balance of power between them.
For about ten years European statesmen attempted to
maintain the system thus set up by means of what has since
come to be known as the " Concert of Europe "—that is,
by means of a series of international congresses where
opportunity was given for the settlement of disputes
between the different States. Soon, however, it became
impossible to satisfy the ambitions of the rulers and peoples
of Europe by this means, and the Concert of Europe broke
up. Wars followed, during which those statesmen, especially
in England, who believed in the " Balance of Power " sought
to prevent any European nation from being overwhelmed
by its enemies. To this end, England supported Austria
against the attacks of Prussia, and then later supported
Prussia against a coalition formed by the rest of Europe
to crush her. Unfortunately neither England nor France
had sufficient strength or courage to prevent the partition
of Poland between Prussia, Russia and Austria, which
constituted a fatal violation of the Balance of Power.
Peace did not return to Europe till 1815, when the whole
continent had been driven to combine for the overthrow of

Napoleon. At the Congress of Vienna in that year the "Concert of Europe" was revived, and for more than thirty years it practically succeeded by means of a series of international congresses in maintaining a stable and balanced system in Europe.

But this "Concert of Europe" was the very thing against which the democratic forces on the continent finally rebelled, for the "Concert" took the form of the so-called "Holy Alliance" between the rulers of Europe, whose object was to prevent popular movements from disturbing the neat and orderly peace which they had created. The system created by the Congress of Vienna began to break down in 1848. Since then the warlike nationalist and democratic movements in Europe, followed by the tremendous economic growth of the European nations, have made it almost impossible to secure any stable balance of power, though a more or less successful attempt to establish such a balance in the affairs of south-eastern Europe was made at the Congress of Berlin in 1878. The two Hague Conferences of 1899 and 1907 did little but reveal the mutual fears and suspicions of the European nations, though many statesmen, especially English and American, laboured sincerely to make the Hague Conventions the guarantee of a lasting peace. But it must be observed that the "Balance of Power," which was originally a distinctly European conception, has now become a world-wide conception. In order to secure a balance of power between the European States it is no longer sufficient to settle European frontiers; it is necessary to settle and, as it were, dovetail into each other the economic interests of the European countries in Africa, Asia, and the Southern Pacific. It is also necessary to define the relations of European countries to the States in North and South America.

What is the conclusion to be drawn from this history ? The idea of the Balance of Power is unsatisfactory. You cannot really " balance " living forces. Nations are not dead masses which can be weighed against each other, but living growths which expand according to obscure natural laws. Human laws can never stop natural growth ; growth can only be stopped by death, and so the Balance of Power seems to necessitate continual conflict. And so, at least twice in the last two centuries, the attempt to maintain a stable European system by a peaceful " Concert of Europe " has broken down. Once, in the Holy Alliance, that Concert itself became an intolerable tyranny. Many men to-day hope to secure peace by re-establishing the Concert of Europe on a democratic basis, but it may well be doubted whether any such system can be permanent, unless there be a radical reform in the mind and character not only of European statesmen but of the European peoples. We shall discuss this later, but meanwhile we may say this at least. A balance of power is an imperfect conception. It is a rough and ready—almost barbarous— policy. The best that can be said for it is that no alternative policy has been devised, or at least none has succeeded. Every one of us who has a spark of idealism believes that the day will come when it shall give place to some more perfect system. But at the present day not only international politics but also home politics are governed by this idea of a balance of power. No democracy has yet been able to establish itself in any country except by virtue of a continual conflict between class and class, between interest and interest, between capital and labour, and international conflicts are but the reflection of the domestic conflicts within each State ; both are continual unsuccessful attempts to reach a stable equilibrium, and

they can only be ended by a true fusion of hearts and
wills.

§ 4. *The Estimation of National Forces.*—It has been
necessary to undertake this long discussion in order to give
a more or less clear idea of the work done by diplomacy
in maintaining a stable international system. Arising out
of this we have now to consider the fourth class of work—
and the most difficult—which the Foreign Office has to
perform. For want of a better name we may call it—

(4) The estimation of national forces. Nations are not
mere agglomerations of individuals ; they have each their
own character, their own feelings, and their own life.
Science has done little to determine the laws of their growth,
but, as we have seen, each nation does grow, reaches out
slowly—almost insensibly—in this or that direction, and
gathers to itself new interests which in their turn give new
impulse to its growth. Perhaps the best simile that we
can use for the foreign policy of the world is that of a
rather tangled garden, where creepers are continually
growing and taking root in new soil and where life is therefore always threatening and being threatened by new life.
The point is that we are dealing with *life*—with its growth
and decay; not with the movements of pieces on a chequer-
board.

Now, the Foreign Office largely exists in order to watch
this growth and, like a gardener, to train and lead it in
directions where it can expand without danger. But for
this work intimate knowledge is necessary—knowledge
not so much of the personal character or policy of those who
govern the different nations, but knowledge of the character,
the economic needs, the beliefs, the feelings, and the
aspirations of the half-dumb millions who form and ultimately determine the life of each nation. The diplomatist

must study every political and social movement which goes on in a nation ; he must estimate the effect which the national system of education is having on the mind of the nation ; he must form an idea of the lessons which the Government of his own country should learn from the government of other countries, whether it be, for instance, lessons in constitutional government or in municipal sanitation ; and he must above all be able to warn his Government of the dangers to his own country which the growth of foreign countries seems to entail, in order that peaceful measures may be taken in time to prevent a collision.

This, then, is a rough account of the actual work of diplomacy. It is not a full account. There are many wrong things done which deserve criticism, but which we have not had space to mention. There is also much self-sacrificing and thankless work done by diplomatists and consuls in distant parts of the world—much seeming drudgery which can hope for no reward—many honourable services rendered to the public of which the public never hears. But the above account will suffice to give a rough idea of the organisation with which we are dealing, and we may now pass on to consider the question of how this organisation should be managed and controlled.

B. The Democratisation of Foreign Policy

This phrase is rapidly becoming a political catchword. As such it requires to be approached with the utmost caution. Before going further it is necessary to test the assumptions underlying it and to inquire how far they really correspond to the facts.

§ 1. *Democracy and Peace.*—First of all, the main assump-

tion made by Englishmen who advocate the democratisation of foreign policy is that international peace would
thereby be assured. True, the extension of the democratic
principle is to many men an end in itself, quite apart from
the question whether it tends to peace. But great masses
of men are not moved to make political demands merely
by theoretical considerations ; it is the pressure of definite
and imminent evils which arouses them to action. In the
case of England the demand for greater democratic control in
the sphere of foreign policy arose in large measure from the
sudden realisation, in the late summer of 1911, at the time
of the so-called Agadir crisis, that war between this country
and Germany was a possibility with which English statesmen and the English people had to reckon. We had felt
the breath of war actually on our cheek, and a large section
of English sentiment revolted from it. A demand was
raised for a democratic policy of peace. Three years later,
on August 3, 1914, when Parliament met to decide the
happiness or sufferings of the quarter of the human race
comprised in the British Empire, the same demand was
voiced in a series of speeches which accurately expressed
the belief that peace was the policy of the people, while
war was the secret aim of their rulers. Mr. T. Edmund
Harvey, M.P., spoke as follows :

" I am convinced that this war, for the great masses of
the countries of Europe, and not for our own country alone,
is no people's war. It is a war that has been made . . . by
men in high places, by diplomatists working in secret, by
bureaucrats who are out of touch with the peoples of the
world, who are the remnant of an older evil civilisation
which is disappearing by gradual and peaceful methods."

Mr. Ponsonby, M.P., spoke in the same sense :

" I trust that, even though it may be late, the Foreign Secretary will use every endeavour to the very last moment, disregarding the tone of messages and the manner of Ambassadors, but looking to the great central interests of humanity and civilisation to keep this country in a state of peace."

Democracy means peace ;— can we accept this assumption ? Contrasts are sometimes illuminating, and it may be well to turn from the Parliamentary debate of August 3 to an article written sixty-two years ago in an English review by the greatest democrat of his time. In April 1852 Mazzini published in the *Westminster Review* an appeal to England to intervene on the Continent in favour of the revolutionary movements in progress there since 1848. The following is an extract from that article :

" The menace of the foreigner weighs upon the smaller States ; the last sparks of European liberty are extinguished under the dictatorial veto of the retrograde powers. England—the country of Elizabeth and Cromwell—has not a word to say in favour of the principle to which she owes her existence. If England persist in maintaining this neutral, passive, selfish part, she will have to expiate it. A European transformation is inevitable. When it shall take place, when the struggle shall burst forth at twenty places at once, when the old combat between fact and right is decided, the peoples will remember that England had stood by, an inert, immovable, sceptical witness of their sufferings and efforts. . . . England will find herself some day a third-rate power, and to this she is being brought by a want of foresight in her statesmen. The nation must rouse herself and shake off the torpor of her Government."

Mr. Ponsonby appealing in the name of the people to Sir Edward Grey to stand aloof from European war; Mazzini appealing in the name of the people to the respectable, peaceable, middle classes of England to forsake Cobden's pacifist doctrines and throw England's sword into the scale of European revolution—it is a strange contrast which serves to remind us that the word "democracy," so lightly bandied about by political parties, has many different meanings and has stood for many different policies. It may be roughly said that it stood for internationalism in 1792, when France claimed as her mission the liberation of all nations under the tricolor; it stood for nationalism in 1848 in the mouth of Mazzini, Kossuth and the German constitutional party; to-day it again stands for internationalism in the more advanced countries of Europe, but are we justified as yet in calling this more than a phase in the development of democratic doctrine? It is a very difficult question, which it would be presumptuous to try to answer offhand; all we have tried to show here is that, on the whole, the assumption as to the peaceful tendencies of a democratic foreign policy is a doubtful one, on which we must to some extent reserve our judgment.

§ 2. *Foreign Policy and Popular Forces.*—The above considerations will help us to appreciate at its true value the second main assumption which lies behind the demand for increased democratic control of foreign policy—namely, the assumption that the stuff of international politics is at present spun from the designs of individual statesmen, and has no relation to the needs of the peoples they govern. Stated thus, this idea will not bear examination for a moment. The doctrine of the "economic interpretation of history," which has received perhaps its most emphatic expression in the teaching of Marxian socialists, is now in one form or another accepted by all thinking men. But "economics" is after all a rough name for the sum of the ordinary needs and efforts of every single human being, and the economic interpretation of history means that the history of the world is in the long run determined by the cumulative force of these humble needs and efforts. This and this alone is the real stuff of international politics. Statesmen may attempt to found systems, but the only real force in international as in domestic politics is the education of the individual man's desires. It is indeed open to any critic to say that our present capitalist economic system is responsible for war because it dams up and diverts from their true channels the needs and the efforts of the mass of mankind. But to this an Englishman may fairly answer that the free trade system under which our capitalist organisation has reached its greatest development was built up by the Manchester School with the sincere and avowed object of introducing universal peace. Cobden avowed this object clearly :

"I see," he said, "in free trade that which shall act on the moral world as the law of gravitation in the universe, drawing men together, thrusting aside the antagonism of race and creed and language and uniting us in the bonds of eternal peace. . . . I believe that the desire and motive for large and mighty empires, for gigantic armies and mighty navies . . . will die away."

Yet, in spite of these aspirations, great wars have come to England, not once, but at least three times, since these words were spoken, and armaments are immeasurably larger than ever before.

Let us understand one thing clearly in connection with the present war. Mr. Ponsonby, in the words already quoted, implored Sir E. Grey to "look to the great central

Q

interests of humanity and civilisation," and to preserve the neutrality of England in those interests. But at the moment at which he spoke the eyes of English statesmen were looking at one thing alone. It was not a question of what French statesmen expected them to do. The British Government had explained quite clearly to French statesmen that they must not expect armed support from England. This fact had been made clear to the French Foreign Office long before in a series of conversations between the statesmen, and it had been embodied in a letter from Sir E. Grey to the French Ambassador. But when the shadow of war actually fell on France these conversations and this letter faded into the background. It was no longer a question of what the French President expected from the King of England. It was a question of what Jacques Roturier, artisan in the streets of Paris, knowing that the Germans were on the frontier and might be dropping their shells into Paris in a fortnight, expected from John Smith, shopkeeper in the East India Dock Road, London, safe behind the English Channel from all the horrors of war. That was, not rhetorically but in all soberness of fact, the real " international obligation " on August 3, 1914 ; for though treaties are made by statesmen they are in the long run interpreted, not by statesmen, but by the public opinion which becomes slowly centred on them—by the hopes and fears of millions of working men and women who have never read the terms of the treaty but to whom it has become the symbol of a friendship on which they can draw in case of need. The magistrate may write the marriage lines, but the marriage becomes what the husband and wife make it—a thing far deeper and more binding than any legal contract.

In the light of these considerations, we can establish

one point of supreme importance in dealing with foreign policy—namely, that the causes of war are very different from the immediate occasions of war. When the British Government, at the outbreak of the present war, published a White Paper containing the diplomatic correspondence between July 20 and August 4, 1914, they were publishing evidence as to the immediate occasion of war—namely the Austrian ultimatum of July 23 to Serbia which brought on the war. In the twelve days which intervened between the delivery of that ultimatum and the declaration of war between England and Germany, the negotiations on which hung the immediate fate of Europe were, it is true, conducted by a few leading statesmen. But it is of little use to argue whether or not these negotiations were conducted ill or well, for they were not the real *cause* of the war. The cause of the war must be sought in the slow development of forces which can be traced back for years, and even for centuries. It was comparatively futile for Parliament to discuss whether this or that despatch or telegram was wise or unwise; the real questions to be asked were—What produced the crowds in Vienna surging round the Serbian Legation at the end of June, and round the Russian Embassy at the end of July; what produced the slow, patient sympathy for the Balkan peoples and hatred for Austria in the heart of millions of Russian peasants; what produced the Servian nationalist movement; above all, what produced that strange sentiment throughout Germany which could honestly regard the invasion of Belgium as justifiable? To answer those questions we have to estimate the force of the most heterogeneous factors in history:—for instance, on the one hand, the slow break-up of the Turkish Empire, extending over more than two centuries, which has allowed the cauldron of the Slavonic Balkan peoples to boil up through the thin crust of foreign domination ; and on the other hand, the gradual development of the whole system of German State education, and the character of the German newspapers, which have turned the eyes of German public opinion in upon itself and have excluded from public teaching and from the formation of thought every breath of fresh air from the outside world, until at last German public sentiment, through extreme and incessant self-contemplation, has lost the calmness and simplicity which were once the strength of the German character. No man can allot the responsibility for these things, spreading as they do over generations ; but assuredly the responsibility does not rest with the half-dozen Ministers for Foreign Affairs who were in power in July 1914.

If we are right in what we have said above, then the phrase " the democratization of foreign policy " takes on a new meaning. It does not mean merely the introduction into foreign policy of any set of democratic institutions ; it means the realisation by both statesmen and people that foreign policy is already in its essence a fundamentally democratic thing, and that the success or failure of any line of action depends not upon the desires of politicians but upon the mighty forces which move and determine the life of peoples.

At present the statesmen do not realise this sufficiently, and hence comes much futile and aimless talking and writing among politicians who fancy that what they say or write to each other in their studies can determine the course of the world. In order to enable diplomatists to discharge all the duties we have already enumerated under the heading of " the estimation of national forces," they need to have a better training and a fuller knowledge of the life and social movements both of their own country and of foreign countries. The Royal Commission on the Civil Service was still considering, when war broke out, how this could be accomplished. It is too long a question to enter on here, but it may safely be said that the more the problem is examined the more does it appear to be, like the wider problem of the whole body of 200,000 civil servants in the United Kingdom, a question of national education, and not a mere matter of Government regulations and democratic institutions. What is required, in the Foreign Office, as in the whole British civil service, has been well expressed by Mr. Graham Wallas in his book *Human Nature in Politics*:

" However able our officials are and however varied their origin, the danger of the narrowness and rigidity which has hitherto so generally resulted from official life would still remain and must be guarded against by every kind of encouragement to free intellectual development."

§ 3. *Foreign Policy and Education.*—But if statesmen do not sufficiently realise the strength of existing popular forces in foreign policy, it is equally true that the people themselves do not realise it. The people of every country are inclined to think that they can alter the destiny of nations by ousting one foreign minister from power and setting up another; they think that speeches and the resolutions passed by congresses can change fundamental economic facts. They think that mere expressions of mutual goodwill can take the place of knowledge, and they forget that no nation can shake itself free in a moment from the historical development which has formed it, just as no man can wholly shake himself free from the character which he has inherited from his ancestors. Indeed all our phrases—our whole attitude of mind—shows how little we, as a people, realise popular forces. We commonly speak, for instance, of Russia as if nothing in that vast country had any influence on foreign affairs except the opinions of a few bureaucrats in Petrograd. Our sympathy for or hostility to Russia is determined by our opinion of the Russian bureaucracy, and we never spare a thought for the hopes and fears and the dumb but ardent beliefs of millions of Russian peasants. We are apt to dismiss them from our minds as ignorant and superstitious villagers tyrannised over by the Tsar, without troubling to enquire narrowly into the real facts of Russian life. We thus make precisely the same mistake that diplomatists too often make. We forget that the masses of peasants who flow every year on pilgrimage to the shrines of their religion constitute a more vital fact in the history of the world than the deliberations of the Duma or the decisions of police magistrates.

Here we have a lesson to learn from Germany, for German statesmen, strangely enough, have taken immense trouble to make their policy a democratic one. The whole German nation is behind them because for years and years they have taught the nation through the schools, the universities, and the press, their own reading of history and their own idea of what true civilisation is. They have adapted their teaching to the fundamental characteristics and to the history of the German people. They have taken pains to ally the interests alike of capital and labour to their policy, and to fuse the whole nation by a uniform national education and by a series of paternal social reforms imposed from above. The real strength and danger of Germany is not what her statesmen or soldiers *do*, but what Germans themselves *believe*. We are fighting not an army but a false idea; and nothing will defeat a false idea but the knowledge of the truth.

When this war is over, whatever its outcome may be, we must try to introduce a new era into the history of the world. But our fathers and our fathers' fathers have tried to do this same thing, and we shall not succeed if we go about the work in a spirit of self-sufficiency and hasty pride. Only knowledge of the truth will enable us to succeed. Knowledge of the truth is not an easy thing; it is a question of laborious thought, mental discipline, the humility which is content to learn and the moral courage which can face the truth when it is learnt. How are we to gain these things?

First of all, by schools, universities, classes—all the machinery of our national and private education.

Then, by the same means as popular government employs in other matters—by discussion, by debates in Parliament, by criticism of the Government. Now, these means are not employed at present partly because it is feared that criticism of the Government in matters of foreign policy will weaken its hands in dealing with foreign nations. This is a just fear if criticism merely springs from the critics' personal likings or prejudices, but no such evil effects need be feared if the criticism springs from deep thought, from knowledge of the facts and from the patience and wisdom which thought and knowledge bring. But partly also effective discussion of foreign politics does not exist because we are more interested in home politics. We really have, if we cared to use it, as much democratic control over the Foreign Office under our constitution as over any Government Department, for the Foreign Office, like every other Department, is under the control of a member of Parliament, elected by the people. But we are more interested in social reform, in labour legislation, and in constitutional reform than in foreign politics; and so it is on questions of home policy that we make and unmake Governments, and when we discuss whether a Conservative or a Liberal Government ought to be in power, we never think what effect the change would have on foreign policy. If the democracy is to take a real part in foreign politics, it must recognise that great responsibilities mean great sacrifices. We must be content to think a little less of our internal social reform, and give more of our attention to the very difficult questions which arise beyond the Channel and beyond the Atlantic Ocean. We must live constantly in the consciousness that the world to-day is one community, and that in everything we do as a people we bear a responsibility not to ourselves alone but to the population of the British Empire as a whole and to the family of nations.

But when we have really set ourselves to understand and discharge the responsibilities of foreign policy, how shall we, the people of this country, make our opinions effective ? How can we be sure that the Foreign Office will carry out a policy corresponding to the considered convictions which we as a people have formed ?

As already stated, we have in our hands the same means of Parliamentary control over foreign policy as over internal policy. Parliament can overthrow a Government whose policy it disapproves, and it can refuse to grant supplies for the carrying out of such a policy. Short of this, the people can express through Parliament its views as to the way in which foreign policy should be conducted, and generally Ministers will bow, in this as in other matters, to the clearly expressed views of Parliament. We have, in fact, recently seen a striking example of this. When after the international crisis of 1911 the country clearly expressed the opinion that no secret engagements should be entered into with any Power which would force Great Britain to go to war in support of that Power, the Prime Minister stated, and has repeated his statement emphatically on several subsequent occasions, that the Government of this country neither had entered, nor would enter, into any such secret engagements, and that any treaty entailing warlike obligations on this country would be laid before Parliament. This has now become a fixed and recognised fact in British policy, and it is not too much to say that, like other constitutional changes under the British system of government, it is rapidly becoming a part of the unwritten constitution of the country.

But many people would like to go beyond this, and lay down that no treaty between Great Britain and another country shall be valid until it has been voted by Parliament. Many countries have provisions of this kind in their constitutions ; for instance, the constitution of the United States provides that all treaties must be ratified by a two-thirds majority of the Senate, and the French constitution contains the following provision :

" The President of the Republic negotiates and ratifies treaties.   He brings them to the knowledge of the Chamber so soon as the interests and the safety of the State permit.

" Treaties of peace and of commerce, treaties which impose a claim on the finances of the State, those which relate to the personal status and property rights of French subjects abroad, do not become valid until they have been voted by the two Chambers.   No cession, exchange, or increase of territory can take place except by virtue of a law."

Such constitutional provisions may be good in their way, and it may be that we should copy them.   But the question is one of secondary importance.   Whether treaties must actually be ratified by Parliament, or merely laid before Parliament for an expression of its opinion, as is commonly done in this country, the Parliament and people of Great Britain will have control over foreign policy just in the measure that they take a keen interest in it. If they take a keen interest no statesman dependent for his position on the votes of the electorate will dare to embody in a treaty a policy of which they disapprove; while if they do not take an adequate interest, no amount of constitutional provisions will enable them to exercise an intelligent control over the actions of statesmen.

The same may be said of another expedient adopted in many countries; namely, the appointment by Parliament of Committees on Foreign Affairs, with power to call for papers and examine Ministers on their policy. Democratic government both in foreign and internal affairs has hitherto rested on the idea that Parliament should have adequate control over the principles on which policy is conducted, but must to a large extent leave the details of administration to the executive departments which are controlled by the Ministers of the Crown. Parliament, whether through committees or otherwise, will never be able to follow or control all diplomatic negotiations, any more than it can control all the details of the administration necessary to carry out a complicated law like the Insurance Act; and Committees of Parliament, however useful, will have no influence unless the people of the country so recognise their responsibilities in foreign politics that they will demand from the men whom they elect to Parliament a judgment and a knowledge of foreign affairs, at least as sound and well based as they now require in the case of internal affairs.

It will be seen that this imposes a very difficult task on

the British electorate. How are they to weigh foreign
affairs and internal affairs against each other ? What are
they to do if they approve the internal policy of a Government, but disapprove of its foreign policy, or *vice versa* ?
Are we, for instance, to sacrifice what we believe to be our
duty in foreign affairs in order that we may keep in power
a Government which is carrying out what we believe to be
a sound policy of internal social reform ? It is here, it
would seem, that some reform is really needed. There is
one solution : namely, to separate the control of domestic
affairs on the one hand and foreign affairs on the other,
placing domestic affairs in the hands of a Parliament and
and a Cabinet who will stand or fall by their internal policy
alone, and entrusting foreign affairs to an Imperial Parliament and an Imperial Cabinet formed of representatives
not of Great Britain alone but of the whole British Empire.
This is an idea which merits the most careful consideration
by the people of the United Kingdom, for it may well be
doubted whether any real popular control of foreign policy
is possible until some such division of functions takes place.

One word in conclusion. If it is true that domestic policy
and foreign policy are separate functions of Government,
it is also true that the domestic policy of a country in the
long run determines its foreign policy. International
peace can never be attained between nations torn with
internal dissensions ; international justice will remain a
dream so long as political parties and schools of thought
dispute over the meaning of justice in domestic affairs.
A true ideal of peace must embrace the class struggle as
well as international war. If we desire a " Concert of
Europe " which shall be based on true freedom and not on
tyranny, it behoves us to realise our ideal first in England,
and to raise our country itself above the political and social

conflicts and hatreds which have formed so large and so
sordid a part of our domestic history for the last decade.

BIBLIOGRAPHY

It is difficult to give a list of books illustrating foreign policy in
general. The lists given in other chapters sufficiently illustrate the
various problems with which foreign policy to-day has to deal.

The diplomacy of a century ago is well illustrated by the *Diaries
and Correspondence of the Earl of Malmesbury.* 4 vols. 1844. (Out
of print.) For the diplomacy of the middle of the nineteenth
century, when the present national forces of Europe were being
created, the following biographies are useful :

Life of Lord Stratford de Redcliffe, by Lane-Poole. 2 vols. 1888.
Life of Lord Granville, by Lord Fitzmaurice. 2 vols. 1905.
Life of Lord Clarendon, by Sir Herbert Maxwell. 2 vols. 1913.
Life of Lord Lyons, by Lord Newton. 2 vols. 1898.
Life of Cavour, by Roscoe Thayer. 2 vols. 1911.
Bismarck's Reflections.

There are many studies of the diplomatic problems of the present
day, but as they deal with history in the making they are to be read
for the general survey they give of forces at work rather than as
authoritative statements. A very comprehensive survey of all the
complexities of international politics will be found in Fullerton's
Problems of Power (1913). 7s. 6d. net.

The actual workings of diplomacy may best be seen in the " White
Books " of diplomatic correspondence, periodically published by the
Foreign Office, such, for instance, as the successive volumes of
Correspondence Respecting the Affairs of Persia. Perhaps the best
idea of the actual labour of foreign relations can be gained by con-
sulting such compilations as Hertslet's *Commercial Treaties*—23 vols.
1827–1905—which are a record of work actually completed.

On the staffing of the Foreign Office and the Diplomatic Service,
see the fifth Report of the Royal Commission on the Civil Service
(Cd. 7748), just published (5½d.).

CHAPTER VII

THE ISSUES OF THE WAR

"March ahead of the ideas of your age, and it will follow you: go with them, and you can feel at ease: remain behind them, and you are lost."—NAPOLEON III.

§ 1. *Is there an Idea behind the War?*—The object of the preceding chapters has been to provide the historic background without which it is impossible to understand either the motives of our opponents or the events which led up to their quarrel. It is now necessary to attempt a survey of the issues raised by the war, both as concerns Europe as a whole and the individual nations which form its component parts. This is a task of no small difficulty, for just as it is true to say that no war in the previous history of mankind has ever been waged on so huge a scale as this, so it is also true to say that the issues raised by it are vaster and more varied than those of any previous European conflict. It is as though by the pressure of an electric button some giant sluice had been opened, unchaining forces over which mortal men can hardly hope to recover control and whose action it is wellnigh impossible to foresee.

Yet complex as is the problem before us, it is essential that we should face it bravely. There is grave danger lest, just as we have been " rushed into " this war (through no fault of ours, as the diplomatic correspondence abundantly proves), so we may at a given moment be " rushed out " of it, without having reached any very clear idea as to what issues are involved, and how far our vital interests have been affected.

The essence of the problem before us is to discover whether there is an Idea behind this war —whether on our own side or on that of the enemy. A dangerous question, this !—a question posed again and again by the jingoes and the fanatics of history, and invariably answered accord- ing to the dictates of their own convenience. And yet a question which we dare not shirk, a question which a Carlyle, a Ruskin, a William Morris would not have hesitated to formulate. Does Britain stand for an Idea ? Is it true that we are fighting in the main for the cause of Liberty and Democracy, for progress in Europe and the world at large ? And if this be really true to-day, how can we best ensure that it shall still be true at the close of this long war, if, as we hope and pray, victory crowns the arms of the Allies ? It was an Idea that nerved Britain for the struggle against Napoleon. It was an Idea that inspired Germany in the great uprising of 1813 against Napoleon. It was an Idea that brought the Balkan League into being and carried its armies in triumph to Salonica and Adrianople. Freedom, Unity, Liberation, such were the forms which that Idea took : the determination of a free people to resist an upstart despot's designs of world- dominion ; the enthusiasm of a divided nation for the dream of national unity ; the longing of races which had but recently won their own freedom, to emancipate their kins- men from an alien and oppressive yoke. In each of these struggles error and even crimes were committed by the victors, and yet it is a thousand times true to assert that the victorious Idea represented in each case the triumph of civilisation. To-day the position is equally clear. In opposing Germany's claim to override international treaty obligations to suit the convenience of her military strategists, in associating ourselves with Belgium and Serbia in their vindication of the rights of the smaller nations, we are not merely resisting a fresh bid for world-dominion on the part of a single power, but are challenging the theory that Might is superior to Right in the political world.

§ 2. *The Aims of British Statesmanship.*—Mr. Asquith on September 19 defined as follows the three main aims of British statesmanship in entering upon war : " (1) To vindicate the sanctity of treaty obligations and what is properly called the public law of Europe, (2) to assert and to enforce the independence of free States, relatively small and weak, against the encroachments and the violence of the strong, and (3) to withstand, as we believe in the best interests not only of our own Empire, but of civilisation at large, the arrogant claim of a single Power to dominate the development of the destinies of Europe." In speaking thus, Mr. Asquith had no intention of placing Britain upon a moral pedestal or of suggesting that we have ever enjoyed a monopoly of political right dealing. Every nation has blots upon its scutcheon ; and the cynic may point to the Irish Union, the destruction of the Danish fleet, the Cyprus Convention, as proofs that we have richly earned the name of " Perfidious Albion." Let us forego the patriotic retort which would fling in Prussia's teeth such incidents as the conquest of Silesia, the partition of Poland, the Ems telegram, the seizure of Kiaochau. But let us, while admitting our shortcomings in the past, nail our colours to the mast and insist that this war shall never degenerate into one of mere revenge or aggrandisement, that the fate of the nations of Europe shall be decided, so far as possible,

in accordance with their own aspirations rather than the
territorial ambitions of dynasties or racial cliques.

Is it, then, possible, when considering the lines of settlement, to lay down any general principles ? The Europe
which we have known has gone beyond recall ;˙ the new
Europe which is coming to birth will be scarcely recognisable
to those who have known its predecessor. Its political,
racial, social, economic outlook will be radically changed.
Let us then meet fate halfway and admit boldly that we
want a new Europe. But let us bear in mind the fiery
process by which a huge bell is forged and the fate which
befell the impatient apprentice who opened the furnace
doors too soon. The Prussian leaders, to whom war is an
ideal and a programme, are entitled, if fortune should
desert them, to manœuvre for a " draw " ; for they would
console themselves with the hope of winning a subsequent
match. But to us, who regard war as a hateful necessity,
from which we do not shrink, but which we did everything
in our power to avert—to us there can be no thought of
relinquishing our task, until there is a reasonable prospect
of a really lasting settlement. We should need no prompt-
ing from our statesmen to realise that this must be " a fight
to a finish." There must be no reversion to the *status quo*,
that accursed device of a worn-out diplomacy, with its inevitable seeds of new quarrels and yet another Armageddon.

Public Law, Nationality, and a general reduction of
armaments (as distinguished from complete disarmament)
are the three foundation stones of the new era, as already
envisaged in the public utterances of those who have some
right to speak for the Triple Entente. Let us then endeavour
to apply these principles to the various problems raised by
the war. It is obvious that their application depends upon
the victory of the Allies. If we are defeated, public law

will have lost its value, for the Germans will have asserted their right to violate its fundamental provisions. The idea of Nationality will have received its death-blow ; for not only will the independence of several of the smaller nations have been destroyed, but Germany will have reasserted her right to dominate her own minor nationalities, and to drain the life-blood of the 26 million Slavs of Austria-Hungary in a conflict with their own Slavonic kinsmen. Finally, all hope of reduced armaments will have been exploded, since the theory of Blood and Iron will have attained its fullest expression in the virtual domination of a single power on land and sea. Regrets or misgivings we may have, but the time for their utterance has long since passed. The British nation must have no illusions ; defeat means the downfall of the Empire, and the reduction of Britain to the position of a second-rate power. Either we shall emerge victorious, or for all practical purposes we shall not emerge at all. Even if *we* shrink from a " fight to a finish," our enemies can be relied upon to persist to the bitter end. It is for this reason only, and not because I underestimate for a moment the vast resources, the splendid organisation, the military valour of Germany, that I restrict myself in the following pages to a consideration of the possible effects of victory rather than of defeat. It would be the height of folly to anticipate victory before it is achieved ; but it is essential that we should be prepared for all possible contingencies, and this involves a careful survey of the various factors in an extraordinarily complicated situation.

§ 3. *Britain and Germany.*—In the forefront of the discussion stands our quarrel with Germany. What are to be our future relations with Germany after the war ? If there is anything in the assertion that we are fighting for

R

the cause of liberty and progress, it can only mean that we are fighting a system rather than a nation—Prussian militarism and bureaucracy, but not German civilisation. We have to go still further and consider the motive powers behind that iron system. Sitting in our little island, we are apt to forget what it means to possess a purely artificial frontier of 400 miles, and to see just beyond it a neighbour numbering 171,000,000 inhabitants, in an earlier stage of civilisation and capable of being set in motion by causes which no longer operate in the western world.

If the final settlement is to be just and lasting, the demands of the victors must be adjusted to the minimum, not the maximum, of their own vital interests. For Britain the central problem must inevitably be : What is to be the position of the German Navy if we are successful in this war ? Is anything even remotely resembling disarmament to be attained unless that Navy is rendered innocuous ? Is it conceivable that even if Britain accepted the *status quo*, a victorious Russia could ever tolerate a situation which secured to Germany the naval supremacy of the Baltic, and the possibility of bottling Russian sea-trade ? Even the opening months of the war have shown what ought always to have been obvious, that sea-power differs from land-power in one vital respect : military supremacy can be shared between several powerful States, but naval supremacy is one and indivisible. In this war we shall either maintain and reassert our command of the sea, or we shall lose it : share it with Germany we shall not, because we cannot.

Again, what is to be the fate of German shipping and German colonies ? Can we not curtail Germany's war navy, while respecting her mercantile marine ? Is it either expedient or necessary to exact the uttermost farthing in the colonial sphere in the event of victory ? It is obvious that just as Germany offered to respect French territory in Europe at the expense of the French colonial empire, so the Allies, if victorious, might divide the German colonies between them. By so doing, however, we shall provide, in the eyes of the German nation, a complete justification of William II.'s naval policy. One of the most widespread arguments among educated Germans (including those friendly to this country) has always been that German colonies and shipping are at the mercy of a stronger sea-power, and that therefore Germany only holds her sea-trade on sufferance. If, as a result of the war, we take from her all that we can, we shall ingrain this point of view in every German. We should thus tend to perpetuate the old situation, with its intolerable competition of armaments, unless indeed we could reduce Germany to complete bank-ruptcy—a thing which is almost inconceivable to those who know her resources and which would deprive us of one of our most valuable customers.

On the other hand, we must of course remember that any extra-European territorial changes depend not merely upon the attitude of Britain and her Allies, but upon the wishes of the Dominions. Even in the event of victory, it is still not London alone that will decide the fate of New Guinea, of Samoa, or of German South-West Africa. The last word will probably be spoken by Australia, New Zealand, and South Africa, and it is improbable that any one of the three will consent to the restoration of territory which they have occupied. It is only in the case of German colonies which border upon British Crown colonies (*e.g.* Togoland, Cameroon, or East Africa) that the decision will rest entirely with the European governments. At this stage it would be absurd to suggest even the bare outlines of a settlement ;

but it is well to emphasize the fact that it involves not only the United Kingdom but the Dominions, and that on its solution depends the future development of the British Empire. In other words, the war can only result in the downfall of the Empire or in the achievement of Imperial Federation and a further democratisation of the central government.

§ 4. *Nationality and the German Empire.*—Finally, there is a still graver question. Is Germany, if defeated, to lose territory *in Europe*? and if so, would it be either possible or expedient to compensate her in other directions for such a loss? The application of the principle of Nationality to the German Empire would affect its territory in three directions—Alsace-Lorraine, Schleswig-Holstein, and Posen. Let us very briefly consider these three problems.

(1) The population of the two provinces of Alsace and Lorraine is mainly German by race and language, but none the less it had become by 1870 almost entirely French in feeling, as the result of its long union with France. The Germans, in reannexing the provinces after the war, were actuated almost equally by reasons of sentiment and strategy. They welcomed the recovery of a section of their race which had been wrested from them by the brutal aggression of Louis XIV. and the dynastic policy of his successor; they also desired to secure their western frontier against the possible attacks of France, which, under the Third Empire, was still most emphatically an aggressive power. In drawing the new frontier they included for purely strategic reasons a small portion of western Lorraine, round the fortress of Metz, which was admittedly as French as Champagne or Picardy. From 1871 till 1911, Alsace-Lorraine was governed as a direct appanage of the Imperial Crown; in the latter year it received a constitution, but

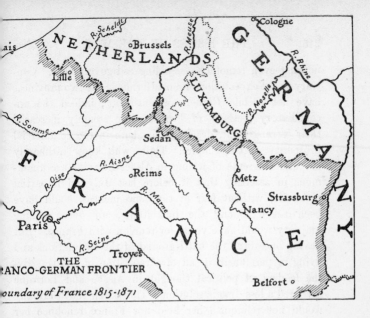

THE
FRANCO-GERMAN FRONTIER
.... Boundary of France 1815-1871

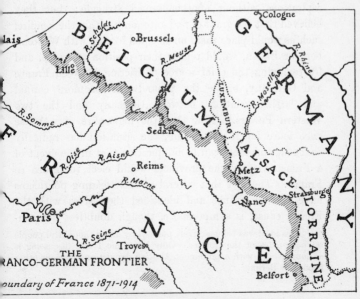

THE
FRANCO-GERMAN FRONTIER
.... Boundary of France 1871-1914

THE FRANCO-GERMAN FRONTIER

nothing even remotely resembling self-government. Contrary to the expectation of most Germans, the two provinces have not become German in sentiment; indeed the unconciliatory methods of Prussia have steadily increased their estrangement, despite their share in the commercial prosperity of the Empire. Those who know intimately the undercurrents of feeling in Alsace-Lorraine are unanimous in asserting that if before last July an impartial plebiscite, without fear of the consequences, could have been taken among the inhabitants, an overwhelming majority would have voted for reunion with France. But having once been the battleground of the two nations and living in permanent dread of a repetition of the tragedy, the leaders of political thought in Alsace and Lorraine favoured a less drastic solution. They knew that Germany would not relinquish her hold nor France renounce her aspirations without another armed struggle; but they believed that the grant of real autonomy within the Empire, such as would place them on an equal footing with Würtemberg or Baden, would render their position tolerable, and by removing the chief source of friction between France and Germany, create the groundwork for more cordial and lasting relations between Germany and the two Western Powers.[1] Now that the nightmare of war has once more fallen upon them, the situation has radically changed, and there can be no question that in the event of a French victory the provinces would elect to return to France. The fact that several of their leading politicians have fled to France and identified themselves with the French cause, is symptomatic, though doubtless not con-

[1] This ideal was being actively pursued by many thoughtful people on both sides of the frontier. Only last June I was discussing it at some length with a prominent Alsatian deputy and various other friends in Berlin.

clusive. That the government of the Republic, if victorious, will make the retrocession of Alsace-Lorraine its prime condition of peace, is as certain as anything can be certain in the seething pot to which triumphant militarism has reduced unhappy Europe. It may, then, seem merely pedantic to refer to an alternative solution ; and yet there is unquestionably a great deal to be said in favour of forming the two provinces into an independent State, or better still, uniting them in federal union with Luxemburg and Belgium. Thus would be realised that " Middle Kingdom " which so many efforts have been made to create, from the days of Charlemagne onwards. Henceforward the fate of Alsace-Lorraine would be neither French nor German ; they would become a neutral clearing-house for the two cultures which have both come to be so inextricably bound up with the life and traditions of the border race. At the same time the most fertile source of friction between France and Germany would be removed, and the two countries would no longer glare at each other across a frontier bristling with fortifications.

(2) The problem of Schleswig-Holstein presents far less difficulty, if treated on a basis of nationality. Much has been written about the enormity of Prussia's treatment of Denmark in 1848 and 1863 ; but the plain truth is that the great majority of the population of the two duchies was as enthusiastic in favour of union with their German kinsmen farther south, as the population of Alsace-Lorraine was reluctant to be torn from France. The whole of Holstein and much the greater part of Schleswig always was, and is, pure German by race. Unfortunately Prussia, in annexing territory which is as German as Kent is English, also acquired a portion of North Schleswig, which is as unquestionably Danish, alike by blood and by sentiment.

Hence a complete revision of frontiers on a racial basis would certainly involve the cession to Denmark of the extreme eastern portions of Schleswig, as far as and including the port of Flensburg.

To-day, however, this question is complicated by strategic considerations, due to the creation of the Kiel Canal as an almost impregnable naval base. The suggestion has already been seriously put forward, that Denmark should be allowed, in the event of Germany's defeat, to extend her territory as far as the north bank of the Canal, which would thus become an international highway for peaceful commerce, possibly under a general guarantee of neutrality. Whether such a present might not prove a very grave embarrassment to Denmark, and whether the guarantee would be more effectual than the treaty which secured Belgian independence, are questions which depend mainly upon the mood of the peoples of Europe after they are tired of shedding each other's blood. But it is well to realise that the question of the Kiel Canal is one which may very possibly lead to a prolongation of the war, and which, as I have already hinted, Russia will not allow to rest, even if Britain should hesitate to complete the work.

(3) The third point at which, on a basis of racial redistribution, a defeated Germany must inevitably suffer territorial loss, is the Polish district on her eastern frontier. The present kingdom of Prussia includes 3,328,750 Poles among its subjects, mainly in the former duchy of Posen, but also in Silesia and along the southern edge of West and East Prussia (known as Mazurians and Kasubians). The pronouncedly anti-Polish policy pursued by the German Government for over twenty years past has aroused deep and insurmountable hatred against Prussia in the heart of the Poles, who even in the days when Berlin was relatively

conciliatory towards them had never relinquished their passionate belief in the resurrection of their country. Above all, the attempt to denationalise the eastern marches by expropriation, colonisation of Germans, and other still cruder methods, has not only been in the main unsuccessful, but it has roused the Poles to formidable counter-efforts in the sphere of finance and agrarian co-operation. This coincided with remarkable changes in Russian Poland, which has rapidly become the chief industrial centre of the Russian Empire. Economic causes have toned down the bitterness which Russia's cruel repression of Polish aspirations had inspired, and to-day Prussia is unquestionably regarded by every Pole as a far more deadly enemy than even the Russian autocracy, the more so as the conviction has steadily gained ground that the Polish policy of Petrograd has been unduly subject to the directions of Berlin. While, then, the Poles look upon the promises from either of these two capitals with pardonable suspicion and reserve, it is certain that to-day such hopes as they may entertain from foreign aid centre more and more upon Russia.

Any attempt to reconstruct the kingdom of Poland, whether as an independent State or, as seems more practicable, as an autonomous unit within the Empire of the Tsar, would inevitably deprive Prussia of the greater part of the Duchy of Posen (except the three or four western " Kreise " or districts, in which the German element predominates), a strip of eastern Silesia from the upper reaches of the Vistula northwards, and a further strip of territory in East Prussia, extending from near the fortress of Thorn along the Mazurian lakes (in fact, the scene of the opening battles of the present war). Polish extremists, however, not content with these indubitably Polish districts, are already laying claim to the lower reaches of the Vistula and to Danzig as the port of the historical Poland; and there is a further tendency in certain Russian circles to regard the whole province of East Prussia as part of the natural spoils of war. And yet it is obvious that the annexation of Danzig,[1] one of the bulwarks of the old Hanseatic League, and of Königsberg, the cradle of the Prussian Crown and of modern German philosophy, would be a flagrant violation of that principle of Nationality which the Allies have inscribed upon their banner. The province of which Königsberg is the capital is to-day, whatever it may have been in the twelfth century, as German as any portion of the German Empire. Moreover, it is the stronghold of Junkerdom, that arrogant but virile squirearchy which still forms the backbone of the old Prussian system; and while it is doubtless the desire to undermine this caste by robbing it of hearth and home that prompts such drastic schemes of conquest, it cannot be too clearly realised that we should not only be guilty of a monstrous injustice in lending our support, but should be sowing the seeds of a new and even thornier problem than that of Alsace-Lorraine. It would, moreover, be a superfluous injustice, since it is perfectly possible to create on broad racial lines a new frontier at least as natural as that which divides Russia and Germany to-day.

Such are the changes which an application of the principle of Nationality involves. Let us then be under no illusions; they are changes such as can only be extracted from a Germany which has virtually ceased to exist as a military power—a contingency which is still remote to-day, and which can only be attained by enormous

---

[1] Strictly speaking, Danzig, though under Polish suzerainty till 1772, has always been a German town enjoying complete autonomy. It shares the fame of Hamburg and Lübeck as one of the greatest of the mediaeval Hansa towns.

sacrifices in blood and resources. It is only by readjust-
ment and compensation in other directions that the German
nation could be induced even to consider a revision of
frontier, and from the nature of things such compensation can only have one meaning—the break-up of Austria-
Hungary.

§ 5. *The Future of Austria-Hungary.*—For many years
this break-up has been foretold by political pessimists
inside and outside the Habsburg dominions, and by many
interested agitators both in Central and in Western Europe.
The present writer, on the other hand, has always regarded
Austria-Hungary as an organism full of infinite possibilities
of progress and culture, a State modelled upon that diversity
of type which Lord Acton held to be the surest guarantee
of liberty. Those who affected to treat it as moribund
under-estimated both the underlying geographical bases
of its existence and its great natural resources; they
emphasised what separates rather than what unites. In
short, they saw the rivalry between the two mottoes
" Divide et Impera " and " Viribus Unitis," and laid
undue stress upon the former. Just because they realised
the extraordinarily complicated nature of the racial problems
involved, they tended to overlook the steady advance made
in recent years by Austria in the conceptions of political
and constitutional freedom. But at every turn Hungary
has been Austria's evil genius : the influence of the Magyar
oligarchy has given a reactionary flavour alike to internal and
to foreign policy, has hampered every reform, and poisoned
the relations of the State with its southern neighbours.

For a short time the aggressive Balkan policy of Count
Aehrenthal, as exemplified in the annexation of Bosnia and
the diplomatic duel with Russia, was hailed as worthy of the
Bismarckian tradition; but it soon became clear that he was

far from being the genius whose advent the Monarchy was so anxiously awaiting. In recent years, then, despite many hopeful signs, and despite increasing activity in almost every sphere of life, a kind of progressive paralysis has taken hold upon the body-politic. Three main causes may be noted —the lack of any great men capable of counteracting the

AUSTRIA-HUNGARY : POLITICAL DIVISIONS

Emperor's lack of initiative, which was always very marked, but has been accentuated by advancing old age ; the superficial and malicious outlook of the capital and the classes which control it ; the alliance between the Magyar oligarchy and the Jewish press and Haute Finance, working in a pronouncedly anti-Slav direction. The wheels still went round, but the machine of State made less and less progress : stagnation and aimlessness were everywhere apparent.

On all sides it was recognised that the existing system had become unworkable, and that a catastrophe could only be averted by speedy reforms. To many far-seeing patriots the last hope of salvation for the State seemed to lie with the late Heir-Apparent, not perhaps as the ideal Prince, but as a man of courage and force of character, possessing the necessary energy to carry through drastic political changes. His removal was a crushing blow to all who still hoped against hope in the regeneration of the Monarchy. His place was filled by a young man, lacking both experience and prestige; never was there less sign of the heaven-born genius who alone could save a desperate situation.

In the life of nations and States, as in that of individuals, there sometimes comes a moment when it is possible to make the " Great Refusal " of which Dante sang ; and " History teaches that those who decline, or prove unworthy of, the leading rôle which is offered to them, are trodden mercilessly underfoot." In closing the German edition of my book with these words, I expressed the conviction that " for a State such as Austria there could only be one choice " ; but unhappily her statesmen have preferred the fatal alternative.[1] " The historic mission of the House of Habsburg is the vindication of equal rights and liberties for all races committed to its charge. The abandonment of this mission would endanger the very existence of a Great Power upon the Middle Danube." [2] Austria has proved

---

[1] In July 1911 I dedicated *The Southern Slav Question* to " that Austrian statesman who shall have the courage and the genius necessary to solve the Southern Slav Question." In April 1913, in publishing a German edition, I added the words, " At the twelfth hour this dedication is repeated." In November 1914 it is unhappily only too evident that that hour has already struck.

[2] See *Racial Problems in Hungary*, concluding sentence.

untrue to this mission, and the inexorable forces of history seem at this moment to be working her destruction. Nations, like individuals, sometimes commit suicide; and those who have most earnestly warned them against such a crime are left as mourners in the funeral procession.

The war-fever which seized upon the populace of Vienna and Budapest last July typified the feelings of the three dominant races in the Monarchy, the Germans, the Magyars, and the Jews; but it is no criterion for the attitude of large masses of the population. In fact, the war has accentuated the centrifugal tendencies which were so marked a feature of recent years, and which the introduction of Universal Suffrage and the annexation of Bosnia arrested but failed to eradicate; a stringent censorship may conceal, but cannot alter, this fact. Disaffection is rife in portions of the army and affects its powers of resistance, while the financial and economic crisis grows from week to week. Cynics have tried to define the mutual relations of Germany and Austria-Hungary by comparing the former to a strong man carrying a corpse upon his shoulders, and the course of the war during the first three months would seem to confirm this view. So far as Austria-Hungary is concerned, its two outstanding features have been the signal failure of the "punitive expedition" against Serbia and the debacle of Auffenberg's army in Galicia. Friendly observers were prepared for a break-down in the higher command and were aware that many Slav regiments could not be relied upon, but they had expected more from the German and Magyar sections of the army and from the very efficient officers' corps, as a stiffening element. It is now known that despite the aggressive policy of its chiefs, the Austro-Hungarian army was far from ready, and that its commissariat and sanitary arrangements utterly broke down.

The evident failure to profit by the experience of two general mobilisations within the previous six years is in itself a proof that there is " something rotten in the state," and it is already obvious that only a complete and crushing victory of Germany can extricate Austria-Hungary from the war without loss of prestige and actual territory. Unless the Russians can be not merely defeated but driven out, it is absolutely certain that they will retain the province of Galicia, or at least the eastern portion, with its Ruthene or Ukrainian population ; unless the Serbian army can be overwhelmed, Bosnia and at least some portion of Dalmatia will fall into the hands of Serbia. This would be an eminently unsatisfactory solution or rather it would be no solution at all, for it would solve neither the Polish, the Ukraine, nor the Southern Slav questions. I merely refer to it as a possible outcome of one form of stalemate ; it is hardly necessary to add that from every point of view stalemate is the result which is most to be dreaded, since it inevitably involves fresh wars in the immediate future. Whatever happens, the effete Dual System in its present form is doomed, for while an Austrian defeat means dissolution, an Austrian victory means the absorption of Serbia and Montenegro, and in either case the balance between Austria and Hungary will be fatally disturbed and a new constitutional arrangement rendered inevitable. It is thus a tragic paradox that while the attempt to bolster up the Dual System was undoubtedly one of the great underlying causes of the war, its first effect is likely to be the collapse of that very system.

The Dual System once abolished, it might seem reasonable to aim at a reconstruction of Austria-Hungary on a modified federal basis. But this was essentially a peace-ideal. The war, far from kindling a common patriotism which in Austria-Hungary was so conspicuous by its absence, has placed a gulf of blood between race and race, and rendered their continued existence under the same roof not only difficult but undesirable. Even in the event of only relative failure on the part of Austria-Hungary a much more radical solution may be expected, while the effect of her complete defeat would be to place the solution of the whole "Austrian problem" in the hands of the Entente Powers and of her own disaffected populations. In that case there are two probable alternatives, one more radical than the other. Both depend to a large extent upon the development of the military situation and upon as yet incalculable economic influences, but it is possible to indicate their broad outlines. Indeed, this is the best means of illustrating the conflicting fears and aspirations which the great conflict has still further intensified in the racial whirlpool of Central Europe. Let us consider the less drastic of the two first.

Austria, as distinguished from Hungary, consists of seventeen provinces, of which Galicia is the largest and most populous; yet there are many Austrians who have long regarded its possession as anything but an unmixed blessing for the Monarchy as a whole, and would scarcely regret its loss. It has always occupied a peculiar autonomous position of its own; its political, social, and economic conditions are at least a century behind those of the neighbouring provinces, and have given rise to many gross scandals. It has been a hot-bed of agrarian unrest, electoral corruption, and international espionage. Instead of paying its own way, it has been financially a heavy drag upon the State, while racially it provides, in the Polish-Ruthene conflict, an object-lesson on the disagreeable fact that an oppressed race can become an oppressor when occasion arises. But the argument which weighs most with the Germans of Austria is that the Poles of Galicia have for a whole generation held in their hands the political balance in the Austrian Parliament, and that the disappearance of the Polish and Ruthene deputies would destroy the Slav majority and correspondingly strengthen the Germans. The Magyars in their turn would no doubt view with some alarm the extension of the Russian frontier to the line of the Carpathians ; but the change would bring to them certain obvious compensations, since it would greatly increase the relative importance of Hungary inside what was left of the Habsburg Monarchy. In short, it is by no means impossible that if the Russians succeed in holding Galicia, Austria-Hungary may show a sudden alacrity to buy peace by disgorging a province which has never wholly fitted into her geographical or political system.

It is obvious that the fate of the small province of Bukovina is bound up with that of Galicia ; and in such circumstances as we have just indicated, it would doubtless be divided between Russia and Roumania on broad ethnographical lines, the northern districts being Ruthene, the southern Roumanian. This, however, must depend upon the attitude of the kingdom of Roumania, to which reference will be made later.

There is one other direction in which Austria could afford to surrender territory, without serious loss save that of prestige. The southern portion of Tirol—the so-called Trentino, the district round the town of Trent—is purely Italian by race, and its union with the kingdom of Italy has long been the chief point in the programme of the Italian Irredentists or extreme Nationalists. It is a poor and mountainous country, which belongs geographically to its southern rather than to its northern neighbour. The pronouncedly Italian sympathies of its inhabitants have complicated the problem of government and have been a permanent source of friction between Austria and Italy. The elaborate fortifications along the existing frontier would have to be sacrificed, but the new racial frontier could soon be made equally satisfactory from a strategic point of view. It should then be borne in mind that at a later stage of the war an attempt may be made by Austria to buy off Italy with the offer of the Trentino. Whether the latter would seriously consider such an offer, if made, will doubtless depend upon future events, but it is clear that Italy, if her diplomatists are sufficiently adroit, has a fair prospect of acquiring the Trentino, whichever side wins, and consequently that a much more tempting bait will be required in order to induce her to abandon her neutrality. These two losses, the one already probable, the other hypothetical, would still leave Austria in the unquestioned position of a Great Power. The problem of her future relations with her Balkan neighbours raises an infinitely more complicated issue. Let us consider the Southern Slav and Roumanian questions, first separately, and then in their bearing upon each other.

§ 6. *The Southern Slav Question.*—The Southern Slav question, as has already been argued in an earlier chapter, can only be treated satisfactorily as an organic whole ; and it may be taken for granted that Austria-Hungary, in the event of victory, will annex the two independent Serb kingdoms, and unite the whole Serbo-Croat race under Habsburg rule. The task of governing them, when once she has overcome their resistance, will be one of extraordinary difficulty, and will involve a complete revision of her own standards of government and administration. Her record and that of Hungary in the

Slavonic South does not inspire one with confidence as to the result. Moreover, it is not too much to assert that the destruction of Serb independence—a task which the present writer unhesitatingly regards as beyond the powers of Austria—will in no way solve the Southern Slav problem, but merely transfer its centre of gravity. The task of Southern Slav liberation would pass to Bulgaria, and Austria-Hungary would be involved in an ever-widening field of hostilities. Hence, even if Serbia's independence were not now inextricably bound up with the success of the British arms, it would still be essential that every effort should be made to heal what has long been an open sore upon the face of Europe. People in this country are only too apt to ignore the question altogether, or at best to say, " Oh yes, of course, if the Allies win, the Serbs will get Bosnia." Those who talk thus have not grasped the elements of the great problem, of which Bosnia, like Serbia itself, is only one section. The idea that to transfer Bosnia alone from Austro - Hungarian to Serbian hands would settle anything whatever, fatally ignores alike the laws of geography and those considerations of national sentiment which dominate politics in South-Eastern Europe. In every respect Bosnia - Herzegovina and Dalmatia complement each other. So long as there were no railways in the Balkans and Bosnia stagnated under Turkish rule, so long as the national consciousness of the Serbo-Croats slumbered or ran in purely provincial channels, the separation between coast and hinterland was possible, though even then un-natural. But with the advent of modern economic ideas the situation radically changed. It was above all the possession of the Dalmatian seaboard that tempted Austria to occupy Bosnia, and so conversely the acquisition of Bosnia by Serbia would at once compel the latter, willy-nilly (quite apart from all racial affinities or sentiments), to aspire to Dalmatia as well.

Geographically, it is inconceivable that to-day Dalmatia should be in different hands from Bosnia-Herzegovina. Herzegovina does actually touch the sea at two places—for a few miles at the swampy mouth of the Narenta below Metković, and for a mile at Castelnuovo-Zelenika, inside the Bocche di Cattaro. It is obvious that to allow Serbia these two outlets, while leaving their surroundings to another State, would create immediate and intolerable friction; whereas to assign the southern half of Dalmatia to Bosnia, but to leave the northern half in other hands, would be keenly resented by the Dalmatians themselves, as an outrage alike upon their national and their local traditions.

When we consider the population of Dalmatia we must apply the rival tests of history and of race. On the grounds of historical sentiment Italy might claim Dalmatia; for its chief towns (Zara, Sebenico, Trau, Spalato, Lesina, Curzola)[1] were Venetian colonies, and not only they but even the Republic of Ragusa, which always maintained an independent existence, were saturated with Italian culture and ideals. But on ethnical grounds Dalmatia is now overwhelmingly Slavonic. In 1900 only 3·1 per cent of its population—in other words, about 15,000 out of a total of 584,000—were Italians, the remaining 97 per cent being Serbo-Croats. The census of 1910 is even more unfavourable to the Italians, probably unduly so. It is, of course, true that the Italian element, though numerically negligible, represents a higher percentage of the educated and cultured

[1] In the West they are only known under their Italian names, but at home they are known as Zadar, Šibenik, Trogir, Split, Hvar, Korčula, and Dubrovnik (Ragusa).

class ; but while this would entitle Italy to demand guarantees for the maintenance of existing Italian schools and
institutions, it cannot conceivably be employed as an argument in favour of an Italian occupation. Not only would it
bring her inevitably into collision with the Southern Slavs
who already are, and are likely to remain, a military power
of no mean order ; it would lead her on into the false and
hopeless path of attempting to assimilate a hostile population
by the aid of an insignificant minority which only exists in
half a dozen towns, and in all the rest of the province is
simply non-existent. The price paid would be the eternal
enmity of all Slavs, the jeopardising of Italian interests in the
Balkans, the sacrifice of many of the benefits which the new
Trans-Balkan railway route (Odessa - Bucarest - Kladovo-
Sarajevo-Spalato) would naturally bring to Italy, a challenge
to one of the finest maritime races in Europe—the Croats
of Dalmatia, Croatia and Istria—a challenge which would
sooner or later involve the creation of a Southern Slav navy
against Italy. So far as Britain is concerned, to separate
Dalmatia from Bosnia is not only to prevent even the
beginnings of a solution of the Southern Slav question, but
to obscure the naval situation in the Mediterranean, to
alienate Russia in a matter in which we have everything to
gain and nothing to lose by accommodating her. But even
when Bosnia and Dalmatia have been united to Serbia and
Montenegro, the Southern Slav problem will still be far from
solution. Dalmatia is alike in constitutional theory and in
political fantasy, though not in sober fact, an integral portion of the Triune Kingdom of Croatia-Slavonia-Dalmatia,
and it is unthinkable that Serbo-Croat opinion could ever
consent to the liberation of the one without the other. No
solution has any chance of permanence which ignores Agram
as the centre of Croat political and religious life, of education,

art and historic memories. The Dalmatian Croats, as the most virile and stubborn element in the race, have always formed the vanguard of political thought, but it is to Agram that they have always turned for the necessary backing, and it is the peasantry of Croatia who have always borne the brunt of every attempt at repression.   Latterly the Dalmatians have been the soul of the student movement, which plays so vital a part in recent political development.

Croatia - Slavonia is a vital part of the problem, indeed from a national point of view perhaps more vital than Bosnia and Dalmatia.   But even this is not enough.   No settlement will be complete which ignores the Slovenes of eastern Istria, Carniola, and southern Carinthia and Styria: they must share the fate of their Croat and Serb kinsmen.

So far, then, as the Southern Slavs are concerned, the triumph of the Allies ought to mean the creation of a new State on the Eastern Adriatic, the expansion of gallant Serbia into Jugoslavia (Jug is the Slav word for south), and the achievement of Unity by the three kindred races, Serbs, Croats, and Slovenes.   On the north it would be comparatively easy to draw a new frontier corresponding to the main requirements of ethnography, geography, and strategy.   With only very slight deviations, this would follow the racial line between Slovenes and Germans from the present Italian frontier as far as the little town of Radkersburg in Styria ; thence, the course of the rivers Mur and Drave as far as the latter's junction with the Danube.   It is only in the Banat—that portion of the great Hungarian plain which faces Belgrade across the Danube— that an artificial frontier will be inevitable, if the Serb districts of Hungary are to be included in the new State and if the Serb capital is to be rendered immune from the dangers of future bombardment.   The weak spot in so

drastic a solution is the inclusion of the Slovene districts,
which—in view of their geographical position, cutting off the
German provinces of Austria from the sea—is unthinkable,
save in the event of a complete collapse of the Monarchy.
All depends upon the number of leaves which are pulled off
the artichoke. If only a few of the outer rows are taken,
a situation may arise in which it would be necessary to
sacrifice the Slovenes and to rest satisfied with the acquisition of Bosnia, Dalmatia, and Croatia—in other words, with
the frontier which at present divides Croatia from Austria
and from Hungary proper. But this, it must be remembered, would leave the work of Southern Slav Unity incomplete, and is only to be regarded as a *pis aller*.

The Slovene section of the Southern Slav problem is
further complicated by the attitude of Italy, who cannot be
indifferent to the fate of Trieste and Pola. On historic
grounds Italy cannot lay claim to Trieste, which has been
a possession of the House of Habsburg since 1386 (400
years longer than Dalmatia). But if as before we apply the
principle of nationality, it is indisputable that Trieste is an
Italian town, though the whole surrounding country up to
the very suburbs is purely Slovene. On the other hand, the
commercial interests of Trieste are entirely bound up with
its hinterland, by which is meant not only the Alpine
provinces, but Upper and Lower Austria and Bohemia on
the one hand and even south Germany (Bavaria) on the
other. Any settlement, then, must be a compromise between national and economic interests. As an ancient
centre of Italian culture, Trieste would welcome the flag of
the Regno upon its municipality, as the surest guarantee
that the town would remain Italian in character to all time.
But any attempt to include Trieste within the tariff system
of the kingdom of Italy would produce fatal results, and the

obvious solution is to proclaim the city as a free commercial port. Of course, from a purely Southern Slav point of view, the fate of the town of Trieste (as distinct from the district) ought to be a matter of complete indifference, though of course the extremists claim it. It is, however, well to bear in mind that the inclusion of Trieste in Italy's tariff system would mean the speedy economic ruin of a great and flourishing commercial centre. Commercially, then, Trieste is unthinkable save either as the port of Austria or as a *porto franco* under Italian suzerainty. So far as Istria is concerned, there would be no insurmountable difficulty in drawing a satisfactory frontier on ethnographical lines ; the western portions, including Capodistria, Rovigno, and Pola, are overwhelmingly Italian, while the interior of the little province and the eastern shore (with Abbazia, Lovrana, etc.) is as overwhelmingly Slavonic (Croat and Slovene mixed). Any redistribution of territory on the basis of nationality must therefore inevitably assign western Istria to Italy, and no reasonable Southern Slav would raise any valid objection. Once more the essential fact to consider is that the acquisition of Trieste and Pola by Italy presupposes the disappearance of Austria-Hungary ; otherwise it is not even remotely possible. Hence it is no exaggeration to assert that the fate of Trieste is one of the central issues in the whole European settlement. Once make Trieste a free port, under the Italian flag, and *ipso facto* the Austro-Hungarian navy ceases to exist, and with it all need for Italian naval activity in the Adriatic. In other words, such a settlement would lead to an almost idyllic reduction of naval armaments in the Adriatic, since both Italy and the new Jugoslavia could afford to restrict themselves to a minimum of coast defence. It is obvious, however, that the dismantlement of Pola—to-day an almost impregnable fortress—would be an essential condition to neighbourly relations between the two, the more so since under such altered circumstances an Italian naval base at Pola could only have one objective.

There is an unfortunate tendency in Italy to misread the whole situation on the eastern Adriatic, to ignore the transformation which the revival of Southern Slav consciousness has wrought in lands which once owned the supremacy of Venice. A short-sighted distrust of the Slav blinds many Italians to the double fact that he has come to stay, and that his friendship is to be had for the asking. The commercial future of Dalmatia, Bosnia, and Serbia is intimately bound up with Italy, and Italy herself will be the chief loser if she closes her eyes to so patent a truth.

The fate of Trieste and Istria is a triangular issue between Teuton, Slav, and Latin. The Italian, if his claims are too ambitious or exacting, may succeed in preventing the Slav from obtaining his share of the spoils, but only by leaving them all in the hands of a still more dangerous rival, in other words, by a crude policy of dog-in-the-manger.

One thing is certain in all this interplay of forces—that it is too late in the day to suppress Southern Slav national consciousness, and that there can never be durable peace and contentment on the eastern Adriatic until the unity of the race has been achieved. It would be premature to discuss the exact forms which the new State would assume ; but when the time comes it will be found that the people of Bosnia-Herzegovina, Dalmatia, Croatia-Slavonia, Istria and Carniola, will acclaim their liberation at the hands of free Serbia and Montenegro. Their watchword, however, will be not conquest from without, but free and voluntary union from within—a union which will preserve their existing political institutions and culture as a worthy contribution to the common Southern Slav fund. The natural solution is a federal union under which the sovereign would be crowned not only as King of Serbia but with the crown of Zvonimir as King of the Triune Kingdom of Croatia-Slavonia-Dalmatia, thus reviving historic traditions dating from the tenth century and never abandoned or forgotten. The Croatian Parliament would continue in Agram, parallel with the Serb Parliament in Belgrade, but both would be represented in a central federal Parliament. The only question is whether the existing provincial divisions should be allowed to survive, the Diets of Bosnia, Dalmatia, Istria, and Carniola thus forming conjointly with the Serbian, Montenegrin, and Croatian Parliaments the units on which the new constitution is based, or whether complete unification should be attempted. The latter would be the ideal arrangement, but in view of the great divergence of local customs and institutions it would probably be premature, and it might therefore be wiser to preserve the smaller units until they were ripe for fusion, rather than to compromise by creating a dual State of Serbia and Croatia.

§ 7. *The Roumanian Question.*—I have dwelt at some length upon the Southern Slav problem, because it is as complicated as it is unfamiliar to public opinion in this country. It has been the *causa causans* of the present struggle, and if neglected or mismanaged at the final settlement, may again plunge Europe into trouble at some future date. Parallel with any solution of the Southern Slav question must come the solution of the Roumanian question, which represents the other half of Austria-Hungary's Balkan policy. The Kingdom of Roumania is, alike in territory, population, and resources, the leading power in the Balkan peninsula, but over five million Roumanians, including the very cream of the race, still live under foreign domination. Of these at least 3,500,000 are in Austria-Hungary, the great majority under the grossly oppressive rule of the Magyars ; and the redemption of Transylvania and the neighbouring counties of Hungary has always been the ideal of all patriotic Roumanians, even of those who looked to a distant future for its realisation. Russia's short-sighted policy in 1878, in annexing the Roumanian province of Bessarabia as a reward for their valiant support at Plevna, drove the Roumanians into the arms of Austria-Hungary, and for a whole generation not even the perpetual irritant of Magyar tyranny in Transylvania could avail to shake the *entente* between Vienna and Bucarest, strengthened as it was by the personal friendship of the Emperor Francis Joseph and King Charles. But the spell was broken by Austria's attitude during the Balkan War. The imperious force of circumstances brought the interests of Roumania and Serbia into line ; for it was obvious that any blow aimed against Serbia's independent existence must threaten Roumania also, just as any weakening of the Serbo-Croat element in the Monarchy must react unfavourably on that of the Roumanians and other nationalities of Hungary. The growth of national feeling within the two neighbour races has proceeded for some time past on parallel lines, and even before the war there were manifest signs that the Roumanians of Hungary, whose economic and cultural progress since the beginning of the century has been very rapid, were at length nearing the end of their patience. The bomb outrage at Debreczen last February—an event which is without parallel in Roumanian history—was the first muttering of the gathering storm. Roumania occupies a position of extreme delicacy. Her natural tendency would be to espouse the cause of the Allies, since they obviously have more to offer her than their rivals. But the somewhat

equivocal attitude of her statesmen has been determined
not merely by an astute desire to win the spoils of war
without making the necessary sacrifice—a policy which is
apt to overreach itself—but also by a very pardonable
anxiety as to the attitude of Bulgaria and Turkey. Roumania
has hitherto been the foremost upholder of the Treaty of
Bucarest, and it is only in the event of drastic territorial
changes farther west that she is likely to consent to its being
torn up. She has made no secret of the fact that she would
not tolerate naked aggression against the Greeks, whether
from the Turkish or Bulgarian side. In view of the political
record of King Ferdinand of Bulgaria and his present Prime
Minister, the Roumanians may perhaps be excused for
adopting an attitude of vigilant reserve ; for their statesmen
suspect that Bulgaria is only waiting until the Roumanian
army has crossed the Carpathians in order to reoccupy the
southern Dobrudja. Certain it is that Roumania, while
declining all temptations to join the central powers, has
also rejected the Russian invitation to occupy the Bukovina,
and has actually approached Hungary with a view to
securing the restoration of Transylvanian autonomy. The
Magyars on their part have tried to buy off Roumania by
introducing the Roumanian language of instruction in many
of the State schools of Transylvania—a wholly inadequate
concession which would none the less have been inconceivable four short months ago. Unfortunately the realisation of Roumanian unity inevitably involves the inclusion in
the new State of considerable Magyar and Saxon minorities,
amounting in all to not less than 600,000 inhabitants.
There are no means of overcoming the hard facts of geography, but it is essential that Roumania, while incorporating
Magyar and Saxon islets in the Roumanian racial sea,
should guarantee the existing institutions of the two races,

and the fullest possible linguistic freedom in church,[1] school, and press.   The Saxons in particular have preserved their identity for over seven centuries in this little corner of the Carpathians, and have contributed far more than their share to the cause of culture and progress in Hungary.   It would be a crying irony of fate if they were allowed to perish in the twentieth century at the hands of those who have pledged themselves to vindicate the rights of smaller nationalities.

It must not be forgotten that the dream of Roumanian Unity can only be fully realised if Russia restores at least a portion of Bessarabia, which contains not less than a million and a quarter Roumanians.   A victorious Russia might well afford such a concession ; for it would involve no strategic dangers and would, especially if conveyed in the graceful form of a wedding dowry, triumphantly efface the last traces of Russophobe feeling that still linger in Roumania.   But it would be absurd to expect such magnanimity on the part of Russia unless Roumania's action is prompt and vigorous.   The abstract theory of nationality must be reinforced by the more practical argument of sterling services rendered to a common cause.

§ 8. *Can the Dual Monarchy be replaced ?*—The result of applying the principle of nationality to the Southern Slavs and Roumanians would thus be to create two powerful national States at the expense of the Habsburg Monarchy ; and here it is well to repeat that such drastic territorial changes are only possible if the military power of Austria suffers an almost complete eclipse.   But even the loss of

[1] The Szekel (Magyar) districts of Transylvania are mainly Calvinist, the Saxons Lutheran to a man, while the Roumanians are divided between the Orthodox and the Roumanian Uniate Churches. Transylvania is also the centre of an interesting sect of Unitarians, who are for the most part Magyar by race.

Galicia, Bukovina, Transylvania, the Trentino, and the
Serbo-Croat provinces would still leave Austria-Hungary
a State of very considerable area, with a population of
32 millions. There is no reason why such a State should
not continue to exist, provided that it retained the necessary
access to the sea at Trieste and Pola, and this would involve the exclusion of the Slovenes from the new Jugo-
Slav State. Under such circumstances it would be possible
to reconstruct the State on a federal basis, with five main
racial units, the Germans, the Czechs and Slovaks, the
Magyars, the Slovenes, and the Italians. Certain un-
important racial minorities would still be left, but these
could unquestionably be dealt with by a law of guarantees,
similar to those which have played so conspicuous a part
in the theory, but sometimes also in the practice, of the
Dual Monarchy. So many severe amputations might,
however, prove too much for the vitality of the patient;
and in any case we may assume that either Austria-Hungary
will be able to prevent the operation, or that the Allies, if
they can once bring matters thus far, will insist upon completing the process by a drastic post-mortem inquiry.
Any sympathetic qualms are likely to be outweighed by
the consideration that a State of this hybrid nature would
tend to be more than ever a vassal of Germany. Moreover,
there can be no doubt that one of the surest means of
bringing Germany to her knees is by crushing her most
formidable ally, and thus tapping some of the sources of her
own military and economic strength. It is safe to assume
that this consideration plays an important part in the
military plans of Russia; and for many reasons—political,
strategic, and economic—a Russian occupation of Bohemia
must be regarded as the essential prelude to a decisive
victory of the Allies. The war has thrown the Dual

Monarchy into the melting-pot; but it is not enough to accept the possibility of its disappearance from the map, it is also necessary to consider what new organisms would take its place. A complete partition would, as we have seen, remove the last obstacle to a unified Southern Slav State. The dreams of Italia Irredenta and Greater Roumania would be realised. Western Galicia and a part of Silesia would be united to autonomous Poland as reconstituted by the Russian Tsar. Eastern Galicia, Northern Bukovina, and the Ruthene districts of Hungary as far as Ungvár and Munkács, would be incorporated in the Russian Empire, though it is to be hoped that an early result of this change would be the grant of a certain modified autonomy, or at least of special linguistic and religious privileges, to the Ukraine population, thus united after centuries of partition in a single body politic.

§ 9. *Bohemia and Hungary.*—But the most striking result of the partition would be the revival of the famous mediaeval kingdoms of Bohemia and Hungary as independent States. Thus would be realised the dream of two races, the Czechs and Magyars, whose national revival forms one of the most romantic incidents of the nineteenth century. But it is difficult to imagine a greater contrast than their respective development. In Bohemia the Czechs, after losing their religious and civic liberty and enduring for two centuries the domination of the Germans, raised themselves once more in the course of two generations, by sheer force of character and tireless industry, to a position of equality, and reorganised their national life on an essentially democratic basis. In Hungary the Magyars, thanks to their central position, their superior political sense, and their possession of a powerful aristocracy, succeeded in concentrating all government and administration in their own hands and reducing the other races of the country, who have always formed a majority of the population, to a state of veritable political helotry. And just as their evolution has been on very different lines, so must be their future fate. In Bohemia all is activity and political progress, in Hungary the sterility of a corrupt and reactionary system, staking the future upon the hollow credit of a long-vanished past. The Czechs are beyond all question the most progressive, the most highly civilised, the most democratic of all Slavonic nations. The stubborn spirit of John Hus is still alive among them to-day, and their recent achievements in music, art, and industry are in every way worthy of the nation which has produced Comenius and Dvořák and first lit the torch of Reformation in Europe. The ancient city of Prague contains all the elements of culture necessary for the regeneration of Bohemia, and the mineral riches and industrial resources of the country are infinitely greater than those of many European States which have successfully led a separate national existence.

But the liberation of the Czechs would not be complete unless their close kinsmen the Slovaks were included in the new Bohemian State; and every reason alike of politics, race, and geography tells overwhelmingly in favour of such an arrangement. The Slovaks, who would to the last man welcome the change, have long suffered from the gross tyranny of Magyar rule. Their schools and institutions have been ruthlessly suppressed or reduced in numbers, their press muzzled, their political development arrested, their culture and traditions—far more truly autochthonous than those of the conquering Magyar invaders—have been discouraged and hampered at every turn. The Slovaks are a race whose artistic and musical gifts, whose innate

sense of colour and poetry have won the sympathy and
admiration of all who know them ; and their systematic
oppression at the hands of the Magyar oligarchy is one of
the greatest infamies of the last fifty years. In this war
Britain has proclaimed herself the champion of the small
nations, and none are more deserving of her sympathy than
the Slovaks. Unless our statesmen renounce that principle
of nationality which they have so loudly proclaimed, the
Slovaks cannot be abandoned to their fate ; for they form
an essential part of the Bohemian problem. Without
them the new kingdom could not stand alone, isolated as
it would be among hostile or indifferent neighbours. In
every way the Slovak districts form the natural continua-
tion of Bohemia and are the necessary link between it and
Russia, upon whose moral support the new State must rely
in the first critical years of its existence.

The main difficulty would be the fate of racial minorities ;
for minorities there still must be, no matter how the frontiers
may be drawn. At first sight the natural solution would
be to pare down Bohemia by assigning to the neighbouring
provinces of Germany the German fringe which almost
completely surrounds the Czech kernel. So far as the
south-west and north-east districts of Bohemia (near
Budweis and along the German Silesian border) are concerned, the historic boundaries might fairly be revised on
ethnographic lines, and in the same way the line of demarca-
tion between Bohemia and Hungary could in the main be
made to follow the racial boundary between Slovak and
Magyar and later between Slovak and Ruthene. But in
the north of Bohemia there are insurmountable objections
to any revision of the historic frontier of the kingdom ; for
not merely is its industrial life concentrated to a very
considerable degree in the German districts, but this fact is

T

responsible for the existence of important Czech industrial minorities, which it would be difficult to sacrifice. So far as there is to be any sacrifice, it must be made by the losers rather than by the winners in this war. But it ought to be possible, under the rule of some carefully selected western prince as ruler of Bohemia, to devise proper administrative guarantees for the linguistic rights of minorities in every mixed district of Bohemia, whether it be Czech or German.

The case of Hungary is different. That the Allies, if victorious, should perpetuate the racial hegemony of the Magyars, and with it many of the abuses which have contributed towards the present war, is as unthinkable as that they should once more bolster up the Turkish regime. If the Habsburg Monarchy should break up, Hungary is fully entitled to her independence. She will become a national Magyar State, but in a sense very different from that which her Jingo politicians have intended—not by assimilating the non-Magyar races of the country, but by losing to the other national States by which she will be surrounded all but the purely Magyar districts of the central plains. Hungary will then be more fully than before a Danubian State; her rich alluvial lands will be developed, and a check will be put upon the unnecessary streams of Magyar emigration which the present political and economic situation favours. The chief gainer by the change will be the Magyar peasantry, who have in their own way been exploited by the ruling oligarchy as cruelly as their non-Magyar neighbours. One result of the war will be to discredit the policy and methods of this oligarchy and to hasten the break-up of the vast latifundia of the great magnates and the Church, and those other drastic land reforms without which Hungary cannot hope to attain her full economic value as the granary of central Europe.

Hitherto the government of the day has secured a parliamentary majority by corrupting and terrorising the
non-Magyar constituencies of the periphery and thus out-
voting the radical Magyar stalwarts of the great plain ;
and with the loss of the Slovak, Ruthene and Roumanian
districts this system would automatically collapse. The
result might be a genuine strengthening of democratic
elements and the dawn of a new era for the Magyar race.

§ 10. *Germany and Austria.*—One final problem connected with Austria-Hungary remains. What is to be the
fate of the German provinces of Austria ? If the map of
Europe is to be recast on a basis of nationality, we obviously
cannot withhold from the great German nation that right
to racial unity which we accord to the Czechs, the Poles
and many minor races. The seven German provinces—
Upper and Lower Austria, Styria, Carinthia, Tirol, Salzburg
and Vorarlberg—reconstituted perhaps as a kingdom of
Austria under the House of Habsburg and augmented by
the German population of western Hungary, would then
become an additional federal unit in the German Empire.
Such an event, it cannot be too often repeated, is inconceivable except as the result of a complete defeat of the
central powers, but if on that assumption Germany loses
Alsace-Lorraine and Posen, the loss would be made good
by the incorporation of German Austria. The result of
this in figures would be the subtraction of six million
inhabitants and the addition of eight million others—a
transaction which need not unduly alarm the British Jingo,
and at the same time might render defeat less galling to
the German patriot.

Whether this fulfilment of the Pan-German aspiration
would meet with unqualified enthusiasm on either side of
the present frontier, is a question on which it is not

altogether easy to answer. The idea of admitting eight million additional Catholic subjects into Germany would certainly arouse misgivings in Prussia, both among the stricter Protestants and among the far more active section of " intellectuals " who merely regard Protestantism as a political asset in the struggle against Latin and Slavonic influences. From a political point of view their admission would unquestionably transform the whole parliamentary situation and force the Imperial Government to revise its whole attitude ; for the Austrian voters would greatly strengthen the two parties to whose existence Prussia has never become reconciled—the Clerical Centre and the Social Democratic Left,—while contributing little or nothing to the parties of the Conservative Junkers or the middle-class " Liberals." In other words, the new element might prove to be an effective leaven which would permeate the whole lump. All the arguments which induced Bismarck to expel Austria from Germany in 1868 would still be upheld by the advocates of " Preussen-Deutschland " (see p. 65), and the Prussian hegemony ; but after an unsuccessful war and territorial losses the chance of making these good by the achievement of national unity would probably sweep away the dissentients, who would no longer represent a triumphant system, but a beaten and discredited caste. The old idea of the " seventy-million Empire," which appealed so strongly to the Liberals of Frankfurt in 1848, should prove irresistible under these circumstances. The influence of Austrian Germans, already so marked in literature, art, music, and above all in political theory, might make itself felt in other spheres also.

Meanwhile, in view of the wild talk in which certain sections of the Press are already indulging, it cannot be too strongly emphasised that only the Germans can reform their political institutions, and that any attempt at external interference will not merely fail lamentably, but produce the very opposite effect from that which is intended. If the German Emperor insists upon confusing the relative positions of the Deity and some of his self-styled vicegerents upon earth, only the German people can restore him to a sense of proportion and modesty. All believers in human progress hope that after this war the monstrous theories of divine right propounded by the House of Hohenzollern will be relegated to the lumber-room of a vanished past. But the sooner references to St. Helena as a residence for deposed emperors are dismissed as arrant nonsense, the better. The future of German dynasties, as of German Unity, rests with the German people itself ; and those who challenge this statement repudiate *ipso facto* the two principles of Nationality and International Law, which we have officially adopted as our programme for the future.

The fate of the German provinces of Austria is one of the central problems raised by this war, since it is the link between the fate of two Empires. The present writer most emphatically disclaims all idea of prophecy ; but he feels that the time has come for outlining some of the possible alternatives which confront the statesmen of " the new Europe." So far as Austria-Hungary is concerned, it is clear that the splendid dream of " a monarchical Switzerland," as conceived by many serious political thinkers, has already died a violent death ; but it would be quite premature to dogmatise on the future grouping of the races of the Dual Monarchy at a moment when its ultimate fate has still to be decided on the field of battle.

§ 11. *Italian Aspirations.*—We have already alluded to Italy's position, in connection with the Southern Slav question, and have pointed out that a settlement which follows even approximately the lines of nationality would assign the Trentino, the town of Trieste (as a free port), and a strip of Western Istria to Italy, but the remainder of the coast from Cape Promontore to the Bojana river to the new " Jugoslavia." There are, however, other directions in which Italy may claim compensation for her friendly attitude towards the Triple Entente. She has already occupied the rocky islet of Saseno, opposite Valona, and in the event of the collapse of Austria-Hungary, she may demand the whole bay of Valona, as the strategic key to the Adriatic, and even a general protectorate of the embryo Albanian State. The establishment of a miniature Gibraltar on the eastern side of the Straits of Otranto is a step which neither France nor Britain would oppose, if Italy should insist upon it; but it may be questioned whether she would not thereby be laying up stores of trouble for a distant future, altogether incommensurate with any possible advantages which might accrue. Indeed, Italy would probably be well advised to abandon all idea of an Albanian adventure (which, originally conceived as a counterstroke to Austrian aggression, would lose its point if Austria disappeared from the scene), to leave the Greeks a free hand in south Epirus, to cede to them Rhodes and the other islands occupied during the Tripolitan War, and then to secure, during the partition of Turkey, the reversion of Cilicia and the Gulf of Alexandretta. It is in any case clear that the Powers of the Triple Entente will raise no objections to such action on the part of Italy, and are resolved to show every consideration to a power whose great and vital interests in the Mediterranean in no way conflict with their own.

§ 12. *The Balkan Situation : Bulgaria and Greece.*—The creation of a Greater Roumania and of a new Southern

Slav State would transform the whole Balkan situation, and therefore obviously involves material concessions to Bulgaria and Greece.

(A) If Roumania succeeds in redeeming her kinsmen across the northern frontiers, she cannot be so ungenerous as to insist upon retaining territory whose population is overwhelmingly Bulgarian, and the least which might be expected from her would be the retrocession to Bulgaria of her bloodless acquisition during the second Balkan War. This means a reversion to the boundary defined under Russian arbitration at Petrograd in January 1913—except outside the fortress of Silistria, where strategic reasons demand its rectification.

It is in the relations of Bulgaria and Serbia, however, that the key to the Balkan situation is to be found. The Serbo-Bulgarian treaty of February 1912, which formed the groundwork of the Balkan alliance, had limited Serbia's sphere of influence to northern Macedonia and referred to the arbitration of the Russian Tsar any disputes arising from conquests to the south of a certain specified line. Serbia was tacitly given a free hand in her attempt to reach the sea in Northern Albania. The action of Austria-Hungary in vetoing her access to the Adriatic forced Serbia to turn her eyes from west to south and to seek her economic outlet to the sea down the valley of the Vardar to Salonica and the Aegean. The cession of Monastir, Ochrida, and the Vardar Valley to Bulgaria would have rendered this impossible, for it would not merely have driven a wedge between Serbia and Greece, but would have placed two customs frontiers, the Bulgarian and the Greek, between Serbia and the sea, instead of only one, the Turkish, as hitherto. Shut in upon all sides, with all hope of expansion blocked by the powerful Dual Monarchy to north and west and by a big Bulgaria to east and south, Serbia would have found herself in a worse position than before the war. The Bulgarians, intoxicated by their victories over the Turks and seduced by the promptings of the Austrian tempter, turned a deaf ear to the arguments of their Serbian allies, and insisted upon their pound of flesh. They failed to realise that the most effective way of inducing the Serbs to evacuate Macedonia was to give them adequate backing in their demand for an Adriatic port. Every fresh intrigue of Sofia with Vienna confirmed Belgrade in its view of the vital necessity for retaining the Vardar Valley. The hoary argument that " circumstances alter cases," appeared anew in the garb of the Bismarckian theory that all treaties are subject to the provision " *rebus sic stantibus* "—a theory which many great international lawyers have unhesitatingly endorsed. In this form it appealed as irresistibly to the Serbs as did the rival shibboleth of " The treaty, the whole treaty, and nothing but the treaty " to the Bulgarians. It is impossible to absolve either side from blame ; for the Serbs, in formally denouncing a treaty into which they had voluntarily entered, were doing exactly what they had so bitterly resented in Austria-Hungary's treatment of Bosnia, while the Bulgarians, in flouting the Tsar whom they had named as arbiter and in attempting to uphold the treaty by brute force and treachery, abandoned the ground of law, and placed themselves openly in the wrong.

The events of the great war have already modified the problem. The one unanswerable argument of the Serbs in declining to surrender Macedonia was the plea that they would then have nothing to offer Bulgaria for her neutrality or her support when their own inevitable day of reckoning with Austria should arrive. In short, Veles, Monastir and Ochrida were widely regarded as a pledge to be held until

Bosnia and Dalmatia could be redeemed, but then to be handed over to the Bulgarians. It is true that the Serbo-Bulgar War of 1913 and the passions which it aroused have converted this feeling into one of reluctance to sacrifice what was bought at such a fearful price. But the moment has now arrived to translate an instinct into a reality. If Southern Slav Unity is to be achieved, a binding promise, under the guarantee of the Entente Powers, must be given to Bulgaria, that, in proportion as the work of Serbo-Croat unification is achieved, the Macedonian frontier will be revised in favour of Bulgaria. It is possible that Bulgaria may prefer a different formula, according to which the Tsar with the approval of his Western Allies should arbitrate upon the original Serbo-Bulgar treaty. Any such concession to Bulgarian sentiment ought not to be resented in Serbia, in view of the great issues involved. It is obvious that Serbia cannot hope to achieve her national unity unless Bulgaria abstains from hostile action, or to consolidate her new position when won unless she can win Bulgaria's active friendship. The latter by her intervention could at any moment turn the scales against Turkey or against Serbia, and it is thus essential that the Allies should treat her now with a generosity proportionate to the callous neglect with which Europe left her to her fate in September 1913.

The tendency to look down upon the Balkan States from the fancied heights of a superior " culture " has never been so marked in France or Britain as in Germany, where the Press is now engaged in comparing their own cultural exploits in Belgium with the lack of culture displayed by the " bandits " and " assassins " of Serbia, and where a man of such scientific distinction as Werner Sombart can describe the heroic kingdom of Montenegro as " nothing but a bad joke in the history of the world ! " [1]   But even here the habit of condescension lingers, and amidst the threatened collapse of Western civilisation it is well to remember the essential distinction between primitive and savage. The Balkan nations have grown to manhood while we slept, and must henceforth be regarded as equals in the European commonwealth.

(B) Such territorial changes as have been outlined above would vitally affect the position of Greece, who is also fully entitled to claim compensation for any serious disturbance of the balance of power. The first and most obvious form which compensation would take is the final occupation of southern Epirus ; no objections will be raised to this by the Entente Powers, and it is probable that Italy has already made her own bargain with the Cabinet of Athens on this very point. It is to be hoped that Italy may also consent to hand over Rhodes and the neighbouring islands to Greece, in return for a free hand in Southern Asia Minor in the event of the Turkish Empire breaking up. By far the thorniest problem is provided by the future ownership of Kavala, which the Treaty of Bucarest assigned to Greece in August 1913, but which from an economic point of view is Bulgaria's port on the Aegean, and as vital a necessity for her future development as it is a superfluous luxury to Greece. The statesmen of Petrograd were not blind to these considerations, but the scale was turned at Bucarest by the active intervention of the German Emperor, who, under the plea of seconding his brother-in-law, King Constantine, skilfully provided a permanent bone of contention between Bulgaria and Greece. His action may not unfairly be compared to that of the Hungarian Premier, Count Tisza, in fomenting the quarrel between Serbia and Bulgaria two months earlier.

[1] *Berliner Tageblatt*, cited by *Observer*, November 8, 1914.

Serbia's cession of Central Macedonia to Bulgaria could not fail to be distasteful to the Greeks, for it would automatically render their tenure of Kavala highly precarious. It is to be hoped, however, that they may be brought to realise that its surrender and the consequent improvement of Greco-Bulgarian relations are in the highest interests of Greece and the whole Hellenic race. Here again, the break-up of the Turkish Empire may enable the Greeks to compensate themselves on the shores of Asia Minor. But the real key to the problem of Kavala, and thus indirectly to the revival of the Balkan League and all the far-reaching effects which that would have upon the fate of Europe, lies in the hands of Britain. It could instantly be solved by the cession of Cyprus to Greece, on condition that Kavala and the valley of the Strymon were restored to Bulgaria. Neither strategically nor economically is Cyprus of any value to Britain ; thirty-five years ago it was taken over by Disraeli " as a sort of fee for opposing Russia," a foolish habit which we had abandoned long before the present war with Turkey. Its population is predominantly Greek, and the Hellenic national movement is steadily gaining ground. Anything that we might gain by its retention is more than counterbalanced by its value as an instrument of barter.

§ 13. *The Future of Turkey.*—The entry of Turkey into the great war marks a further stage in the winnowing process from which we hope that a regenerated Europe will emerge. Two of the main causes of the war are the Turk and the Magyar, whose effete and tyrannous systems have each in its own manner and degree long kept South-Eastern Europe in a ferment of unrest and reaction. It is a matter of profound regret that two infinitely more virile and progressive races, the German and the Jew, should be fighting their battles for them, and indeed bolstering up causes which would otherwise speedily collapse by reason of their own inward rottenness. It is the Triple Alliance which has made it possible for the iniquitous racial hegemony of the Magyars to survive in Hungary; it is the joint policy of Vienna, Budapest, and Berlin which has hampered the progress of the Balkan States, and above all the development of every Slavonic nation; and in this their most valuable allies have been the Jewish Press and the Jewish *haute finance* of Germany, Austria and Hungary. Just as we hope and believe that one result of this war will be the emancipation of Germany and German "culture" from the corroding influences of militarist doctrine, so there are good grounds for hoping that it will also give a new and healthy impetus to Jewish national policy, grant freer play to their many splendid qualities, and enable them to shake off the false shame which has led men who ought to be proud of their Jewish race to assume so many alien disguises and to accuse of anti-Semitism those who refuse to be deceived by mere appearances. It is high time that the Jews should realise that few things do more to foster anti-Semite feeling than this very tendency to sail under false colours and conceal their true identity. The Zionist and the orthodox Jewish nationalist have long ago won the respect and admiration of the world. No race has ever defied assimilation so stubbornly and so successfully, and the modern tendency of individual Jews to repudiate what is one of their chief glories suggests an almost comic resolve to fight against the course of nature.

These cryptic tendencies of pseudo-national as opposed to national Judaism have played a great part in the Young Turkish movement and the destruction which it is bringing upon Turkey. The Committee of Union and Progress at first enjoyed the moral and financial support of many men, both Christians and Jews, to whom its methods and secret currents were a sealed book. For a time the Young Turks, like the Magyars farther west, deceived foreign opinion by claptrap phrases from the repertory of modern democracy. But " murder will out," and the Committee—despite the tiny group of able, and in certain cases honourable, men who control its destinies—has gradually been revealed in its true colours, as a parasitic growth upon the body politic, preserving the worst faults of the old regime and blending with it much of the decadence which lies like froth along the backwaters of Western civilisation.

Since 1908, then, the fate of Turkey has passed from the control of the Turk and is being decided by an alien clique of infidels, renegades, political freemasons [1] and Jews, in whose hands the Caliph is a helpless tool, and to whom the teachings of Christ and of Mohammed are mere worn-out superstitions. In fact, the Committee is in its essence non-Turkish and non-Moslem. In the name of a secret society, based openly upon the subversive ideas of the wilder French Jacobins, and not shrinking from assassination as a convenient political weapon, a Jehad or Holy War is to be preached against the British Empire, and the most sacred interests of Islam are to be exploited in the interests of Germany. What bitter irony is in the fact that William II., who risked universal war to avenge the murder of his friend, the Archduke Francis Ferdinand, should now find himself closely allied with Enver Pasha, the military adventurer who barely two years ago foully assassinated his own commander-in-chief, Nazim Pasha, and who therefore represents everything that is

[1] Not to be confused for a moment with the very different form of freemasonry which prevails in this country.

anathema to the Prussian War Lord with his exaggerated
ideas of military discipline and personal loyalty !

The die has been cast, and even those who most regret
Turkey's action cannot shut their eyes to the fact that it
inevitably raises the whole question of Constantinople and
the Dardanelles. If Germany should emerge victorious,
Turkey is likely to fall under a more or less veiled German
protectorate. In the event of the victory of the Allies,
Turkey may continue to exist as an Asiatic power, but there
is little doubt that she will be eliminated from Europe.
The only real question is, Who is to replace her ? Bulgaria
will, it is to be hoped, recover Adrianople and the Enos-
Midia line, of which she was so cruelly robbed last year.
The fact that the Turks on their re-entry systematically
wiped out the entire Bulgarian population of northern
Thrace does not weaken, but enormously strengthens, the
case for its restoration. But to offer Constantinople to
Bulgaria would be a fatal gift. She has absolutely no historic claim to the great city of the Caesars (Tsarigrâd, as it is
rightly known to every Slav) ; nor is there even any considerable Bulgarian population which could rally round the new
government. The administrative task is obviously far
beyond the powers of a small peasant state, most of whose
present leaders were born under a foreign yoke. Nor is
Greece a serious candidate for the vacant post. The Greeks,
of course, unlike the Bulgarians, have a definite claim,
based on the traditions of the Byzantine Empire, and there
is a large Greek population in the city—at present close
upon 350,000, though their numbers are likely to be materially reduced before this war is over. But in their case also
Constantinople would be a fatal gift. The resources even
of the enlarged Hellenic kingdom would inevitably prove
unequal to the task. Moreover, it must not be forgotten

that a Greek occupation would be opposed on many grounds
by the entire commercial community of every other nation
in Europe.

In some ways the ideal arrangement would be that
Roumania should assume the administration of the city,
as trustee for a reconstituted Balkan League, with proper
guarantees for the commercial rights of all the Powers.
But it is to be feared that such a solution would please
nobody, perhaps not even Roumania herself. A league
of the five Balkan kings, with Roumania as *primus inter
pares,* is the dream of a remote future, and until it can be
realised, Constantinople cannot assume its natural position
as capital of the Balkan peninsula.

§ 14. *Russia and Constantinople.*—In short, as matters
stand to-day, there is only one power which can replace the
Turks as master of Constantinople, and that power is Russia.
The Russians could not of course incorporate the city in
their empire for reasons of geography ; and this fundamental fact destroys at a blow the numerous objections
which might have told against the occupation, if Constantinople had been contiguous to the Russian dominions. It
would obviously be necessary to establish a special autonomous administration under a Russian governor. It is by
no means impossible that Russia would be satisfied with the
expulsion of the Turks and the internationalisation of
Constantinople as a free port under a Christian prince or
a commission of the Powers. But, though admirable in
theory, such a solution would give rise to endless complications and disputes. Unless the Western Powers can
trust Russia sufficiently to leave her in full possession, they
must make up their minds to bolstering up the impossible
Turk for a further period of years. Such a surrender to the
unreasoning and ignorant prejudices of a previous genera-

tion would be a sure prelude to the collapse of our alliance with Russia, which it is the vital interest of all British patriots to uphold at all costs. Happily, "the fear of Russia," as of a strange and unknown colossus, is dying out, vague fancies inevitably yielding to the hard logic of facts. The Disraeli policy in the Near East must give place once and for all to the broader conceptions of Gladstone, tempered by the cautious statesmanship of Salisbury. The greatest of the Christian Powers must be allowed to replace the cross upon the dome of Saint Sofia. The religious appeal of such a change is clear enough, nor need there be any anxiety on economic grounds. There is nothing to prevent Constantinople from becoming a free port under the Russian flag, and filling a similar place to that which the free port of Trieste would occupy under the flag of United Italy. Indeed it may be confidently assumed that the change would give an extraordinary impetus to trade in the whole eastern Mediterranean. The recent history of Batum and Baku is a faint indication of what might be expected.

The fate of the Dardanelles cannot be separated from that of the capital; both must be in the same hands. At the same time a reasonable compensation for their cession to Russia would be the dismantlement of their forts. In any case, whatever their fate may be, it is clear that an end must be put to the galling restrictions upon Russia's Black Sea fleet. The essential point to bear in mind is that if the war goes well with the Allies, and if Russia expresses a definite desire to occupy Constantinople and the straits, resistance on our part would be alike difficult, pointless, and undesirable. Those who oppose have no arguments, so long as the special international needs and conditions of the city are properly recognised and guaranteed. With true Oriental fatalism, the Turk has always regarded his ultimate disappearance from Europe as a certainty; the superstition which led the inhabitants of Stamboul to prefer burial across the straits in Asia has its parallel in the alarm aroused in the bazaars by the Young Turks' decision to exterminate the pariah dogs which have for centuries supplied the place of scavengers in the streets of the capital. To-day the prophecy which made their removal the prelude to the departure of their masters seems on the point of fulfilment, and all who believe in the retributive justice of history will re-echo Mr. Asquith's hope that the fall of Ottoman rule will remove " the blight which for generations has withered some of the fairest regions of the world."

§ 15. *Asiatic Turkey*.—What then will be the subsequent fate of the Turks if they are once driven " bag and baggage " across the straits. The Sultan will doubtless transfer his capital to Brussa, or even to Konieh. But can the Khalifate survive such a loss of prestige on the part of the Ottoman dynasty ? It would be altogether premature to discuss in anything approaching detail the vast issues of the fate of Turkey's Asiatic dominions, but it is necessary to indicate that even after settling the fate of the straits we shall still be confronted by issues of appalling magnitude. It is the conjunction of the spiritual and temporal power in a single person which has given the Khalifate its importance, and its expulsion from the Golden Horn would transform its whole political status. Above all, it is necessary to reckon with the Arab nationalist movement which is already a reality and a factor of permanent importance. Here, too, the principle of nationality must be applied, though in a very different sense, for national feeling is of course at a much earlier stage of development among the Arabs than in Central Europe. Hitherto they have accepted the Khalifate of the House of Othman, though without en-

U

thusiasm ; but recent events are likely to bring to a head the resentment with which they view the spectacle of the Khalif as the helpless tool of a clique which in no way represents Islam. Will they repudiate him and restore the Khalifate to some more authentic descendant of the Prophet ? Is there to be an independent Arab power ? Will it be practicable to create a central authority amid the virtual anarchy of so vast and primitive a country ? Or will Britain, as the chief Mahommedan power, be obliged to assume a loose protectorate over Arabia and Mesopotamia ? If so, will she share this with the French in Syria, and will Lebanon be able to preserve its autonomy ? Only the course of events can provide an answer to such questions ; only one fixed point emerges from the surrounding uncertainty—the firm pledge of the British Government that the Holy Places of Islam shall be respected.

Even this does not exhaust the possibilities of the immediate future. Is Palestine to become a Jewish land ? In recent years there has been a steady emigration of Moslem and Christian and an equally marked Jewish immigration, and among other factors in the movement the potentialities of Jewish nationalism in the United States deserve especial notice. America is full of nationalities which, while accepting with enthusiasm their new American citizenship, none the less look to some centre in the Old World as the source and inspiration of their national culture and traditions. The most typical instance is the feeling of the American Jew for Palestine, which may well become a focus for his *déclassé* kinsmen in other parts of the world. The Jews quite realise that they can have no exclusive claim to the possession of such a religious centre as Jerusalem, and it is clear that whatever happens to the Holy Land as a whole, the city itself must be subject to an impartial administration, which would be neither Jewish, Catholic, Orthodox, Protestant nor Moslem in any exclusive sense, but would secure free play to the religious and educational aspirations of them all. Herzl himself, the founder of modern Zionism, dreamt of Jerusalem as the shrine of all religions and never looked forward to the day when it would be a purely Jewish city.

Lastly, what is to be the fate of Asia Minor ? There can be no question that the Russians must be allowed to occupy and retain the whole of Turkish Armenia. They will thus be conferring a benefit upon humanity and ending one of the most grinding and barbarous tyrannies that the modern world has ever seen ; the progress made by the Armenians under Russian rule during the past twenty years is a happy augury for the future of this race when once united in common allegiance to the Tsar, under a wise system of local autonomy. But will the Ottoman Empire be able to survive when shorn of its European possessions, of its Armenian and Arab populations ? Will not Italy demand her share of the spoils, and side by side with the French in Syria assume in friendly rivalry the protectorate of Cilicia from a point east of Adalia as far as the gulf of Alexandretta ? Will it be possible to arrest the process of disintegration even at this stage ? Will not Greece attempt to annex Smyrna and at least a portion of its hinterland, or has she not at least as good a title as any other competitor ? Here, again, it would be absurd to attempt any answer for the present, but we must at least be prepared for the possibility of a transformation as rapid and as overwhelming in Asiatic Turkey as that which freed the Balkans from the Turkish nightmare two short years ago. In Asia, as in Europe, the war is the prelude to a new era, and Britain is faced with the alternative of weakly abandoning her Imperial mission or assuming still greater responsibilities. " The Turkish Empire has committed suicide, and dug with its own hand its grave," and to Britain will fall more fully than ever before the leadership of the Mahommedan world. The loyalty and devotion of the Moslem community in India can best be repaid by the most scrupulous and sympathetic attention to the interests of Islam throughout the world.

§ 16. *Russia and Poland.*—It is no mere accident that Germany, Austria-Hungary, and Turkey should be ranged on the same side in the great European struggle ; for they represent, each in its own way, those false conceptions of nationality which have so long envenomed the public life of Europe, and which, for want of better words, have been described as Germanisation, Magyarisation, and Turkification. It would, however, be flagrantly untrue to suggest that those three States enjoyed a monopoly of racial intolerance ; for the ideas on nationality which dominated official Russia under the old absolutist regime and which so rapidly regained the upper hand under Stolypin and the triumphant bureaucracy, struck at the very root of tolerance and political liberty. But recent years have revealed a subtle change of attitude. The policy of Russification had not been abandoned ; indeed in Finland and the Ukraine it survived in its most odious form. But it was none the less possible to detect a growing note of interrogation even among the bureaucracy, and still more an increasing movement of impatient protest on the part of thinking Russians. Without in any way ignoring what has happened in Persia, we have every right to point to the essential fact that Russia has of her own accord raised the question of nationality and thus set in motion vast forces which are already shaking Europe to its foundations. In proclaiming as one of her foremost aims the restoration of Polish Unity, Russia did not, it is true, commit herself to any concrete project of autonomy. But whether her action represents genuine feeling on the part of the Tsar and his advisers, as M. Gabriel Hanotaux so positively asserts, or whether it was originally a mere manœuvre to prevent the Polish question being raised against her, it is at least certain that Russia has entered upon a new path from which it will be very difficult if not impossible to recede. The Russian Poles, under the leadership of M. Dmowski, have rallied loyally round the Tsar ; and there are many signs that the long-deferred Russo-Polish *rapprochement* is at length on the point of fulfilment. Here economic interests play their part, for in recent years the district between Warsaw and Lodz has become one of the chief industrial centres of the Russian Empire, and its annexation to Austria or to Prussia would place a tariff wall between it and the South Russian markets upon which it chiefly depends. The Poles of Galicia, having enjoyed the utmost liberty under Austrian rule, have naturally been almost immune from the discontent so noticeable among their kinsmen in Russia and Prussia, and have indeed for a generation past formed the backbone of all parliamentary majorities in the Austrian Reichsrat. But even among them the first faint signs of Russophil feeling have been noticeable in the last two years. This is partially due to the encouragement given by the Austrian Government to the Ruthenes in Galicia, but also to the disintegrating effect of universal suffrage upon the Polish political parties, the growth of democratic tendencies at the expense of the Austrophil nobility, and the consequent increased influence of the Poles of Warsaw. Though the Polish parties in Galicia issued declarations of loyalty to Austria at the beginning of the war, and though their *franc-tireurs* are fighting in the Austrian ranks, there is a growing perception of the fact that the only serious prospect of attaining Polish Unity lies in a Russian victory. Austria, they argue, might, if successful, unite the Russian and Austrian sections (at the expense of the former's economic future !), but never the Prussian; and Prussia, out of loyalty to her ally, could at best add *Russian* Poland to her own territory : Russia alone can hope, in the event of a victory, to unite all three fragments in a single whole. However profoundly they may differ on points of detail, all Poles agree that the first essential is the attainment of that unity without which they may at any moment become, as now, the battleground of three great Empires, and which provides the key with which they themselves can unlock the portals of their future destiny. Should their dream be fulfilled, the valley of the Vistula, restored to geographical unity, may soon play an important part in the political and economic life of Europe.

Russia, then, is faced by one of the greatest choices in history. An opportunity will present itself after this war, for solving her own racial question which has in the past presented scarcely less grave embarrassment than the parallel problem of Austria-Hungary, and which, if left unsolved, may at no distant date endanger the unity and welfare of the Empire. The grant of Polish autonomy, the restoration of the Finnish constitution, the recognition of the special position of the Ukraine or Ruthene language and cultural traditions, the relaxation of linguistic restrictions among the lesser races of the Empire, and the adoption of a humaner attitude towards the Jews of the Pale—these are steps which follow logically from the proclamation of the Grand Duke Nicholas, and indeed from the alliance with the Western Powers. Incidentally much will depend upon the attitude adopted by the Russian Government towards its new Catholic subjects. Its relations with the

Vatican will require to be placed upon an entirely new footing, and due respect must be accorded to the Uniate Catholic Church of the four million Ruthenes of Galicia. In this respect the Concordat signed a few weeks before the outbreak of war between Serbia and the Vatican should form a very valuable precedent for the whole future relations of the Catholic and Orthodox Churches, relations which are likely to assume increasing importance in the not too far distant future. And here it is worth while to emphasise, for the benefit of those who still regard Russia with misgiving or dislike, the indisputable fact that it is just the most democratic and enlightened of the smaller Slavonic States, and the most intellectual and enlightened politicians and thinkers in those States, who have always looked with the greatest confidence and enthusiasm to Russia, and who to-day are most unanimous in welcoming her as the herald of a new era of humanity and progress.

§ 17. *General Aims.*—It would lead us much too far afield to consider the possible effects of the war upon colonial development and upon the political and commercial development of the Far East. Here again, the central fact to remember is that we may, indeed, that we must, defeat Germany or perish in the attempt, but that a nation of 65 million inhabitants cannot be effaced or permanently reduced to impotence. After the war the two nations will have to live peaceably side by side once more, and repair so far as possible the wreckage to which this gigantic struggle has reduced their political, social, and commercial intercourse. Any peace settlement will be good only so far as it avoids placing obstacles in the path of so difficult an achievement. It will be the first duty of our statesmen to watch over the alliance between Russia and the Western Powers, sealed as it is by the fiery ordeal of war, and to neutralise the occult influences which are even now working to undermine it, to the advantage of interests which are anything but British. But it will also be their duty to create a situation which, while safeguarding the Empire's vital interests, shall not render improved relations with the central European Powers impossible from the very outset. It is one thing to abandon our allies and friends, it is quite another thing to perpetuate a feud which, though converted by circumstances into a struggle between two unanimous nations, was in the first instance the work of mischievous if powerful minorities.

The final settlement will inevitably bring many disappointments and errors in its train. We can best guard against such a result by preparing ourselves for all eventualities and giving the most careful consideration to each of the many problems at issue. Our obvious aim must be a settlement which shows some reasonable prospect of permanence, and this can best be achieved if we respect so far as possible the wishes of the populations concerned. The principle of Nationality is not a talisman which will open all gates, for in some parts of Europe the different races are so inextricably intermingled as to defy all efforts to create ethnographic boundaries. This does not, however, affect the central fact that Nationality is the best salve for existing wounds, and that its application will enormously reduce the infected area. But if the peoples are to make their wishes felt there must be a regeneration of diplomatic methods throughout Europe. Attempts will be made to revive the pernicious principles of the Congress of Vienna, by which a few autocrats and aristocrats carved out the fate of millions according to their dynastic appetites or fancies, and thus tied a whole series of unnecessary knots for subsequent wars to sever. A healthy and informed

public opinion—especially in the West—must watch over
the doings of those who represent it at the fateful Congress,
according loyal support to their declared policy, but
promptly checking the reactionary tendencies which are
certain to reveal themselves. It is still unhappily possible
for the arrogant impatience of a single ruler or the persistent intrigue and misrepresentation of an ambassador
to embroil the European situation. Unless the nations
in council can devise some practical checks upon irresponsible meddling, the flower of their manhood will have
massacred each other in vain. The antecedents of Sir
Edward Grey, and more especially his attitude during the
crisis which led to war, justify us in the hope that his entire
influence will be employed in the right direction when the
decisive moment arrives, and that he will insist upon such
crucial questions as the reduction of armaments, the substitution of " citizen " for " conscript " armies, the control
of armament firms and their occult influence, the effective
extension of arbitration and the elimination of impossible
time-limits, being discussed in all seriousness, and not merely
dismissed with a few ironic platitudes and expressions of
hypocritical goodwill. We must not be unduly discouraged
if some of these ideals prove impossible of realisation, for
it would be childish to suppose that when the great war is
over the nations will at once convert their swords into
ploughshares and proclaim for the first time in history the
sway of Right over Might. But it is obvious that in a world
which has long ceased to be merely European, the European
Powers cannot long continue with impunity such inter-
necine strife, and that unless some real shape and substance
can be given to the Concert of Europe—so long and so
justly a byword among all thinking men—our continent
(and with it these islands) will inevitably forfeit the leader-

ship which has hitherto been theirs and surrender the direction of the world's affairs into the hands of the extra-European powers. It will be remembered that Sir Edward Grey, in a last despairing effort to preserve peace,[1] broached the idea of " some more definite rapprochement between the Powers," and though admittedly " hitherto too Utopian to form the subject of definite proposals," it may be hoped that the enormous difficulty of the task will not deter him from pleading before the future Congress the outraged cause of international goodwill.

[1] White Paper, No. 101.

CHAPTER VIII

SOCIAL AND ECONOMIC ASPECTS OF THE WAR

"And the economic ravages of war are also much greater with civilised nations than with barbarians. A war nowadays may have stern, fearful consequences, especially through the destruction of the ingenious credit system."—TREITSCHKE.

"Those who have fallen have consecrated deaths. They have taken their part in the making of a new Europe, a new world. I can see signs of its coming in the glare of the battlefield. The people will gain more by this struggle in all lands than they comprehend at the present moment. . . . A great flood of luxury and of sloth which had submerged the land is receding, and a new Britain is appearing. We can see for the first time the fundamental things that matter in life and that have been obscured from our vision by the tropical growth of prosperity."—MR. D. LLOYD GEORGE.

IT is obvious that a great war must profoundly disturb every side of the national life of the peoples taking part in it, and that these disturbances must react upon neutral States. The exact character and extent of these changes, however, are by no means easy to understand, and the present chapter does not pretend to offer an exhaustive treatment of them. It is impossible to appreciate the full significance of the immediate social and economic reactions of the war, whilst an attempt to state the ultimate effects of the war leads us along the slippery paths of prophecy. Nevertheless, we are not likely to grasp the importance of the various phenomena which have followed so closely upon the heels of the declaration of war, nor to adapt ourselves to the new situation which will arise out of the war, unless we give our attention to the things which are happening around us.

Unfortunately we can gain little guidance from the past. The South African War inevitably disturbed the normal course of our industrial life, but it involved us in conflict with a nation of relatively little general economic importance ; and so, costly and prolonged though it was, it bears no comparison in its magnitude and in the character of its main issues to the present war in Europe. The Crimean War of sixty years ago, though waged between four European nations—Great Britain, France, Turkey, and Russia—cost Great Britain much less in money than the Boer War ; the issues so far as this country was concerned were not so momentous ; and industry and commerce, though important, were not then nearly so highly developed and complicated as they are now. The Napoleonic wars, though comparable to the present war in fundamental importance, lasted for a generation, which the war of to-day can hardly do ; the effects of the wars with Napoleon were complicated by the Industrial Revolution ; the industrial system and the commercial fabric erected on it were then only in process of formation and the power of the people was small.

These differences enable us to see the new factors which have come into play during the past century. The present war is being fought under conditions which were non-existent during the struggle with Napoleon—conditions which on the one hand add to the waste and loss and misery of war, but on the other give rise to the hope that many of its evil consequences may be averted. Firstly, industry and commerce are world-wide ; the remotest countries are bound together by economic ties ; invisible cords link the

Belgian iron worker with the London docker and the Clyde shipwright, the Californian fruit grower with the Malay tin miner and the German dye worker. The economic effects of modern warfare, therefore, reverberate throughout the whole world, and widespread dislocation ensues. In the next place, the gigantic scale on which war between great powers is conducted, though it tends to shorten the duration of wars, increases the intensity of the shock to human society.

But besides these new material conditions, modern warfare is carried on under the eyes of more enlightened peoples than in the past. The struggle which is now being pursued is the first great war watched by a conscious or at any rate partly conscious democracy. It is the first modern war waged (except in our own case) by national armies constituting practically the entire fit male population. The masses of the people have in most civilised countries some measure of political power. And though to the elector diplomacy and the conduct of foreign affairs are a closed book, war once declared is war by the people ; and their voice must be heard in matters connected with it and arising out of it. Then, further, in the past the aftermath of war was in many ways as horrible as war itself, whilst the period during war witnessed an enormous amount of privation and suffering among non-combatants almost as ghastly as that of the battlefield. This was due not so much to inaction resulting from callousness as to unwise action and ignorance. During the past century political science and economic inquiry have made vast strides, and consequently the injurious social effects of warfare may be minimised, though not averted ; and a considerable body of public opinion, far more enlightened than during any previous European war, is almost certain to exercise some pressure in the direction of wise and far-reaching action both during the war and after it is ended. These considerations must be borne in mind in discussing both the present position and possible future developments.

It is clear that four great European Powers and some smaller ones cannot engage in war without shaking the fabric of European civilisation to its foundations. The tramp of fifteen million armed men is the greatest social and economic fact of the present day, and indeed of the present generation. These millions of combatants have to be clothed, fed, armed, transported, and tended in health and in sickness; they are non-producers for the time, consuming in large quantities the staple commodities of life, and calling in addition for all the paraphernalia of war; sooner or later, they will desire to return to the plough and the mine, the factory and the railroad. These two facts alone are of tremendous importance. But besides this, the activity of those who stay at home is called into play in a thousand different ways, and economic and social life leave their well-trodden paths in answer to the imperious call of national necessity. Social institutions of all kinds are inevitably led into new fields of thought and action, and States are driven to untried experiments in communal activity. The usual channels of thought dry up, the flood of new ideas and of old ideas throbbing with a new life rushes on unconfined, here in the shallows, there in the deeps, presently to overflow into the old channels, cleansing their beds and giving them a new direction, and linking up in fruitful union but remotely connected streams. When fighting ceases and there comes the calm of peace, society will tend to revert to its normal functions, based on peace; but the society of yesterday can never return. Social life cannot be the same as it was before, not merely because those activities called forth by the war may persist in some form, but because of the growth of new ideas under the stimulus of the war. The struggle will almost certainly set in progress trains of thought not only connected with questions of war and peace, but with the wider questions of human destiny.

Coming to a closer view of the question, we must distinguish between the immediate effects of the war which are already in evidence and the ultimate effects which will but begin to unfold themselves after the return of peace. Some of the latter results will grow out of the immediate effects ; others will be more directly due to the events following on the conclusion of the war. It will also be advisable to distinguish between the economic reactions of the war, and the broader social consequences. At such an early stage it would be presumptuous and tempting Providence to attempt to forecast the future in any detail or to try to trace the play and interplay of the various forces going towards the making of the future. This chapter will be concerned with broad tentative generalisations on quite simple lines.

One of the things which struck the intelligent working man during the early days of the war was the rapidity with which the State acted in the face of the crisis. In next to no time large measures of State control and action were put successfully into operation and those who had advocated co-operative action in the past with but indifferent success were amazed at the swiftness with which the nation can act in the hour of need. The drastic action of the State cannot be better illustrated than by the steps which were taken to meet the sudden commercial deadlock which the war precipitated. A discussion of these financial measures will at the same time enable us to understand how, through credit, war strikes at the industry and trade of the modern world.

A. State Action in Industry and Commerce

The Austrian ultimatum to Servia was followed by the paralysis of the world's international system of finance. Before the end of July many important stock exchanges were closed, and by the 31st the London Stock Exchange for the first time in its history was also compelled to close. The remittance market collapsed and with it the fabric of international trade. Widespread bankruptcy and ruin seemed imminent ; so serious did the state of affairs become that moratoria were declared not only in several European countries but in parts of America, and in many continental countries specie payments were suspended. In a word, the possibility of war had thrown the delicately poised credit system of the commercial world out of gear ; the declaration of war had brought it to a standstill. Into an explanation of its working it is not possible to enter ; it is sufficient for our immediate purpose to realise that the foreign exchange machinery by which the supply of commodities from other countries becomes practicable on a large scale was for a time altogether unworkable. London as the financial centre of the world has immense sums owing to it and in its turn owes large sums. The ultimate effect of the collapse of credit, which depends on confidence, was that London could neither receive nor make payment. The big finance houses, who had " accepted " bills of exchange and rendered themselves liable to meet the payments for the things they represented, on the understanding that the means to pay them were to be promptly despatched, found that these means were not forthcoming ;

their own resources were far from sufficient to meet these payments. Utter ruin stared them in the face. At home also a run on the banks seemed probable, which would have meant ruin to large numbers of people. In this grave crisis the State acted with commendable promptness. The bank holiday was extended; State notes for 10s. and £1 were issued; a moratorium was declared, legalising the postponement of the due payment of debts, with certain exceptions; the Bank of England under a guarantee from the Government that the latter would meet the loss, began discounting, or buying for cash, approved bills of exchange accepted before war was declared, many of which are hardly likely to be met by the people liable for payment. These steps were taken swiftly and boldly and allayed the panic. But more was needed; such measures were not in themselves sufficient to put the machinery of foreign exchange into operation again and the suspension of this method of settling international indebtedness was having serious effects. To carry on international trade, and to supply ourselves with the produce on which the very existence of the community depends, without the machinery, is a thousand times more difficult than to conduct our home trade by means of direct barter. Without going into technical details, it may be said that the purchase of bills by the Bank of England, whilst relieving the last holder from loss, did not extinguish the liability of persons whose names had appeared on the bills as acceptors, endorsers and drawers. This was true of traders and commercial people not only in this country but also in other parts of the world. In the face of these liabilities, in most cases unexpected, it was hardly likely that they would increase their liabilities under new bills. Consequently the remittances coming to London shrank to next to nothing.

As bills of exchange—or their equivalent—are the means by which both importers and exporters get paid for their goods, the difficulty of getting paid naturally began to have a serious effect on trade. As the figures of foreign trade during August show, cargoes were being held up. It was clear, therefore, that if this country were to continue to receive supplies of corn and meat, of cotton and wool, of hides and timber, something further must be done. The question the Government had to decide was what steps could be taken to safeguard the food of the people, and to avoid a crushing volume of unemployment through the lack of the raw materials of industry. The produce was there ; what was needed was to start the flow of the particular kind of currency—" credit money "—which would expedite exchange. The course taken by the State was to advance money to the large bill bankers or " accepting houses " in London to allow of the due payment of the enormous number of bills falling due in the three months succeeding the outbreak of war. The audacity of the step will be understood when it is realised that probably something like £300,000,000 of bills fall due over a period of three months.[1] The necessary money was lent without security, the Government promising not to demand repayment until twelve months after the end of the war. A proportion of this advance will be in the nature of a loss, though how much it is quite impossible to say. By this measure, in the event of the bills not being met by those who have promised to pay them—the acceptors—the liability which would ordinarily have fallen upon the drawers and endorsers through whose hands the bills had passed has been removed. The State has advanced to the com-

[1] Mr. J. M. Keynes (*Economic Journal*, Sept. 1914) estimates the aggregate value of outstanding bills in London at £350,000,000.

mercial community a huge sum of money, risking the total loss of some part of it, in order to set in motion the machinery of international exchange. Further steps, however, were taken. The general moratorium expired on November 4. Useful as it had been, it still left many traders in financial difficulties because of the impossibility of collecting debts owing to them in enemy and other countries. The Government, therefore, appointed a committee representing the Treasury, the Bank of England, the Joint Stock Banks, and the Association of Chambers of Commerce of the United Kingdom to authorise advances in approved cases to British traders carrying on an export business in respect of debts outstanding in foreign countries and colonies, including unpaid foreign and colonial accepted bills which cannot be collected for the time being. It is safe to say that no Government ever took such gigantic measures to meet a great crisis.[1] The Prime Minister, speaking at the Guildhall on November 9, 1914, summarised as follows the effects of the steps taken : " The foreign exchanges are working in the case of most countries quite satisfactorily, and the gold reserves at the Bank of England, which were 40 millions on July 22, and which had fallen on August 7 to 27 millions, now stand at the unprecedented figure of 69½ millions. The central gold reserve of the country after three months of the war amounts to £80,000,000, almost exactly twice the amount at which it stood at the beginning of the crisis. The bank rate, which rose, as you know, to 10 per cent, has now come down to 5, a figure, I think, not in excess of that at which it stood this time last year. Food prices have been kept

---

[1] In addition to these various financial measures, the State has lent Belgium £10,000,000 and the Union of South Africa £7,000,000, whilst it has also guaranteed £5,000,000 of the new Egyptian cotton loan.

at a fairly normal level, and though trade has been curtailed in some directions, unemployment has been rather
below than above the average."

But this is by no means the only example of State action.
The Government has established temporarily a State-aided
system of marine insurance, by undertaking 80 per cent of
the war risk, in order to encourage overseas trade. It has
given substantial aid to the joint-stock banks " for the sole
purpose that they might be fit to aid in every way possible
the country's trade and finance." [1] It made arrangements
for the direct purchase of forage and vegetables, etc., from
farmers.[2] It took over the control of the railways. When,
owing to panic, there was a rush for the purchase of food-
stuffs, which was used to force up prices unduly, the Government intervened to prevent exorbitant charges. Particularly interesting is the action of the State regarding sugar,
two-thirds of our supply of which comes from Germany
and Austria. In the days immediately following the
declaration of war wholesale prices were trebled. The
Government, therefore, decided to take upon itself the task
of ensuring an adequate supply of sugar, and a Royal Commission was appointed. The leading refiners were approached
and an arrangement was made with the whole body of
refiners that they should stand aside from the market for
raw sugars, leaving it free for the operations of the Government. The Royal Commission pledged the refiners to
buy their sugar from the Commission, *i.e.* from the State ;
sugar was to be offered to them at a fixed price, and the
refiners were to sell the refined product to the dealers also

---

[1] *Round Table*, Sept. 1914, p. 705.

[2] This was done through the Board of Agriculture for the War
Office. On the other hand, in the purchase of clothing, boots,
blankets, etc., the War Office approached the producers directly
instead of through the Board of Trade.

at a fixed price sufficient to yield the refiners a fair profit on manufacture. As a result of the corner, a big rise in the price of sugar, which is not only an important domestic commodity but the raw material of several industries, was averted. This merits the description given of it in *The Nation*—" a really dashing experiment in State Socialism." [1] On the other hand, it has done nothing to increase the world's supply of sugar, but has merely commandeered a part of the existing stock. The aid of the State has been invoked in other directions. Already the Government has assisted experimental cultivation of beet in this country. The suggestion has been made that the State should build two beet-sugar factories, which would cost about £200,000 each; in this way it is suggested that our home supply of sugar would in the future be assured, and that agriculture would benefit considerably.[2]

Sir Charles Macara has put forward a scheme of State aid for the cotton industry. Owing to the war, a third of the total cotton crop (usually taken by the continental countries) was thrown on the market. Prices naturally fell, and there was a danger that the cotton planters might not be able to pay the debts they had contracted to enable them to grow their crops, in which case there would be a likelihood of the land being used for other saleable commodities, and the efforts which have been made in the past to increase the cotton crop would be nullified. In the meantime, the surplus cotton on the market created an uncertainty regarding prices, and buying came to a standstill, with the result that the position of the industry as a whole became

---

[1] It was reported in the Press on October 8, 1914, that the Home Secretary had purchased 900,000 tons of sugar at about £20 per ton, the transaction involving an outlay of about £18,000,000.

[2] See an article by Mr. Robertson Scott in *The Nineteenth Century*, October 1914.

very critical. The suggestion of Sir Charles Macara is that the Governments of this country and the United States, acting in conjunction, should take the temporarily unsaleable surplus of raw cotton off the market and store it for use in years when the crop is short. In other words, it is proposed to establish a permanent national cotton reserve. It is estimated that the cost of the scheme would mean an outlay of sixty to seventy millions sterling. If the plan were put into operation, however, it is claimed that it would restore confidence, prevent the wholesale stoppage of mills, and at the same time establish a cotton reserve to counteract the fluctuations of crops in the future.[1] These matters need but to be stated as examples of the remarkable adaptability of the State and the possibility of drastic action under the pressure of imperative needs.[2]

The course of events has shown the temporary collapse of economic individualism in the face of the European crisis. The economic system, which works during times of peace, could not meet successfully the crushing effects of a

---

[1] It should be pointed out that the serious condition of the cotton industry is not due to the war. The overstocking of the Eastern and Indian markets during the trade boom of 1913, together with the financial crisis in India last year, has reduced the demand for cotton goods. The war has merely emphasised a depression which had already fallen on the industry. Sir Charles Macara's scheme, whilst it may be desirable on other grounds, cannot compensate for the shrinkage in the demand for Lancashire products. The Government, it is interesting to note, have commissioned certain firms in Alexandria " to buy cotton extensively from small proprietors at a reasonable rate, on Government account, to be stored until the arrival of more prosperous times " (Press Association Telegram, *Daily Press*, Nov. 2, 1914).

[2] The voluntary gifts of different parts of the Empire should not be overlooked. Besides these other steps have been taken. The Australian Government, for example, in order to induce farmers to extend the area of cultivation, has guaranteed " a fixed minimum price of 4s. " for all wheat grown on the newly cultivated land. (Reuter's Correspondent, *Daily Press*, Oct. 27, 1914).

European war. It lacked not only adequate resources but the necessary power of corporate action and co-ordination. Immediate State action seemed to be the only way to avert disaster. In a month, Britain came nearer than ever before to being a co-operative commonwealth. It has been realised that industry and commerce are not primarily intended as a field for exploitation and profit, but are essential national services in as true a sense as the army and navy. The complexity of the modern economic world and the large individual gains which have been made in it have obscured the fact that the economic structure exists to serve the needs of the community. It was recognised by the Government, at any rate to some extent, that the success of our armies in the field would be nullified if, in the economic sphere, the production of commodities and services were seriously diminished and if their interchange were hampered in a large degree. People have felt that the spinner, the miner, the weaver, the machinist, are all by following their occupations performing a valuable service to the community. How far this attitude of mind will persist after the war, when normal conditions in industry and commerce gradually return, remains to be seen.

B. Immediate Social and Economic Effects of the War

1. *Foreign Trade.*—The effects of the war on industry and commerce will be complicated and far reaching. The British and German Empires together transact about two-fifths of the international trade of the world, the British Empire doing over a quarter and Germany almost exactly an eighth. Between them they own over half the merchant shipping of

the world. A war in which they are both engaged, therefore,
must have serious consequences not only to these countries
themselves but to the countries with whom they carry on
business relations, and through them, in a lesser degree, to
all other commercial countries. But this is not all : France
has a foreign trade amounting to £615,000,000 a year ;
Belgium's is valued at £326,000,000, Russia's at £275,000,000,
and Austria-Hungary's at £256,000,000. Besides a gigantic
foreign trade there is a domestic trade, which is on a
larger scale than the external trade of these countries.
Let us consider in more detail the case of Germany. Half
her foreign trade is transacted with the nations now engaged in the great war. The trade of Britain, Russia, and
France with the German Empire is now at a standstill,
except possibly for a very small amount transacted viâ
neutral countries ; her trade with Austria-Hungary must
seriously decline. Moreover, her imports from neutral
countries and her exports to them have dwindled very
considerably, and must remain small as long as British
naval supremacy continues. More than one half of Germany's total imports are raw materials for manufactures,
about two - thirds of her exports being manufactured
goods. Assuming that she continues o conduct foreign
trade through Norway and Sweden, Denmark, Holland,
Switzerland, and Austria - Hungary, the volume will
be small, and even if her whole trade with neutral
countries could be maintained she would still be without the trade of her enemies. For example, in 1913
this country sold goods to the value of £40,000,000 to
Germany and purchased from her goods to the value of
£80,000,000.[1]

[1] The following list indicates some of the chief articles of trade
between the two countries :

In Great Britain, economic activity has been developed
on the assumption of continued peace. In Germany, however, though there were those who would " base all economic
policy on an imaginary permanent peace," [1] the Government has had in view the possibility of war. " Every
conscientious Government," writes von Bülow, " seeks to
avoid [war] so long as the honour and vital interests of the
nation permit of so doing. But every State department
should be organised as if war were going to break out to-
morrow. This applies to economic policy as well." [2] It
is with this idea in mind that the German Government
has striven to maintain the importance of agriculture.
" Economic policy must foster peaceful development ; but
it must keep in view the possibility of war, and, for this
reason above all, must be agrarian in the best sense of the
word." [3] It is held that in the event of war the home
market in Germany would be an important factor in maintaining intact the fabric of industry. " The home market,"
we are told, " is . . . of very great importance. It would be
called upon to replace the foreign market if in time of war
our national frontiers should be wholly or partly closed.
But in the home market agriculture is by far the most

German Imports into the United Kingdom, 1912.		British Exports to Germany, 1912.	
	£ million.		£ million.
Sugar	6·2	Cottons and yarn .	8·3
Cottons and yarn . .	5·9	Woollens and yarn .	6·6
Iron and steel and		Coal, coke, etc. . .	4·4
manufactures . .	5·7	Herrings. . . .	2·4
Woollens and yarn .	2·6	Ironwork . . .	2·1
Machinery . . .	2·4	Machinery . . .	2·1
Glass and Manufactures	1·1		

It is not true, as Dr. R. G. Usher says, that Germany is " literally
self-sufficing " (*Pan Germanism*, p. 65).

[1] *Imperial Germany*, by Prince Bernhard von Bülow, p. 221.

[2] *Ibid.* p. 220. See also Bernhardi, *Germany and the Next War*,
pp. 157-159 and 260 *et seq.*   [3] *Imperial Germany*, pp. 220-221.

important customer of industry ; only if agriculture is able to buy, if it earns enough itself to enable others to earn too, will it be able, in critical times, to consume a part of the products which cannot be disposed of abroad. The old proverb, " If the peasant has money then every one else has too," is literally true, as soon as industry is forced, to a greater extent than is necessary in times of peace, to find its customers at home." [1] " As in time of war industry is dependent on the buying power of agriculture, the productive power of agriculture is a vital question for the nation." [2]

The importance of agriculture in Germany is undoubtedly great ; it may be, as Bülow says, that " the value of its produce is equal to that of the produce of industry, or even surpasses it." [3] But if the demand for it were to shrink because the industrial population lost their work through a shortage of raw materials or in any other way, agriculture would also suffer. The population at present engaged in agriculture will in times of peace buy up to the practical limits of its purchasing power, and is hardly likely, especially in the early stages of a war, to " consume a part of the products which cannot be disposed of abroad," except in so far as they buy German goods (the production of which the declaration of the war may have seriously impeded), instead of commodities produced abroad. But it is questionable whether they will be able to maintain their aggregate purchasing power. Prince Bülow ignores the fact that production for the home market will be hampered by the possible non-arrival of foreign raw materials in war time; yet Germany imported raw cotton to the value of over £29,000,000 in 1913. Her foreign purchases of hides and skins amounted to over £22,500,000 and of wool to £10,000,000. With even

[1] *Imperial Germany*, p. 219. [2] *Ibid.* p. 221.
[3] *Ibid.* p. 217.

a partial suspension of imports of these and similar commodities, industries dependent on foreign products must be
severely hit; unemployment must increase and the purchasing power of the urban workers diminish. The agricultural community must suffer also, and in all likelihood
will not be able to take their normal share of goods off the
market. It is true, of course, that Germany buys large
quantities of food - stuffs from abroad, and that home
produce will be required to take their place; but they
cannot be grown immediately; in the interval, industrial
disorganisation must result, and before agriculture can
begin to profit by the lack of foreign supplies the harm will
have been done. Moreover, agriculture must be impeded,
as, owing to the size of the German Empire, the transport of
troops must seriously interfere with the conveyance of
goods to the larger centres of population. It would seem,
therefore, that the policy of developing German agriculture at the same time that her dependence on foreign
commerce is increasing is not an effective reply to the
British Navy. The position in Germany then is that she
must for the present be satisfied with a much smaller amount
of imported food-stuffs and of the raw materials of industry;
and that in any case, even if the industrial machine could
be kept at work, there will be practically no outlet for
goods abroad. Commercially isolated, she must, therefore,
suffer an industrial and commercial collapse. On the other
hand, the total volume of unemployment, which would have
been enormous during the first weeks of the war, has of
course been considerably reduced by the withdrawal of
great masses of men to join the colours, and by the stimulus
which the war has given to industries supplying the needs
of the German armies. Then also Rotterdam, through
which Germany does a great deal of its trade, remains open,

whilst a fraction of her foreign trade is being carried on
through Denmark, Scandinavia, and Switzerland. Nevertheless, the amount of economic distress within a very few
weeks after the outbreak of war, especially in the large
towns, was considerable even on the showing of German
newspapers.[1] The amount of distress was increased and
intensified by steadily rising prices. As the rise has taken
place not only in commodities of which there is a shortage,
but in others such as sugar, it may be concluded that it is
due largely to the inflation of the currency, owing to the
adoption of the fatally easy expedient of issuing large
masses of paper money.

Austria-Hungary, which is not an advanced industrial
country, will not suffer quite so keenly, though even here
the German newspapers admit that trade has come almost
to a standstill.[2] In the western theatre of war the fighting

[1] " Let us imagine," says Bernhardi, " the endless misery which
a protracted stoppage or definite destruction of our oversea trade
would bring upon the whole nation, and in particular on the masses
of the industrial classes who live on our export trade " (*Germany and
the Next War*, p. 232).

According to *The Times* (Sept. 18, 1914) the German nautical
newspaper *Hansa* on Sept. 12 admitted that England had captured
many millions of marks worth of German shipping, and that " the
cessation of business will cost our shipowners many millions more."
" It will hold up the development of our shipping trade for years."
The *Neue Freie Presse* of Vienna on Sept. 11 admitted that the
activity of the exporters in Germany had been crippled. According
to *The Times* (Oct. 7), the German Socialist paper *Vorwaerts*, stated
that " the state of want has reached an alarming extent, even though
we are now only at the beginning of the catastrophe which has be-
fallen the people of Europe." " Masses of unemployment grow every
month."

[2] " The shortage of raw materials, notably cotton, wool, jute, and
petroleum, is greatly restricting production in many branches of
manufacture in Austria-Hungary. According to official estimates,
the supplies of some of the most necessary raw products are barely
sufficient for two more months. Factories are closing down, and
the number of unemployed is steadily increasing " (Reuter's telegram
from Venice, Oct. 21, 1914).

has centred largely round the Franco-Belgian Coalfield, on or near which stand on both sides of the frontier many industrial towns. Lille, Nancy, Epinal, Belfort, Reims, Amiens, and Valenciennes on one side, and Liège and Charleroi on the other, are all of economic importance. Even apart from the actual destruction due to the war which in some of these towns has been serious, the mere presence of the contending armies will have a more or less paralysing effect on industrial and commercial life in both France and Belgium.[1] The position in Belgium, however, is much more serious than in France. It may best be described in the words of Professor Sarolea, written after a visit of five weeks to his native country. " Other belligerent nations may suffer from unemployment. In Belgium alone there has been created a whole nation of unemployed. In other countries trade and industry are dislocated. In Belgium they have come to a complete standstill. Out of a population of eight millions, seven millions are under the heel of the invader. Railwaymen are starving, for railways have ceased to work. Office clerks are starving, for banks and offices are closed. Public officials are starving, for no salaries can be paid. . . . Journalists and printers are starving, for newspapers and books have ceased to appear. Mill hands and coal miners and ironworkers are starving, for mills and coal mines and iron works are closed." [2] Bad as this is, the condition of affairs is somewhat relieved so far as France and Belgium are concerned by the fact that the seas are open to them, but even then we must add

---

[1] For example, the probable number of French factories in a position to produce sugar in 1914–15, will be 82 or 83 as against 206 during the year 1913–14 (*Times*, Nov. 3, 1914).

[2] Letter to the Press dated Sept. 12, 1914. Mr. J. H. Whitehouse, M.P., who visited Belgium says, " The whole life of the nation has been arrested."

these areas to Germany and Austria-Hungary as regions where industry and trade are at the best severely hampered, regions all of which are important factors in the markets of Europe, and whose commercial paralysis will re-echo through the whole commercial world.

The most fortunately situated combatants in Europe are Russia and Great Britain. The former, covering half the area of Europe, has almost limitless resources, and is much more easily capable of being self-supporting than any of the other Great Powers engaged in the war. This country still has the seas open to it.[1] The State subsidy to marine insurance has encouraged overseas trade, and the re-establishment of the remittance market has removed an obstacle to the flow of exports and imports. Still, it is true that the financial world cannot recover all at once. " It is like a man whose nervous system has been shattered by a great shock. Tonics and stimulants may save him from complete collapse, but real recovery is a matter of months and even years." [2] Further, the work hitherto done and the services performed for Germany and Austria are now no longer called for; our allies in the west of Europe are suffering acutely from the immediate economic effects of

---

[1] According to an Admiralty statement, corrected up to Sept. 23, 1914, 12 British ships had been sunk by German cruisers, 8 had been sunk by mines, whilst a few fishing boats had been destroyed. British ships detained and captured by Germany numbered 86, with a total tonnage of 229,000. On the other hand, 387 German vessels had been detained or captured, the total tonnage being 1,140,000. According to *The Times* (Oct. 9, 1914), up to date 1·6 per cent of the tonnage registered in the United Kingdom had been lost. The figures for Germany and Austria were 18 and 13 per cent respectively. The Committee which prepared the State War Insurance Scheme estimated that the loss during the first six months of the war might be about 10 per cent of all British steamers employed in foreign trade.

[2] *Round Table*, Sept. 1914, p. 704.

the war and the large destruction of capital ; our neutral customers have not escaped scot-free. It would seem, therefore, that in spite of the British command of the seas, production must necessarily be seriously curtailed and that, therefore, the volume of unemployment must be very considerable. On the other hand, though production in France, Belgium and Russia may diminish in many directions, what goods they do produce for export will find no market in Germany and Austria-Hungary and a proportion of them will find their way to this country. Such commodities will not only be valuable as food and raw material for industry, but will set up a flow of British goods in payment for them. Further, the production of commodities needed for the prosecution of the war, will increase the volume of employment. Goods of all kinds are required not only for the British armies but for the Allies generally. The manner and extent to which these factors have influenced unemployment will be considered presently.

Now the demand for the goods hitherto supplied by Germany to her foreign customers, though abated, will still continue. As we have seen, she cannot for the present supply them. By whom will she be superseded ? [1] The Government of this country early in the war took steps to co-operate with British traders in an attempt to obtain some share of this trade, and the United States also strove to make the fullest use of the opportunity. In this country goods previously imported from Germany will, if still needed, either be bought from the next cheapest importer or produced at home. Commodities which we have in the past

[1] Towards the end of August, the tin-plate and steel-sheet trade in this country which had suffered badly on the outbreak of war revived, and " several mills were reopened, owing to the obtaining of orders which formerly went to Germany " (*Board of Trade Labour Gazette*, Sept. 1914, p. 330),

produced for German consumption are not now required from us. If they continue to be made, it must be for other countries. In other words, whether the volume of British foreign trade remains the same or not, a proportion of it will be diverted into new channels during the progress of the war. In a less degree, the trade of other states will be deflected from its accustomed channels. Beyond this, special influences will be felt in the case of certain new countries, as for example Canada. " Canada's annual balance of trade is probably about £60,000,000 against her : £30,000,000 being the excess of her trade imports over her trade exports and the remaining £30,000,000 representing her annual payment on money borrowed. She has balanced her account hitherto by borrowing very large sums of money. Now she will be unable to do that any longer. Nor will she at present, at any rate, obtain the immigrants on which she is counting to enable her to pay her interest. She cannot redeem the balance due by the export of gold. The burden would be too great in any case, and moreover she has suspended specie payments. A part of the balance due may be covered by the higher value of her exports, such as wheat. The remainder she can only meet either by increasing her exports or by reducing her imports. The latter she has already begun to do." [1] This new readjust-ment may be accompanied by great economic loss ; in any case the dislocation will be harmful for the time, not only to the new countries, but to the countries with whom they trade. It is clear that foreign trade generally will during the war gradually be readjusted to the new conditions of the times. To what extent the various streams of the world's trade will be directed into new channels it is impossible to say ; the readjustment will be partly tem-

[1] *Round Table*, Sept. 1914, pp. 708-9.

porary, and partly permanent.[1] This redistribution of production, if it leads to production under less favourable conditions than before, will tend to raise prices, and thereby probably diminish the power to buy other commodities. If it leads to the substitution of a well organised and well paid industry by an industry of a less skilled kind, there will be in effect a net lowering of wages. The widespread effects of the war on industry and commerce must, therefore, have a profound effect on the whole of the economic world.

2. *Unemployment and Short Time.*—We are now able to understand how the war has affected the individual workman. As we have seen, the panic caused by the outbreak of war and the collapse of the remittance market meant in many industries the holding up of production and the stoppage of the workman's wages. If it had not been possible to restart the machinery of exchange, starvation would have walked through the land, and the industries dependent on foreign raw material would have closed down altogether. As it was, the inevitable dislocation increased the amount of unemployment.[2] Whereas the trade union percentage [3] of unemployment amongst their members was only 2·8 at the end of July, it had reached 7·1 by the end of August. This figure, however, is considerably below the percentage of unemployed during many periods of trade depression ; the average for the whole of 1908 was 7·8 and for 1909, 7·7, whilst during the month of March 1912 it rose to 11·3 as a result of the coal strike.

[1] This, of course, does not mean that Great Britain will " capture " German trade and increase its foreign commerce by the amount of its value.

[2] Note that unemployment prior to the war was showing a tendency to increase.

[3] It should be observed that these figures relate only to about a million trade unionists, no non-unionists being included. Further, they ignore short time.

The volume of unemployment during August varied considerably from trade to trade. In the cotton industry, which, however, appeared to be in for a bad time anyhow, 17·7 per cent of the trade union members were returned as unemployed during August 1914, whilst in coal mining the percentage was 1·3. As compared with the previous month of July, there was a general decline in all industries except shipbuilding, which benefited by increased activity on Government work. The contraction in the volume of employment was specially marked in the case of tin-plate works and in the textile, furnishing and woodworking, and pottery trades. Again, in the trades where the Government scheme of compulsory unemployment insurance applies, the volume of unemployment at the end of July was 3·6 per cent, but at the end of August it had reached 6·2 per cent or double the volume recorded in August 1913.[1] Beyond this, there was during the month of August, an enormous amount of short time ; in several industries for which particulars are available, thousands of workpeople were working half-time or less.[2] The rise which took place

[1] The gradual increase during the month may be observed from the weekly returns :—Aug. 7, 4·0 per cent; Aug. 14, 5·1 per cent; Aug. 21, 5·8 per cent; Aug. 28, 6·2 per cent.

[2] The Board of Trade receives monthly reports from employers and others in different industries. These returns, though they do not cover the whole of the industries, are sufficiently reliable to indicate the widespread character of short time. During August 1914, in slate quarries and china clay works, " there was a good deal of short time and some unemployment in consequence of the war " ; in tin-plate and sheet-steel works, " short time was very general. In some cases discharges were obviated by the sharing of work at the mills remaining open. The decrease in employment is to be attributed to the effects of the war, and in particular to the general restriction of the European market " ; some branches of the engineering trade, particularly agricultural and textile machinery, and the motor car and cycle trades, were " disorganised by the war ; many discharges took place and a large amount of short time was worked."

in the price of certain food-stuffs especially during the first
part of August intensified the evil by reducing " real "
wages.

During the month of September, however, employment
revived.[1] Besides Government work in shipbuilding yards,
certain branches of the woollen industry were working at
full pressure on the production of blankets and cloth for
uniforms; the leather and boot and shoe industries on some
sides received an impetus from the large orders placed for
army boots; hosiery and knitted goods were required in large
quantities. Speaking generally, industries whose products

In the miscellaneous metal trades, except in the manufacture of
articles required for military and naval purposes, " much short time
was reported." In the cotton industry, " the trade as a whole was
working less than three days a week, and large numbers of workpeople were entirely unemployed." In the woollen trade, " about
60 per cent of the workpeople covered by the returns received were
on short time, including over 20 per cent who were working half-time
or less." The returns showed a decrease of " 21·5 per cent in the
amount of wages paid compared with a month ago." In the worsted
industry, " about 65 per cent of the workpeople covered by the
returns were working short time during the month, including over
30 per cent who were working only half time or less." The returns
showed a decrease " of 26·5 per cent in the amount of wages paid
compared with a month ago." In the linen trade " short time was
reported generally." In the hosiery industry, " short time was
reported by firms employing over 40 per cent of the operatives
covered by the returns." In the silk trade " a great deal of short
time was worked in all the districts." In the levers and curtains
branches of the lace industry " the majority of the operatives . . .
were only working half time, and large numbers were altogether unemployed." In the carpet trade " short time was general, most districts
working only half the usual hours." In the furnishing trades
" short time was worked in almost every district." " Short time
was very generally reported " in printing. In the glass trades " short
time was reported in several districts." In the potteries " most of
the firms " were running short time (see the *Board of Trade Labour
Gazette*, Sept. 1914).

[1] The percentage of unemployment at the beginning of October
in the trades compulsorily insured against unemployment was 5·1,
as compared with 6·3 at the beginning of the previous month.

were required for the army and navy were strained to the extent of their resources. But each industry supplies a large variety of goods of many different grades, and machinery and works equipment cannot always be easily converted to the production of other classes of commodities ; so that even in the woollen and boot trades, for example, the whole industries were not uniformly busy. The many industries, however, to which the war brought no orders, enjoyed but a slight recovery, and in some cases none at all. As the month of September proceeded, the news-papers triumphantly referred to the fall in the percentage of unemployment. The truth is that the decline was by no means general or uniform, but was brought about, not so much by the gradual revival of normal activity, but by the rush of Government orders. For instance, the cotton industry remained in the trough of a deep depression, and the furniture and piano making trades profited little. Further, no account was taken of the prevalence of short time, though over a large field it was widespread especially amongst women. What the real position of the labour market was after we had been at war two months, cannot be precisely determined, but it was certainly more serious than the Board of Trade percentage would seem to indicate.[1]

[1] "Certain confidential statistical enquiries on a large scale are said to support the inference to be drawn from the figures published by the Board of Trade, that at least 10 per cent of the fifteen million wage-earners in the United Kingdom are not at work at all, whilst quite as large a proportion are on short time. But out of more than a million men whose services the employers have thus temporarily dispensed with, some nine hundred thousand are being clothed, or are going to be clothed, in khaki, and given Government pay. Thus the actual unemployment among men is, except in (certain) black patches, only sporadic and scarcely more than we are accustomed to. Very different is the situation of the women wage-earners. Of these apparently half a million are now unemployed, and twice as many are working only short time. Though the industrial situation is considerably better than would have been predicted for the end of

The month of October saw a further recovery and a more normal state of affairs. The percentage of unemployment in insured trades continued to decline ; [1] but whilst the number of men on the Labour Exchange registers fell (from 28,664 on October 2 to 24,690 on October 30), the number of women registered remained almost stationary. At the end of three months from the beginning of the war the condition of men's employment was about normal ; but women were suffering from excessive unemployment, whilst short time was still common in many industries in which women are largely employed.

The large volume of unemployment, which it had been anticipated would accompany a great war, was avoided, partly because of prompt State action in maintaining the fabric of commerce and finance, and therefore the supply of raw materials, and partly because of the large demand for commodities for the Army and Navy—a war demand vastly in excess of that in any previous war. In other words, State intervention and the Navy have placed Great Britain in a much superior economic position to that of her adversaries.

3. *Trade Unions, Co-operative Societies and Distress.*— Before the outbreak of the war there were signs that the wave of industrial activity which reached a high point in 1913 was receding, and that unemployment was beginning to increase ; but the trade unions did not anticipate that the ordinary ebb and flow of trade was to be disturbed by a great war. Within a very short time after the declaration of war, the trade unions experienced a heavy drain on

---

the second month of a world war, it was, in fact, worse than it has been at any time during the past quarter of a century " (*New Statesman*, Oct. 3, 1914).

[1] The percentages are as follows : Oct. 2, 5·11 ; Oct. 9, 4·80 ; Oct. 16, 4·46 ; Oct. 23, 4·29 ; Oct. 30, 4·16.

their funds in respect of unemployment benefit. It is, of course, obvious that the accumulated funds of trade unions were never intended as a subsidy to the community during a time of war, which is what, in point of fact, they became. It is true that the unions made efforts to conserve their resources in various ways, not least by advising their younger members without dependants to join the army ; it is true also that most of them profited under Section 106 of the National Insurance Act by the State refund of one-sixth of their payments to their unemployed members ; but these measures—and others—were inadequate to maintain the unions in a sound financial condition, and many unions trembled on the verge of bankruptcy.[1] Such a condition of affairs was viewed with apprehension not only by the trade union movement, but by the State, with the result that at the beginning of October the Government subsidy of one-sixth was under certain conditions increased.[2] But

[1] Speaking generally, it cannot be said that the trade unions faced the crisis with either wisdom or courage. Their attitude, on the whole, was one of utter bewilderment. The lack of the power of adaptability to new circumstances, together with the fact that sufficient pressure was not brought to bear upon the Government in the first weeks of the war, accounts for the unfortunate position in which the trade unions found themselves.

[2] The scheme applies only to unions suffering from abnormal unemployment. There are also conditions that they "should not pay unemployment benefit above a maximum rate of 17s. per week, including any sum paid by way of State unemployment benefit," and that they "should agree while in receipt of the emergency grant to impose levies over and above the ordinary contributions upon those members who remain fully employed." The amount of the emergency grant in addition to the refund of one-sixth already payable will be either one-third or one-sixth of the expenditure on out-of-work pay, depending on the amount of the trade union levy. Under special conditions the grant is to be retrospective. It is, therefore, possible for trade unions to be subsidised so far as unemployment benefit is concerned, to the extent of one-half their payments. But this scheme does nothing to assist trade unions (of which there are many) which get no unemployment benefit.

even with this assistance, many unions will undoubtedly experience considerable difficulty in avoiding financial disaster. Speaking generally, the trade union movement as a whole will emerge from the war in straitened circumstances. Some unions may have collapsed, and amongst others the movement in favour of amalgamation may have received an impetus owing to financial embarrassments.

The decrease in earnings accompanying short time, and their total stoppage in the case of unemployment, mean amongst the workers a restriction of purchasing power. The shrinkage in the total wages bill, especially in Lancashire, must lead to a diminution in the income of small traders and the co-operative societies. Where trade is very bad the societies will be severely hit; smaller purchases will mean smaller profits, which, where there is no large reserve to fall back upon, will in turn mean the declaration of a smaller dividend. The "divi" received by the workers will be less, and the purchases which the thrifty housewife of the north usually makes with it in the way of clothing and replacement of household articles will be less also; where the "divi" has been left in the society, it will in a large number of cases be used to supplement the scanty wages earned on short time, or to provide the necessaries of life where the breadwinner is altogether unemployed. In places where times become very bad, the co-operative societies during the war, and for some time after, will suffer because of the conversion of the cash orders which ordinarily go to the "co-op" into credit orders at the shop round the corner. On the whole, however, the co-operative societies will probably come better out of the war than many classes of small shop-keepers. The small tailors, drapers, earthenware dealers, etc., and others who sell all but indispensable commodities, will see a shrinkage in their sales, especially if prices rise. The co-operative societies will also lose in this respect, but they will lose less on the whole, owing to the fact that a good deal of their capital is used in the sale of food-stuffs, the consumption of which will be restricted last. But admitting this, they cannot expect to escape unscathed, and the blow they suffer will be felt on other sides of their activity, such as their educational work, the income for which usually fluctuates with the prosperity of the societies.

The diminution of the purchasing power of the working people because of the restriction of the national wages bill, however, may be minimised by common action. The National Relief Fund and the Women's Employment Fund are intended really for this purpose. The establishment of women's training workshops and of maintenance grants on condition of attendance at schools and classes are steps in the same direction. The Government has increased the disgracefully low payments made to dependants of soldiers on active service, and its scale of pensions for widows of soldiers and sailors and for those totally or partially disabled in the performance of military or naval duties. Arrangements have been made for the payment of allowances of half wages up to a maximum of £1 a week to dependants of sailors employed on insured British merchant ships captured or detained by the enemy. More important from the point of view of industry as a whole are the steps which have been taken to minimise the effects of a diminution in the volume of employment by the development of new openings. The Government through the Board of Trade took the lead in the attempt to secure a share of the trade hitherto done by Germany and Austria. Special efforts were made to develop the manufacture of toys, and other industrial experiments were begun by the Central Committee on Women's Employment. The Government appointed a Chemical Products Supply Committee with a view to stimulating the production of dyes and drugs at home. These proposals are in the main an attempt to divert the trade of foreign countries, especially Germany, into British channels. The second line of action is fuller provision of home needs which cannot be satisfied by foreign producers, but are essentially domestic. Such needs are housing, public parks, roads, etc. Between August 4 and September 21, 1914, the Local Government Board received over 600 applications from local authorities for powers to borrow money amounting in all to over £2,500,000. About a fifth of this amount it was intended to expend on housing. During this period the Board sanctioned loans amounting in the aggregate to more than £3,500,000, as compared with rather under £2,000,000 in the same period in 1913. The Road Board arranged to put in hand the construction of certain new highways arranged for before the beginning of the war. In addition, in the first seven weeks of the war, the Board arranged to make grants amounting to about £450,000 in aid of new road construction and road improvements in many different parts of the country, which will involve a total expenditure of about a million sterling. The Development Commission began to consider schemes for the construction of light railways, for the improvement of the navigation of rivers, etc., in order that work of this kind should be ready to be put into operation when the necessity arose. The Board of Agriculture has urged that where practicable the acreage under wheat should be increased. This suggestion is, of course, valuable, but will not greatly affect the industrial situation. Even if the schemes sanctioned by the Local Government Board and those adopted by the Road Board were put into operation immediately, which is almost impossible, they would not make a very appreciable difference to the total wages bill of the country. But perhaps it is thought by the Government that the state of employment is not sufficiently grave to warrant a greater expenditure at the present time. In spite of the insistence on forestalling destitution, there is still among local authorities much confusion of charity and relief work with anticipation of future needs calling for employment through the ordinary channels of trade. On the whole the Government has not met the domestic problems of the war with the unanimity and boldness which has characterised its actions in the actual prosecution of the war and in dealing with the financial crisis.

4. *The New Spirit.*—The broader social effects which showed themselves in the early days of the war are illustrated by the remarkable growth of State Socialism. The nation became a community, united in a single purpose; breaches which many imagined to be permanent, cleavages which were thought to be fundamental, no longer existed. None was for a party; all were for the State. The three political parties formed a Parliamentary Recruiting Committee, and altogether impossible teams of people appeared on public platforms with a common aim; Mr. Ben Tillett, in words that might have fallen from the lips of a Tory ex-Cabinet minister, declared that " every resource at our command must be utilised for the purpose of preserving our country and nation "; the anti-militarist trade union movement earnestly appealed to those of its members who were ex-non-commissioned officers to re-enlist; the Queen and Miss Mary MacArthur were members of the same committee. This unanimity, which has pushed into the background for the present causes of difference, has led the

vast majority of people to submit cheerfully to the will of
the State.   The unity of to-day must necessarily make its
influence felt even when the reason of its existence has
passed away.   In the meantime it is assisting in the growth
of a new spirit which the war itself has fostered.   The
social outlook of the people and their attitude towards the
larger problems of life is changing, and patriotism has
taken a deeper meaning.

So far we have devoted our attention to some of the
immediate effects of the war.   But on the return of peace
there will be new influences at work, the immediate and
ultimate effects of which will powerfully affect the course
of future development.   The European War will mark an
era in international politics.   It may also stand as a land-
mark in the history of the social and economic life of
Western Europe.   It is not unlikely that in this respect it
will surpass in its importance all the wars of the past.   The
reasons are to be found in the magnitude and costliness of
the war, the highly developed character and the inter-
relatedness of foreign commerce, the possibility of new
industrial forces coming into play, and the influence of the
war on the political and social ideas of the European
peoples.   It may be that in this country the war will let
loose economic forces destined to modify industrial organisation very profoundly ; and that social forces, especially
on the Continent, will be liberated to work towards fuller
political freedom.   These things lie in the veiled future,
and prophecy is dangerous.   We may, however, turn to
consider some of the probable effects the war will leave
behind it.

C. AFTER THE WAR

1. *General Effects.*—When the war comes to an end, an immediate revival of commercial relations between the combatant States and a general revival of foreign trade cannot be reasonably expected. After the Napoleonic Wars, English manufacturers, assuming the eagerness of continental peoples to buy their goods, were met with the obvious fact that impoverished nations are not good customers. When peaceful relations are resumed in Europe, we shall recognise very vividly the extent to which industry and commerce on the Continent have been closed down. Even assuming that British production continues, Germany, Belgium and Austria will have little to send us in exchange. The closing of the overseas markets of Germany, and the consequent shrinkage in production, the disruption of normal industrial life by the withdrawal of millions of men to join the colours, and the abnormal character of existing trade, due to the needs of the armies in the field, are not conditions favourable to the easy resumption of normal commercial relations. The dislocation of the mechanism of industry and commerce in Europe, on a much larger scale than ever before—a mechanism which has with growing international relations and interdependence become more complicated and more sensitive in recent years—cannot be immediately remedied by a stroke of the pen or the fiat of an emperor. The credit system upon which modern industry and commerce are built depends upon mutual confidence. This confidence will not be restored among the combatant nations immediately on the cessation of war ; it will require time to grow. Further, Europe during the war has been spending its substance and must emerge much poorer. This applies not only to combatant States, but to neutral countries,

some of which have floated loans to meet the abnormal expenditure thrown upon them by prolonged mobilisation. The capital and credit of a large number of people will have suffered great loss or have vanished into thin air. Houses, shops, and buildings of all kinds, produce manufactured and unmanufactured, bridges, ships, railway stations and stock of enormous value will have been destroyed. The community will have been impoverished, not only by the expenditure of great armies and the destruction of wealth, but by the utilisation for immediate consumption of wealth which would have been used as new capital, and by the withdrawal of probably close upon fifteen million men from production during the period of the war. Even if we assume that the world has lost the production of only twelve million men,[1] the loss is enormous. If each man were capable of producing, on the average, wealth to the value of £100 per year, the loss of production per year during the continuance of the war would be about £1,200,000,000. The effect of these factors will be heightened by the fact that the millions of men whose needs during the war have been satisfied by their non-combatant fellow-countrymen will be thrown upon their own resources. And though Europe will still need to be fed and clad and housed, the effectual demand of the population for the goods and services it needs, a demand which it is able to satisfy because of its possession of exchangeable wealth, will be smaller than before the war. The demand will be more or less stifled until the credit system is re-established and mutual confidence restored, and until industry and commerce have adjusted themselves to the new situation. The volume of employment in this country during the war will have been swollen by temporary

[1] The number must be larger than this, as the mobilisation of the armies of neutral states should be taken into account.

demands for war supplies which will cease when the war ends; foreign trade will be uncertain; a larger number of soldiers will be thrown on the labour market than ever before. It would seem, therefore, that in the absence of special steps, the volume of unemployment at the close of the war will be a good deal greater than during the progress of the war.[1]

It is just conceivable, though one hopes not probable, that the economic effects of the war will be complicated by the imposition of war indemnities. The indemnity is really a means of obtaining booty from a vanquished State, and has been looked upon as a justifiable means of further humiliating an already beaten enemy. It has been pointed out,[2] however, that the advantages derived from an indemnity are not an unmixed gain. The indemnity recoils on the heads of those who impose it. It is unnecessary here to enter into a consideration of the detailed effects of huge payments by defeated nations; though it may be remarked that the ramifications of such payments are so intricate and often so incapable of measurement, whilst other economic influences are at work at the same time, that it is impossible to draw an accurate conclusion as to the net advantage or disadvantage of indemnities to the State which levies them. But the point to be borne in mind is that the addition of a great debt to the already large burden of an unsuccessful war reacts upon all countries with which the defeated state enters into business relations. The losses due to this

[1] It is thought by some that the war will be followed by a short boom, when Europe will make good the necessities of industry and civilised life, but it is at least doubtful whether there will be a rapid reproduction of these commodities, owing to the conditions, already described, which will obtain at the close of the war. In any case, however, it will be merely a flash in the pan, and there will follow the gloom of a deep depression, unless there is clear-sighted State action.

[2] See Norman Angell, *The Great Illusion*, Part I. chap. vi.

cause will not necessarily be counterbalanced by gains from increased trade with the country receiving the indemnity; and even if they were, the latter trade might be of a different character. In any case, countries not parties to the indemnity will be affected by it in some way or other; war indemnities, like wars, do not pass by neutral countries and leave them untouched.

It is important to remember that, though modern warfare is much more costly and more exhausting than in the past, there is another side to the matter. Society has also gained remarkably in its powers of recuperation. The blight of war is not as terrible as might be expected. The accumulated knowledge, the vastly increased productivity of industry, and the high organising ability, which have made the modern industrial and commercial world, will not be obliterated by the war. And though there will be difficulties in the way of their full operation when peace returns, they will aid powerfully in shortening the period of recovery. The forces which have transformed mediaeval into modern cities in a few short years will still exist. Though they can hardly be expected to overcome all the many factors likely to restrain economic activity, they may be relied on to stimulate the revival of normal economic life. Indeed, the knowledge of science and the faculty of organisation are likely to be applied more extensively than in the past to productive processes.

After the war, when the States of Europe begin to tread the paths of peace again, one of the first things to be done will be to repair as far as possible the damage done by the war. Take Belgium as an extreme example; leaving aside the irreparable destruction of historic buildings and priceless treasures, there are many million pounds' worth of houses and farm buildings, shops, warehouses, factories, public buildings, ships, railway stations, and bridges to be replaced. This work will take precedence over other kinds of production. Sugar, motor cars, glass, etc , will still be manufactured, but chiefly in order to buy the requisite raw materials and finished goods for the replacement of the wealth destroyed by the ravages of the war. Speaking generally, Belgium will probably consume less food than ordinarily, wear less clothes, and consume less luxuries. Savings, which would normally have been devoted to new industrial developments, will be needed to make good the losses in existing industrial establishments. It is clear, therefore, that the economic growth of Belgium will be retarded in a great degree.[1] The same holds good of Germany, though probably not to the same extent unless the theatre of war is extended to cover a considerable part of the Empire. In the case of our own country, provided it remains free from invasion, there will not be such a large replacement of lost wealth and capital destroyed by the war, except in the case of shipping ; but in common with other States there will be the war to pay for, and certain obligations to meet regarding the maimed and the relatives of the slain. Taxation will be heavy, and therefore, on this ground alone the accumulation of new capital will be retarded. Industrial organisation, having been re-arranged and modified to meet the requirements of the war period, will not resume its old form without a good deal of creaking and jolting. And even if it could, it will not be able to face the new conditions arising out of the war at all rapidly. There is every prospect, therefore, of a time of great difficulty after the war is over, before the normal course of

[1] If Germany be required to compensate Belgium for the damage done, these effects will in large part disappear ; though the burden would still remain. The difference would be that it would be more widely distributed.

industrial and commercial activity is fully resumed. In all likelihood, we shall find that the relative importance of our various industries will have altered to some extent, and that the nature of our trade will have been modified also. Then also the relative positions of our home and foreign trade may shift ; in other words, if the war lasts sufficiently long for new industries to develop and become efficient, they may survive the competition of foreign goods after the war ; in which case, the goods which have hitherto been produced to buy the foreign goods will not now be required for foreign trade. It may be that on the return of peace, some European States, in order to give their industries an opportunity to recover from the effects of the war, will inaugurate new tariffs ; there is, indeed, a strong possibility that on these grounds, and because of the dependence of the United Kingdom on the products of Germany, the Tariff Reform Movement here may be electrified into life.

2. *Possible Industrial Developments.*—But industrial changes will not be confined to the direction and form which economic activity will take. As has been suggested above, there may be far - reaching changes in the methods of production. It has been said that " there is only one way by which the wealth of the world will be quickly replaced after the war and that is by work. The country whose workers show the greatest capacity for productiveness will be the country which will most rapidly recuperate." [1] The question goes deeper than the replacement of wealth. The position after the war will be that production will be retarded because of the diminution in the rate of accumulation of new capital since the beginning of the war ; there will be a certain amount of leeway to make up. Consequently, there will be every incentive

[1] *Round Table*, Sept. 1914, p. 708.

towards the greatest possible efficiency in production. It is here that the workers are likely to be affected. Has labour reached its maximum efficiency? It has been shown by the application of what is called " scientific management," that the output of labour can be increased to a remarkable extent. For instance, instead of shovelling 16 tons a day, a man can shovel 59 tons; a man loading pig-iron increased his total load per day from $12\frac{1}{2}$ to $47\frac{1}{2}$ tons; the day's tale of bricks laid has been raised from 1000 to 2700. The list could be extended to cover operatives working at machines. In the endeavour to screw up industry to a maximum of production, it is not likely that the expedients of " scientific management " will long remain untried. Already the system is making considerable headway in the United States, and it is not altogether unknown in this country. It is not possible to enter into a full explanation of the methods of " scientific management." Briefly, by a process of scientific selection it puts each worker in the job for which he is best fitted, and teaches him exactly how to use the most efficient tools with which he would be provided. The method of teaching may be illustrated from Mr. F. W. Taylor's own example : " Schmidt started to work, and all day long and at regular intervals, was told by the man who stood over him with a watch, ' Now, pick up a pig and walk. Now sit down and rest. Now walk—now rest,' etc. He worked when he was told to work, and rested when he was told to rest, and at half-past five in the afternoon had his $47\frac{1}{2}$ tons loaded on the car." [1] By elaborate experiments the exact shape and size of a shovel is determined ; by long observation useless and awkward movements of a workman are eliminated or replaced by the correct movements giving the

[1] *Scientific Management*, by F. W. Taylor, p. 47.

maximum return for the minimum of effort. In this way, and by a bonus on wages, a largely increased output is obtained. It is clear that the adoption of such methods gives the " scientific manager " great power ; it also seems inevitable that the workman should degenerate into an automaton ; it is obvious that in the hands of employers ignorant of the principles underlying it, and seeing merely a new and highly profitable method of exploitation, it will be open to serious abuse, as experience has already shown in America.

So far the tremendous significance of " scientific management " has not been fully recognised. Properly understood, it is the complement to the industrial revolution, which by the more extensive use of machinery, etc., increased the efficiency of capital. The present movement aims at a similar increase in the efficiency of labour as an agent of production. The new revolution in industry has as yet merely begun, because employers, in spite of the motive of self-interest, are conservative ; but it will receive an enormous impetus from the conditions arising out of the war. Like the introduction of machinery and factory industry a century and a half ago and onward, it may be accompanied by widespread evils and cruel exploitation. Indeed, there is every likelihood that the methods will be distorted and misused. By their careful application there is no doubt that the output of the labourer can be increased without the expenditure of greater effort than before, but even then there would be the tendency towards becoming de-humanised. This, however, might be overcome by shorter hours and higher wages, which would raise the standard of comfort and widen the worker's interests. Unwisely used, " scientific management " will become an instrument for shackling the worker, and increasing at a great rate the wealth of the capitalist. It will be freely admitted that anything that will increase the productivity of the labourer, and therefore the wealth of the community, is advantageous, provided there is an equitable distribution of the product, and that the effects on the working members of the State are not socially injurious. But the hidden evils that may manifest themselves are very real, and it is important that not only the workers, but the State should be prepared to save the good and prevent the evil. There will, however, be large numbers of employers of labour who will not avail themselves of the new-fangled methods, and who will endeavour to increase production by the old policy of " driving." And even without driving, wage-earning labour under present conditions may be carried on under circumstances unfavourable to industrial efficiency, and for hours inimical to the welfare of the community and actually injurious to industrial productivity. In the future the State will be more closely concerned with industry and commerce than hitherto ; there will probably be a more clearly defined State policy aimed at the encouragement of production. Its view will be wider than that of the individual employer, and we may expect therefore, providing there is no serious reaction after the strain of the war, that the State will impose working conditions which will favour maximum production in the long run. It will be to the interest of the community to maximise the efficiency of the industrial system ; and enlightened statesmanship will overhaul our existing code of industrial laws to achieve this object as far as possible, as well as to guard the community against the evils inherent in a misapplication of the principles of " scientific management." [1]

[1] See an article on " Next Steps in Factory and Workshop Reform," by Arthur Greenwood, in the *Political Quarterly* for September 1914.

After the war, unemployment is likely to increase. The work of new production will be put into operation only gradually; there will be every inducement to economise the use of labour as far as possible; wages during the depression will most probably fall; there will be disaffection in the ranks of the trade unionists; the possible consolidation of industries into the hands of fewer employers will increase the strength of the masters; the funds of the trade unions will be depleted by the heavy strain on their resources, and subject to a further drain after the war. The outlook of the trade union movement is, therefore, far from bright. It will be generally agreed that the bankruptcy or serious impoverishment of the unions of this country would be nothing less than a national disaster; but unless action of some kind is taken, they will become greatly weakened and almost impotent, and one great bulwark against unjust encroachments upon the rights of labour will be removed.

It is not improbable, however, that the community will indirectly assist the trade unions by the steps taken to mitigate the evils which the war will leave in its train. The army instead of being immediately disbanded may be gradually dismissed over a period of, say, five years; the widows and dependants of soldiers and sailors, and those who have returned maimed and crippled from the war, may be adequately provided for, and, together with children of twelve and thirteen, kept off the labour market; the larger schemes of the Development Commission may be put into operation; the legal minimum wage may be extended to all low-paid trades. In these and other ways the community may deal comprehensively with the problems it has to face. The difficulties of the aftermath period will call for both clear-sighted action and public spirit; and if it is to be bridged over successfully, the transition from a war to a peace footing must be gradual; the community must continue its state of mobilisation in order to meet the enemy within the gates. Provided the united wisdom of the nation is thrown into the task, the evil after-effects of the war may be, if not altogether avoided, restricted within narrow limits. At the bottom, therefore, the future course of events depends upon the temper and spirit of the people at the close of the war.

3. *Social Effects and the New Outlook.*—The European conflict will probably exercise a strong sobering influence upon the minds of the people. The gravity of the crisis, whatever victories may crown our arms, will be reflected in the gravity of the people. A new dignity, a greater self-respect, a deeper earnestness may arise among the mass of the people, to which the conduct of our soldiers in the field will contribute. High qualities of leadership win their admiration; but for them they claim no credit. The army is officered for the most part by people of a higher social standing, whose qualities they will willingly admit; but the social gulf debars them from gaining inspiration from their achievements. In the case of the rank and file, largely drawn from their own class, the effect is different. The Tommy is flesh of their flesh and blood of their blood. The qualities he displays reflect credit upon his class. The working man is not unmindful of the high opinion in which the British private has been held by a line of continental soldiers from Napoleon to Bernhardi. The exploits of his fellows in the field have given the lie to stories of deterioration; and working people are experiencing a sense of pride in their class which may have no inconsiderable effect on their attitude regarding social developments in the future.

Already the national temper has not submitted without protest to the disgraceful sweating of our troops merely because their patriotism has led them to sacrifice their lives, which are beyond all money payment. But the feeling in favour of the war and the spirit of trust in the Government has, up to the present, overridden serious criticism. The result has been that the Government has often remained inactive when action was needed and has acted unwisely and ignorantly at times ; for example, in the case of the Local Government Board circular, stating that the Army Council are prepared to issue allowances through the Soldiers' and Sailors' Families Association or the Local Representation Committees. It has been said that " the whole system is an outrage on democratic principles. The State sweats its servants and then compels them to take the niggardly wages it allows them from a charitable society." [1] This type of action may pass muster during a time of stress, but whether the spirit of the people will accept it after the war is over and there are the dependants of the slain to be maintained and the permanently crippled to be provided for is a different matter. Not merely justice, but the new pride of the people will rebel against it. These are but phases of the larger social problem. There is the question of poverty in all its ramifications. For the moment, economic injustices and social evils have fallen into the back of people's minds, and the new and abnormal causes of destitution are calling forth special measures of assistance. After the war, the ever-present deep-seated poverty will reassert its presence, and in the hearts of many people the question will arise as to whether the community which courageously and whole-heartedly fought the enemy without the gates will turn

[1] *The Nation*, Sept. 19, 1914.

with equal courage and determination when the time comes to fight the enemy within the gates. The experiences of the war time, the willingness to embark on great projects in face of a national crisis, will not be forgotten, but will inspire in social reformers the hope that the country may also face the internal national peril in a similar spirit. The national—as opposed to the individual—poverty which the war will cause may itself be a force making for good. As Mr. Lloyd George well said, "A great flood of luxury and of sloth which had submerged the land is receding and a new Britain is appearing. We can see for the first time the fundamental things that matter in life, and that have been obscured from our vision by the tropical growth of prosperity." [1] There seems a prospect of an era of social growth and regeneration following the war. In other European countries there may be equally important developments. It may well be that in the event of German defeat the democratic movements of that country will gain a great impetus from the blow given to the Prussian hegemony. In Russia there is an expectation of a new freedom. At the first meeting of the Duma after the opening of hostilities the Labour Party declared its opinion that "through the agony of the battlefield the brotherhood of the Russian people will be strengthened and a common desire created to free the land from its terrible internal troubles."

It must be admitted, on the other hand, that there is a possibility of a period of reaction and torpor after the strain of the war; the country will be seriously impoverished, and there will be a heavy burden of taxation in spite of some probable relief from the burden of armaments. Still, social evils and injustices will be more obvious than

---

[1] Speech at the Queen's Hall, London, Sept. 19, 1914.

ever. There will be many new national and imperial problems clamouring to be faced. The intellectual ferment which has had its source in the war will remain at work to widen the mental outlook and deepen the social consciousness. On the whole, it will probably be true to say that, though circumstances may postpone it, there will sooner or later arise a great movement pledged to cleanse our national life of those features which bar the way to human freedom and happiness.

It also seems undeniable that the deep interest taken by large numbers of people in the war will rouse them to a sense of the importance of problems of government and of foreign policy. The working men's committees on foreign affairs of half a century ago, which have left no trace behind them, may be revived in a new form, and the differentiation of economic and social questions from political and foreign problems may be obliterated. The importance of the gradually widening area of vision among the more thoughtful section of the people can hardly be exaggerated. In no respect is the broadening of outlook more discernible than in the sphere of imperial affairs. Hitherto the Empire to the working man has been regarded as almost mythical. In so far as it did exist, it was conceived as a happy hunting ground for the capitalist exploiter. The spontaneous assistance given to the mother country by the colonies and dependencies has convinced him of the reality of the Empire, and vaguely inspired him with a vision of its possibilities as a federation of free commonwealths. In other words, the British Empire, contrasted with that of Germany, is gradually being recognised as standing for Democracy, however imperfect its achievements may be up to the present. Consequently, the return of peace will see a deeper interest in imperial questions ; indeed, it is not too much to say that there will be an imperial renaissance, born of a new patriotism, "clad in glittering white." The change of heart which is taking place in the people of this country, through the opening of the flood-gates of feeling and thought by the unsuspecting warrior in shining armour, may bring a new age comparable in its influence on civilisation with the great epochs of the past. To-day is seed-time. But the harvest will not be gathered without sweat and toil. The times are pregnant with great possibilities, but their realisation depends upon the united wisdom of the people.

BOOKS

In order to understand the machinery of international trade, reference should be made to Hartley Withers' *Money Changing* (5s.), or Clare's *A.B.C. of the Foreign Exchanges* (3s.) ; an outline of the subject will be found in any good general text-book on Economics. On the financial situation, see articles on "Lombard Street in War" and "The War and Financial Exhaustion" (*Round Table*, September and December 1914) ; "War and the Financial System, August 1914," by J. M. Keynes (*Economic Journal*, September 1914) ; and articles in the *New Statesman* on "Why a Moratorium ?" (August 15, 1914), and "The Restoration of the Remittance Market" (August 29, 1914). Norman Angell's *The Great Illusion* (2s. 6d.) should be consulted for an examination of the relations between war and trade. The most accessible book dealing with the foreign trade of the European countries is the *Statesman's Year-Book*, published annually at 10s. 6d. The chapters reprinted from the *Encyclopaedia Britannica* are also useful. A valuable article on "The Economic Relations of the British and German Empires," by E. Crammond, appeared in the *Journal of the Royal Statistical Society*, July 1914. The same writer published an article on "The Economic Aspects of the War" in *The Quarterly Review* for October 1914 (6s.). A grasp of the economic development of Germany may be obtained from W. H. Dawson's *Evolution of Modern Germany* (5s.) and the same writer's *Industrial Germany* (Nation's Library, 1s.). Mr. F. W. Taylor's *Scientific Management* (5s.) and Miss J. Goldmark's *Fatigue and Efficiency* (8s.) explain scientific management. A short account is also given in Layton's *Capital and Labour* (Nation's Library, 1s.).

The course of unemployment in this country may be traced from the returns published each month in the *Board of Trade Labour Gazette* (monthly, 1d.). Proposals for dealing with possible and existing distress during the war are to be found in a pamphlet on *The War and the Workers*, by Sidney Webb (Fabian Society, 1d.). For the possible use of trade unions as a channel for the distribution of public assistance, see an article in *The Nation* for September 5, 1914, and Mr. G. D. H. Cole's article on " How to help the Cotton Operative " in *The Nation* for November 7, 1914. The same paper published two suggestive articles on " Relief or Maintenance ? " (September 19 and October 3). The situation which has arisen in the woollen and worsted industries owing to the large demand for cloth for the troops is dealt with in an article on " The Government and Khaki," by Arthur Greenwood in *The Nation* for November 28, 1914. Reference may be made to the official White Paper on Distress ; other official documents of note are the following :

" Separation allowances to the Wives and Children of Seamen Marines, and Reservists." Cd. 7619. 1914. ½d.

" Increased Rates of Separation Allowance for the Wives and Children of Soldiers." Cd. 7255. 1914. ½d.

" Return of Papers relating to the Assistance rendered by the Treasury to Banks and Discount Houses since the Outbreak of War on August 4, 1914, and to the Questions of the Advisability of continuing or ending the Moratorium and of the Nature of the Banking Facilities now available." H.C. 457 of 1914. 1d.

" Report, dated April 30, 1914, of a Sub-Committee of the Committee of Imperial Defence on the Insurance of British Shipping in Time of War, to devise a scheme to ensure that, in case of war, British Steamships should not be generally laid up, and that Oversea Commerce should not be interrupted by reason of inability to cover war risks of Ships and Cargoes by Insurance, and which would also secure that the insurance rates should not be so high as to cause an excessive rise in prices." Cd. 7560. 1914. 2½d.

The Government has issued a *Manual of Emergency Legislation* (3s. 6d.) containing the statutes, proclamations, orders in council, rules, regulations, and notifications used in consequence of the war ; the appendices contain other documents (the Declarations of Paris and of London, the Hague Convention, etc.).

CHAPTER IX

GERMAN CULTURE AND THE BRITISH COMMONWEALTH

" Peace cannot become a law of human society, except by passing through the struggle which will ground life and association on foundations of justice and liberty, on the wreck of every power which exists not for a principle but for a dynastic interest."—MAZZINI in 1867.

"The greatest triumph of our time, a triumph in a region loftier than that of electricity or steam, will be the enthronement of this idea of Public Right as the governing idea of European policy ; as the common and precious inheritance of all lands, but superior to the passing opinion of any. The foremost among the nations will be that one which, by its conduct, shall gradually engender in the minds of the others a fixed belief that it is just."—GLADSTONE.

§ 1. *The Two Issues.* — The War of 1914 is not simply a war between the Dual Alliance and the Triple Entente : it is, for Great Britain and Germany especially, a war of ideas—a conflict between two different and irreconcilable conceptions of government, society, and progress. An attempt will be made in this chapter to make clear what these conceptions are, and to discuss the issue between them as impartially as possible, from the point of view, not of either of the combatant Powers, but of human civilisation as a whole.

There are really two great controversies being fought out between Great Britain and Germany : one about the

348

ends of national policy, and another about the means to be adopted towards those or any other ends. The latter is the issue raised by the German Chancellor's plea—not so unfamiliar on the lips of our own countrymen as we are now tempted to believe—that " Necessity knows no law." It is the issue of Law and " scraps of paper " against Force, against what some apologists have called " the Philosophy of Violence," but which, in its latest form, the French Ambassador has more aptly christened " the Pedantry of Barbarism." That issue has lately been brought home, in its full reality, to the British public from the course of events in Belgium and elsewhere, and need not here be elaborated. Further words would be wasted. A Power which recognises no obligation but force, and no law but the sword, which marks the path of its advance by organised terrorism and devastation, is the public enemy of the civilised world.

But it is a remarkable and significant fact that the policy in which this ruthless theory is embodied commands the enthusiastic and united support of the German nation. How can this be explained ?

It must be remembered in the first place that the German public does not see the facts of the situation as we do. On the question of Belgian neutrality and the events which precipitated the British ultimatum, what we know to be a false version of the facts is current in Germany, as is evident from the published statements of the leaders of German thought and opinion, and it may be many years before its currency is displaced.

This difficulty should serve to remind us how defective the machinery of civilisation still is. One of the chief functions of law is, not merely to settle disputes and to enforce its decisions, but to ascertain the true facts on which alone a settlement can be based. The fact that no tribunal exists for ascertaining the true facts in disputes between sovereign governments shows how far mankind still is from an established " rule of law " in international affairs. Not only is the Hague powerless to give and, still more, to enforce its decision on the questions at issue between the European Powers. It has not even the machinery for ascertaining the facts of the case and bringing them to the notice of neutral governments and peoples in the name of civilisation as a whole.

But apart from divergent beliefs as to the facts, it is remarkable that thinking Germany should be in sympathy with the spirit and tone of German policy, which led, as it appears to us, by an inexorable logic to the violation of Belgian neutrality and the collision with Great Britain.

But the fact, we are told, admits of easy explanation. Thinking Germany has fallen a victim to the teachings of Treitschke and Nietzsche—Treitschke with his Macchiavellian doctrine that " Power is the end-all and be-all of a State," Nietzsche with his contempt for pity and the gentler virtues, his admiration for " valour," and his disdain for Christianity.

This explanation is too simple to fit the facts. It may satisfy those who know no more of Treitschke's brilliant and careful work than the extracts culled from his occasional writings by General von Bernhardi and the late Professor Cramb. It may gratify those who, with so many young German students, forget that Nietzsche, like many other prophets, wrote in allegory, and that when he spoke of valour he was thinking, not of " shining armour," but of spiritual conflicts. But careful enquirers, who would disdain to condemn Macaulay on passages selected by undiscriminating admirers from his *Essays*, or Carlyle for his frank admiration of Thor and Odin and the virtues of Valhalla, will ask for a more satisfying explanation. Even if all that were said about Treitschke and Nietzsche were true, it would still remain an unsolved question why they and their ideas should have taken intellectual Germany by storm. But it is not true. What is true, and what is far more serious, both for Great Britain and for Europe, is that men like Harnack, Eucken, and Wilamowitz, who would repudiate all intellectual kinship with Macchiavelli and Nietzsche—men who are leaders of European thought, and with whom and whose ideas we shall have to go on living in Europe—publicly support and encourage the policy and standpoint of a Government which, according to British ideas, has acted with criminal wickedness and folly, and so totally misunderstood the conduct and attitude of Great Britain as honestly to regard us as hypocritically treacherous to the highest interests of civilisation.

That is the real problem ; and it is a far more complex and difficult one than if we had to do with a people which had consciously abandoned the Christian virtues or consciously embarked on a conspiracy against Belgium or Great Britain. The utter failure of even the most eminent Germans to grasp British politics, British institutions, and the British point of view points to a fundamental misunderstanding, a fundamental divergence of outlook, between the political ideals of the two countries. It is the conflict between these ideals which forms the second great issue between Germany and Great Britain ; and on its outcome depends the future of human civilisation.

§ 2. *Culture.*—What is the German ideal ? What do German thinkers regard as Germany's contribution to human progress ? The answer comes back with a monotonous reiteration which has already sickened us of the word.

It is *Kultur*, or, as we translate it, culture. Germany's contribution to progress consists in the spread of her culture.

Kultur is a difficult word to interpret. It means " culture " and a great deal more besides. Its primary meaning, like that of " culture," is intellectual and aesthetic : when a German speaks of " Kultur " he is thinking of such things as language, literature, philosophy, education, art, science, and the like. Children in German schools are taught a subject called *Kulturgeschichte* (culture-history), and under that heading they are told about German literature, German philosophy and religion, German painting, German music and so on.

So far, the English and the German uses of the word roughly correspond. We should probably be surprised if we heard it said that Shakespeare had made a contribution to English " culture " : but, on consideration, we should admit that he had, though we should not have chosen that way of speaking about him. But there is a further meaning in the word *Kultur*, which explains why it is so often on German lips. It means, not only the product of the intellect or imagination, but the product of the disciplined intellect and the disciplined imagination. *Kultur* has in it an element of order, of organisation, of civilisation. That is why the Germans regard the study of the " culture " of a country as part of the study of its history. English school children are beginning to be taught social and industrial history in addition to the kings and queens and battles and constitutions which used to form the staple of history lessons. They are being taught, that is, to see the history of their country, and of its civilisation, in the light of the life and livelihood of its common people. The German outlook is different. They look at their history in the light of the achievements of its great minds, which

are regarded as being at once the proof and the justification
of its civilisation.   To the question, " What right have you
to call yourselves a civilised country ? " an Englishman
would reply, " Look at the sort of people we are, and at
the things we have done," and would point perhaps to the
extracts from the letters of private soldiers printed in the
newspapers, or to the story of the growth of the British
Empire ; a German would reply (as Germans are indeed
replying now), " Look at our achievements in scholarship
and science, at our universities, at our systems of education,
at our literature, our music, and our painting ; at our
great men of thought and imagination : at Luther, Dürer,
Goethe, Beethoven, Kant."

   Kultur then means more than " culture " : it means
culture considered as the most important element in civilisation.
It implies the disciplined education which alone, in the
German view, makes the difference between the savage and
the civilised man.   It implies the heritage of intellectual
possessions which, thanks to ordered institutions, a nation
is able to hand down from generation to generation.

   We are now beginning to see where the British and
German attitudes towards society and civilisation diverge.
Broadly, we may say that the first difference is that
Germany thinks of civilisation in terms of intellect while
we think of it in terms of character.   Germany asks,
" What do you know ? "   " What have you learnt ? "
and regards our prisoners as uncivilised because they cannot
speak German, and Great Britain as a traitor to civilisation
because she is allied with Russia, a people of ignorant
peasants.   We ask, " What have you done ? "   " What
can you do ? " and tend to undervalue the importance of
systematic knowledge and intellectual application.

   But we have found no reason as yet for a conflict of

ideals. Many English writers, such as Matthew Arnold, have emphasised the importance of culture as against character ; yet Matthew Arnold's views were widely different from those of the German professors of to-day. If their sense of the importance of culture stopped short at this point, we should have much to learn from Germany, as indeed we have, and no reason to oppose her. What is there then in the German admiration for culture which involves her in a conflict with British ideals ?

§ 3. *Culture as a State Product.*—The conflict arises out of the alliance between German culture and the German Government. What British public opinion resents, in the German attitude, is not culture in itself, about which it is little concerned, but what we feel to be its unnatural alliance with military power. It seems to us wicked and hypocritical for a government which proclaims the doctrine of the " mailed fist " and, like the ancient Spartans, glories in the perfecting of the machinery of war, to be at the same time protesting its devotion to culture, and posing as a patron of the peaceful arts. It is the Kaiser's speeches and the behaviour of the German Government which have put all of us out of heart with German talk about culture.

This brings us to a fundamental point of difference between the two peoples. The close association between culture and militarism, between the best minds of the nation and the mind of the Government, does not seem unnatural to a modern German at all. On the contrary, it seems the most natural thing in the world. It is the bedrock of the German system of national education. Culture to a German is not only a national possession ; it is also, to a degree difficult for us to appreciate, a State product. It is a national possession deliberately

handed on by the State from generation to generation,
hall-marked and guaranteed, as it were, for the use of its
citizens. When we use the word " culture " we speak of
it as an attribute of individual men and women. Germans,
on the other hand, think of it as belonging to nations as a
whole, in virtue of their system of national education.
That is why they are so sure that all Germans possess
culture. They have all had it at school. And it is all the
same brand of culture, because no other is taught. It is
the culture with which the Government wishes its citizens
to be equipped. That is why all Germans tend, not only
to know the same facts (and a great many facts too), but
to have a similar outlook on life and similar opinions about
Goethe, Shakespeare and the German Navy. Culture, like
military service, is a part of the State machinery.

Here we come upon the connecting link between culture
and militarism. Both are parts of the great German system
of State education. " Side by side with the influences of
German education," wrote Dr. Sadler in 1901,[1] " are to be
traced the influences of German military service. The two
sets of influence interact on one another and intermingle.
German education impregnates the German army with
science. The German army predisposes German education
to ideas of organisation and discipline. Military and
educational discipline go hand in hand. . . . Both are
preserved and fortified by law and custom, and by administrative arrangements skilfully devised to attain that end.
But behind all the forms of organisation (which would
quickly crumble away unless upheld by and expressing
some spiritual force), behind both military and educational
discipline, lies the fundamental principle adopted by
Scharnhorst's Committee on Military organisation in

[1] *Board of Education Special Reports*, vol. ix. p. 43.

Prussia in 1807 : ' All the inhabitants of the State are its defenders by birth.' "

At last we have reached the root of the matter. It is not German culture which is the source and centre of the ideas to which Great Britain is opposed : nor yet is it German militarism. Our real opponent is the system of training and education, out of which both German culture and German militarism spring. It is the organisation of German public life, and the " spiritual force " of which that organisation is the outward and visible expression.

§ 4. *German and British Ideals of Education.*—Let us look at the German ideal more closely, for it is worthy of careful study. It is perhaps best expressed in words written in 1830 by Coleridge, who, like other well-known Englishmen of his day (and our own) was much under the influence of German ideas. Coleridge, in words quoted by Dr. Sadler, defines the purpose of national education as " to form and train up the people of the country to obedient, free, useful, and organisable subjects, citizens and patriots, living to the benefit of the State and prepared to die in its defence." In accordance with this conception Prussia was the first of the larger States in Europe to adopt a universal compulsory system of State education, and the first also to establish a universal system of military service for its young men. The rest of Europe perforce followed suit. Nearly every State in Europe has or professes to have a universal system of education, and every State except England has a system of universal military service. The Europe of schools and camps which we have known during the last half century is the most striking of all the victories of German " culture."

Discipline, efficiency, duty, obedience, public service ; these are qualities that excite admiration everywhere—in the classroom, in the camp, and in the wider field of life. There is something almost monumentally impressive to the outsider in the German alliance of School and Army in the service of the State. Since the days of Sparta and Rome, there has been no such wonderful governmental disciplinary machine. It is not surprising that " German organisation " and " German methods " should have stimulated interest and emulation throughout the civilised world. Discipline seems to many to be just the one quality of which our drifting world is in need. " If this war had been postponed a hundred or even fifty years," writes a philosophic English observer in a private letter, " Prussia would have become our Rome, worshipping Shakespeare and Byron as Pompey or Tiberius worshipped Greek literature, and disciplining us. Hasn't it ever struck you what a close parallel there is between Germany and Rome ? " (Here follows a list of bad qualities which is better omitted.) . . . " The good side of it is the discipline ; and the modern world, not having any power external to itself which it acknowledges, and no men (in masses) having yet succeeded in being a law to themselves, needs discipline above everything. I don't see where you will get it under these conditions unless you find some one with an abstract love of discipline for itself. And where will you find him except in Prussia ? After all, it is a testimony to her that, unlovely as she is, she gives the law to Germany, and that the South German, though he dislikes her, accepts the law as good for him." And to show that he appreciates the full consequences of his words he adds : " If I had to live under Ramsay MacDonald (provided that he acted as he talks), or under Lieutenant von Förstner " (the hero of Zabern), " odious as the latter is, for my soul's good I would choose him : for I think that in the end, I should be less likely to be irretrievably ruined."

Here is the Prussian point of view, expressed by a thoughtful Englishman with a wide experience of education, and a deep concern for the moral welfare of the nation. What have we, on the British side, to set up against his arguments ?

In the first place we must draw attention to the writer's candour in admitting that a nation cannot adopt Prussianism piecemeal. It must take it as a whole, its lieutenants included, or not at all. Lieutenant von Förstner is as typical a product of the Prussian system as the London policeman is of our own ; and if we adopt Prussian or Spartan methods, we must run the risk of being ruled by him. " No other nation," says Dr. Sadler, " by imitating a little bit of German organisation can hope thus to achieve a true reproduction of the spirit of German institutions. The fabric of its organisation practically forms one whole. That is its merit and its danger. It must be taken all in all or else left unimitated. And it is not a mere matter of external organisation. . . . National institutions must grow out of the needs and character (and not least out of the weakness) of the nation which possesses them."

But, taking the system as a whole, there are, it seems to me, three great flaws in it—flaws so serious and vital as to make the word " education " as applied to it almost a misnomer. The Prussian system is unsatisfactory, firstly, because it confuses external discipline with self-control ; secondly, because it confuses regimentation with corporate spirit ; thirdly, because it conceives the nation's duty in terms of " culture " rather than of character.

Let us take these three points in detail.

The first object of national education is—not anything national at all, but simply education. It is the training of individual young people. It is the gradual leading-out (e-ducation), unfolding, expanding, of their mental and bodily powers, the helping of them to become, not soldiers, or missionaries of culture, or pioneers of Empire, or even British citizens, but simply human personalities. " The purpose of the Public Elementary School," say the opening words of our English code, " is to form and strengthen the character and to develop the intelligence of the children entrusted to it." In the performance of this task external discipline is no doubt necessary. Obedience and considera-tion for others are not learnt in a day. But the object of external discipline is to form habits of self-control which will enable their possessor to become an independent and self-respecting human being—and incidentally, a good citizen. " If I had to *live under* Ramsay MacDonald, or the Prussian Lieutenant," says our writer, " I would choose the latter, for my soul's good." But our British system of education does not proceed on the assumption that its pupils are destined to " live under " any one. Our ideal is that of the free man, trained in the exercise of his powers and in the command and control of his faculties, who, like Wordsworth's " Happy Warrior " (a poem which embodies the best British educational tradition) :

> . . . Through the heat of conflict, keeps the law
> In calmness made, and sees what he foresaw.

Neglect for the claims of human personality both amongst pupils and teachers is the chief danger of a State system of education. The State is always tempted to put its own claims first and those of its citizens second—to regard the citizen as existing for the State, instead of the State for its citizens. It is one of the ironies of history that no man was more alive to this danger than Wilhelm von Humboldt, the gifted creator of the Prussian system of education. As the motto of one of his writings he adopted the words, "*Against the governmental mania, the most fatal disease of modern governments*," and when, contrary to his own early principles, he undertook the organisation of Prussian education he insisted that "headmasters should be left as free a hand as possible in all matters of teaching and organisation." But the Prussian system was too strong for him and his successors, and his excellent principles now survive as no more than pious opinions. The fact is that in an undemocratic and feudal State such as Germany then was, and still largely is, respect for the personality of the individual is confined to the upper ranks of society. "I do not know how it is in foreign countries," says one of Goethe's heroes,[1] "but in Germany it is only the nobleman who can secure a certain amount of universal or, if I may say so, *personal* education. An ordinary citizen can learn to earn his living and, at the most, train his intellect; but, do what he will, he loses his personality. . . . He is not asked, "What are you?" but only, "What have you? what attainments, what knowledge, what capacities, what fortune? . . . The nobleman is to act and to achieve. The common citizen is to carry out orders. He is to develop individual faculties, in order to become useful, and it is a fundamental assumption that there is no harmony in his being, nor indeed is any permissible, because, in order to make himself serviceable in one way, he is forced to neglect everything else. The blame for this distinction is not to be attributed to the adaptability of the nobleman or the weakness of the common citizen. It is due to the constitution of society itself." Much has changed in Germany since Goethe wrote these words, but they still ring true. And

[1] Wilhelm Meister's *Lehrjahre*, Book v. chapter iii.

they have not been entirely without their echo in Great Britain itself.[1]

But man cannot live for himself alone. He is a corporate being; and, personality or no personality, he has to fit into a world of fellow-men with similar human claims. The second charge against the German system is that it ignores the value of human fellowship. It regards the citizens of a country as " useful and organisable subjects " rather than as fellow-members of a democracy, bound together by all the various social ties of comradeship and intercourse.

The Prussian system, with its elaborate control and direction from above, dislikes the free play of human groupings, and discourages all spontaneous or unauthorised associations. Schoolboy " societies," for instance, are in Germany an evil to be deplored and extirpated, not, as with us, a symptom of health and vigour, to be sympathetically watched and encouraged. Instead, there is a direct inculcation of patriotism, a strenuous and methodical training of each unit for his place in the great State machine. We do not so read human nature. Our British tendency is to develop habits of service and responsibility through a devotion to smaller and more intimate associations, to build

[1] The contrast which has been drawn in the preceding pages, as working-class readers in particular will understand, is between the *aims*, not the achievements, of German and British education. The German aims are far more perfectly achieved in practice than the British. Neither the law nor the administration of British education can be acquitted of " neglect for the claims of human personality." The opening words of the English code, quoted on p. 359 above, are, alas! not a statement of fact but an aspiration. We have hardly yet begun in England to realise the possibilities of educational development along the lines of the British ideal, both as regards young people and adults. If we learn the lesson of the present crisis aright, the war, so far from being a set-back to educational progress, should provide a new stimulus for effort and development.

on a foundation of lesser loyalties and duties. We do not conceive it to be the function of the school to *teach* patriotism or to *teach* fellowship. Rather we hold that good education *is* fellowship, *is* citizenship, in the deepest meaning of those words ; that to discover and to exercise the responsibilities of membership in a smaller body is the best training for a larger citizenship. A school, a ship, a club, a Trade Union, any free association of Englishmen, is all England in miniature. " To be attached to the subdivision, to love the little platoon we belong to in society," said Burke long ago, " is the first principle, the germ, as it were, of public affections. It is the first link in the series by which we proceed towards a love to our country and mankind. . . . We begin our public affections in our families. No cold relation is a zealous citizen. We pass on to our neighbour-hoods, to our habitual provincial connections. These are inns and resting-places . . . so many images of the great country, in which the heart found something which it could fill." [1]

There is one fairly safe test for a system of education : What do its victims think of it ? " In Prussia," says Dr. Sadler, " a schoolboy seems to regard his school as he might regard a railway station—a convenient and necessary establishment, generally ugly to look at, but also, for its purpose efficient." The illustration is an apt one : for a Prussian school is too often, like a railway station, simply a point of departure, something to be got away from as soon as possible. " In England a boy who is at a good secondary school cares for it as an officer cares for his regiment or as a sailor cares for his ship," or, we may add, as a Boy Scout cares for his Troop.[2]

[1] *Reflections on the French Revolution*, pp. 292, 494 (of vol. iii. of *Collected Works*, ed. 1899).

[2] *Special Reports*, ix. p. 113. Dr. Sadler's article deals with secondary schools only. Unfortunately, no one can claim that the

Democracy and discipline, fellowship and freedom, are in fact not incompatible at all. They are complementary : and each can only be at its best when it is sustained by the other. Only a disciplined and self-controlled people can be free to rule itself, and only a free people can know the full meaning and happiness of fellowship.

§ 5. *German and British Ideals of Civilisation.*—Lastly, the German system regards national " culture " rather than national character as the chief element in civilisation and the justification of its claim to a dominant place in the world. This view is so strange to those who are used to present-day British institutions that it is hard to make clear what it means. Civilisation is a word which, with us, is often misused and often misunderstood. Sometimes we lightly identify it with motor cars and gramophones and other Western contrivances with which individual traders and travellers dazzle and bewilder the untutored savage. Yet we are seldom tempted to identify it, like the Germans, with anything narrowly national ; and in our serious moments we recognise that it is too universal a force to be the appanage of either nations or individuals. For to us, when we ask ourselves its real meaning, civilisation stands for neither language nor culture nor anything intellectual at all. It stands for something moral and social and political. It means, in the first place, the establishment and enforcement of the Rule of Law, as against anarchy on the one hand and tyranny on the other ; and, secondly, on the basis of order and justice, the task of making men fit for free institutions, the work of guiding and training them to recognise the obligations of citizenship, to sub-ordinate their own personal interests or inclinations to the

---

idea of fellowship is as prominent in English elementary schools, or even in all secondary schools, as the quotation might suggest.

common welfare, the "commonwealth." That is what is meant when it is claimed that Great Britain has done a "civilising" work both in India and in backward Africa. The Germans reproach and despise us, we are told,[1] for our failure to spread "English culture" in India. That has not been the purpose of British rule, and Englishmen have been foolish in so far as they have presumed to attempt it : England has to learn from Indian culture as India from ours. But to have laid for India the foundations on which alone a stable society could rest, to have given her peace from foes without and security within, to have taught her, by example, the kinship of Power and Responsibility, to have awakened the social conscience and claimed the public services of Indians in the village, the district, the province, the nation, towards the community of which they feel themselves to be members, to have found India a continent, a chaos of tribes and castes, and to have helped her to become a nation—that is not a task of English culture : it is a task of civilisation.

Law, Justice, Responsibility, Liberty, Citizenship—the words are abstractions, philosophers' phrases, destitute, it might seem, of living meaning and reality. There is no such thing as English Justice, English Liberty, English Responsibility. The qualities that go to the making of free and ordered institutions are not national but universal. They are no monopoly of Great Britain. They are free to be the attributes of any race or any nation. They belong to civilised humanity as a whole. They are part of the higher life of the human race.

As such the Germans, if they recognised them at all, probably regarded them. They could not see in them the binding power to keep a great community of nations

[1] For evidence of this see Cramb's *Germany and England*, p. 25.

together.   They could not realise that Justice and Responsibility, if they rightly typify the character of British rule, must also typify the character of British rulers ; and that community of character expressed in their institutions and worked into the fibre of their life may be a stronger bond between nations than any mere considerations of interest. Educated Indians would find it hard to explain exactly why, on the outbreak of the war, they found themselves eager to help to defend British rule.   But it seems clear that what stirred them most was not any consideration of English as against German culture, or any merely material calculations, but a sudden realisation of the character of that new India which the union between Great Britain and India, between Western civilisation and Eastern culture, is bringing into being, and a sense of the indispensable need for the continuance of that partnership.[1]

It is just this intimate union between different nations for the furtherance of the tasks of civilisation which it seems so difficult for the German mind to understand.   " Culture," with all its intimate associations, its appeal to language, to national history and traditions, and to instinctive

[1] The reader will again understand that it is British aims rather than British achievements which are spoken of.   That British rule is indispensable to Indian civilisation is indeed a literal fact to which Indian opinion bears testimony; and it is the conduct and character of generations of British administrators which have helped to bring this sense of partnership about.   But individual Englishmen in India are often far from understanding, or realising in practice, the purpose of British rule.   Similarly, the growth of a sense of Indian nationality, particularly in the last few years, is a striking and important fact. But it would be unwise to underestimate the gigantic difficulties with which this growing national consciousness has to contend.   The greatest of these is the prevalence of caste-divisions, rendering impossible the free fellowship and social intercourse which alone can be the foundation of a sense of common citizenship.   Apart from this there are, according to the census, forty-three races in India, and twenty-three languages in ordinary use.

patriotism, is so much simpler and warmer a conception :
it seems so much easier to fight for Germany than to fight
for Justice in the abstract, or for Justice embodied in the
British Commonwealth. That is why even serious German
thinkers, blinded by the idea of culture, expected the break-
up of the British Empire. They could imagine Indians
giving their lives for India, Boers for a Dutch South Africa,
Irishmen for Ireland or Ulstermen for Ulster ; but the
deeper moral appeal which has thrilled through the whole
Empire, down to its remotest island dependency, lay beyond
their ken.

Let us look a little more closely at the German idea of
national culture rather than national character as the chief
element in civilisation. We shall see that it is directly
contrary to the ideals which inspire and sustain the British
Commonwealth, and practically prohibits that association
of races and peoples at varying levels of social progress
which is its peculiar task.

" Culture," in the German idea, is the justification of
a nation's existence. Nationality has no other claim.
Goethe, Luther, Kant, and Beethoven are Germany's title-
deeds. A nation without a culture has no right to a " place
in the sun." " History," says Wilamowitz in a lecture
delivered in 1898, " knows nothing of any right to exist
on the part of a people or a language without a culture.
If a people becomes dependent on a foreign culture " (*i.e.*
in the German idea, on a foreign civilisation) " it matters
little if its lower classes speak a different language : they,
too . . . must eventually go over to the dominant language.
. . . Wisely to further this necessary organic process is a
blessing to all parties ; violent haste will only curb it and
cause reactions. Importunate insistence on Nationality
has never anywhere brought true vitality into being, and

often destroyed vitality ; but the superior Culture which,
sure of its inner strength, throws her doors wide open, can
win men's hearts." [1] In the light of a passage like this, from
the most distinguished representative of German humanism,
it is easier to grasp the failure of educated Germany to
understand the sequel of the South African War, or the
aspirations of the Slav peoples, or to stigmatise the folly
of their statesmen in Poland, Denmark, Alsace-Lorraine,
and Belgium. " Importunate insistence on Nationality "
—the words come home to us now with a new meaning when
we learn that in Belgium, now perforce " dependent on a
foreign culture," babies are registered under German names
and newspapers printed in " the dominant language," and
that already " forty newspaper vendors in Brussels have
been sentenced to long terms of hard labour in German
prisons for selling English, French, and Belgian newspapers." [2] " Our fearless German warriors," writes the
leading German dramatist, Gerhart Hauptmann,[3] " are
*well aware of the reasons for which they have taken the field.
No illiterates will be found among them.* Many of them,
besides shouldering their muskets, carry their Goethe's
Faust, some work of Schopenhauer, a Bible, or a Homer
in their knapsacks." Such is a serious German writer's
idea of the way in which civilisation is diffused !

With such a philosophy of human progress as this,
German thinkers and statesmen look out into the future
and behold nothing but conflict—eternal conflict between
rival national " cultures," each seeking to impose its
domination. " In the struggle between Nationalities,"

[1] *Speeches and Lectures,* pp. 147-148 (1913 edition).
[2] Daily Papers, October 12, 1914 (Exchange Telegram from
Rotterdam).
[3] Letter quoted in the *Westminster Gazette.*

writes Prince Bülow,[1] in defence of his Polish policy, putting into a cruder form the philosophy of Wilamowitz, " one nation is the hammer and the other the anvil ; one is the victor and the other the vanquished. It is a law of life and development in history that where two national civilisations meet they fight for supremacy."

Here we have the necessary and logical result of the philosophy of culture. In the struggle between cultures no collaboration, no compromise even, is possible. German is German : Flemish is Flemish : Polish is Polish : French is French. Who is to decide which is the " more civilised," which is the fitter to survive ? Force alone can settle the issue. A Luther and Goethe may be the puppets pitted in a contest of culture against Maeterlinck and Victor Hugo. But it is Krupp and Zeppelin and the War-Lord that pull the strings. As Wilamowitz reminds us, it was the Roman legions, not Virgil and Horace, that stamped out the Celtic languages and romanised Western Europe. It is the German army, two thousand years later, that is to germanise it. It is an old, old theory ; Prussia did not invent it, nor even Rome. " You know as well as we do," said the Athenians in 416 B.C. to the representatives of a small people of that day,[2] " that right, as the world goes, is only in question between equals in power, while the strong do what they can and the weak suffer what they must " ; and they went on, like the Kaiser, to claim the favour of the gods, " neither our pretensions nor our conduct being in any way contrary to what men believe of the gods, or practise amongst themselves." There is, in fact, to be no Law between Nations but the Rule of the Stronger.

§ 6. *The Principle of the Commonwealth.*—Such seems to

---

[1] *Imperial Germany*, p. 245 (1st ed.).
[2] *Thucydides*, Book v. 89 and 105.

many the meaning of the present European situation—a stern conflict between nations and cultures, to be decided by force of arms. The bridges between the nations seem broken down, and no one can tell when they will be repaired. The hopes that had gathered round international movements, the cosmopolitan dreams of common action between the peoples across the barriers of States and Governments, seem to have vanished into limbo; and the enthusiastic dreamers of yesterday are the disillusioned soldiers and spectators of to-day. Nationality, that strange, inarticulate, unanalysable force that can call all men to her tents in the hour of crisis and danger, seems to have overthrown the international forces of to-day, the Socialists, the Pacifists, and, strongest of all, the Capitalists, as it overthrew Napoleon and his dreams of Empire a hundred years ago. What Law is there but force that can decide the issue between nation and nation? And, in the absence of a Law, what becomes of all our hopes for international action, for the future of civilisation and the higher life of the human race?

But in truth the disillusionment is as premature as the hopes that preceded it. We are still far off from the World-State and the World-Law which formed the misty ideal of cosmopolitan thinkers. But only those who are blind to the true course of human progress can fail to see that the day of the Nation-State is even now drawing to a close in the West. There is in fact at present working in the world a higher Law and a better patriotism than that of single nations and cultures, a Law and a patriotism that override and transcend the claims of Nationality in a greater, a more compelling, and a more universal appeal. The great States or Powers of to-day, Great Britain, the United States, France, and (if they

2 B

had eyes to see it) Russia, Germany and Austria-Hungary, are not Nation-States but composite States—States compacted of many nationalities united together by a common citizenship and a common law. Great Britain, the United States, the German Empire, and Austria-Hungary bear in their very names the reminder of the diverse elements of which they are composed; but France with her great African Empire, and Russia with her multitudinous populations, from Poland to the Pacific, from Finland to the Caucasus, are equally composite. In each of these great States nations have been united under a common law; and where the wisdom of the central government has not " broken the bruised reed or quenched the smoking flax " of national life, the nations have been not only willing but anxious to join in the work of their State. Nations, like men, were made not to compete but to work together; and it is so easy, so simple, to win their good-hearted devotion. It takes all sorts of men, says the old proverb, to make a world. It takes all sorts of nations to make a modern State. " The combination of different nations in one State is as necessary a condition of civilised life as the combination of men in society. . . . It is in the cauldron of the State that the fusion takes place by which the vigour, the knowledge, and the capacity of one portion of mankind may be communicated to another. . . . If we take the establishment of liberty for the realisation of moral duties to be the end of civil society, we must conclude that those States are substantially the most perfect which, like the British and Austrian Empires, include various distinct nationalities without oppressing them." So wrote Lord Acton, the great Catholic historian, fifty years ago, when the watchwords of Nationality were on all men's lips, adding, in words that were prophetic of the failure of the

Austrian and the progress of the British Commonwealth of Nations: " The coexistence of several nations under the same State *is a test* as well as the best security *of its freedom.* It is also one of the chief instruments of civilisation ; and, as such, it is in the natural and providential order, and indicates a state of greater advancement than the national unity which is the ideal of modern liberalism." [1]

Of the Great Powers which between them control the destinies of civilisation Great Britain is at once the freest, the largest, and the most various. If the State is a " cauldron " for mingling " the vigour, the knowledge, and the capacity " of the portions of mankind—or if, to use an apter metaphor, it is a body whose perfection consists in the very variety of the functions of its several members— there has never been on the earth a political organism like the British Empire. Its 433 million inhabitants, from Great Britain to Polynesia, from India and Egypt to Central Africa, are drawn from every division of the human race. Cut a section through mankind, and in every layer there will be British citizens, living under the jurisdiction of British law. Here is something to hearten those who have looked in vain to the Hague. While international law has been brought to a standstill through the absence of a common will and a common executive, Great Britain has thrown a girdle of law around the globe.

§ 7. *The Future of Civilisation.*—What hopes dare we cherish, in this hour of conflict, for the future of civilisation ?

The great, the supreme task of human politics and statesmanship is to extend the sphere of Law. Let others labour to make men cultured or virtuous or happy. These are the tasks of the teacher, the priest, and the common

[1] Essay on Nationality, in *The History of Freedom and other Essays,* pp. 290, 298.

man. The statesman's task is simpler. It is to enfold
them in a jurisdiction which will enable them to live the
life of their souls' choice. The State, said the Greek philosophers, is the foundation of the good life; but its crown
rises far above mere citizenship. "There where the State
ends," cries Nietzsche,[1] echoing Aristotle and the great
tradition of civilised political thought, "there *men begin*.
There, where the State ends, look thither, my brothers!
Do you not see the rainbow and the bridge to the Overman?"
Ever since organised society began, the standards of the
individual, the ideals of priest and teacher, the doctrines
of religion and morality, have outstripped the practice of
statesmanship. For the polestar of the statesman has not
been love, but law. His not the task of exhorting men to
love one another, but the simpler duty of enforcing the law,
"Thou shalt not kill." And in that simple, strenuous,
necessary task statesmen and political thinkers have
watched the slow extension of the power of Law, from the
family to the tribe, from the tribe to the city, from the city
to the nation, from the nation to the Commonwealth.
When will Law take its next extension? When will warfare, which is murder between individuals and "rebellion"
between groups of citizens, be equally preventable between
nations by the common law of the world?

The answer is simple. When the world has a common
will, and has created a common government to express and
enforce that will.

In the sphere of science and invention, of industry and
economics, as Norman Angell and others have taught us,
the world is already one Great Society. For the merchant,
the banker, and the stockbroker political frontiers have been
broken down. Trade and industry respond to the reactions

[1] *Also sprach Zarathustra*, Speech xi. (end).

of a single, world - wide, nervous system. Shocks and panics pass as freely as airmen over borders and custom-houses. And not " big business " only, but the humblest citizen, in his search for a livelihood, finds himself caught in the meshes of the same world-wide network. " The widow who takes in washing," says Graham Wallas,[1] in his deep and searching analysis of our contemporary life, " fails or succeeds according to her skill in choosing starch or soda or a wringing machine under the influence of half a dozen competing world-schemes of advertisement. . . . The English factory girl who is urged to join her Union, the tired old Scotch gatekeeper with a few pounds to invest, the Galician peasant when the emigration agent calls, the artisan in a French provincial town whose industry is threatened by a new invention, all know that unless they find their way among world-wide facts, which only reach them through misleading words, they will be crushed." The Industrial Revolution of the past century, steam-power and electricity, the railway and the telegraph, have knit mankind together, and made the world one place.

But this new Great Society is as yet formless and in-articulate. It is not only devoid of common leadership and a common government ; it lacks even the beginnings of a common will, a common emotion, and a common consciousness. Of the Great Society, consciously or un-consciously, we must all perforce be members ; but of the Great State, the great World-Commonwealth, we do not yet discern the rudiments. The economic organisation of the world has outstripped the development of its citizen-ship and government : the economic man, with his far-sighted vision and scientific control of the resources of the world, must sit by and see the work of his hands laid in

[1] *The Great Society* (1914), p. 4.

ashes by contending governments and peoples. No man can say how many generations must pass before the platitudes of the market and the exchange pass. into the current language of politics.

§ 8. *The Two Roads of Advance : Inter-State Action and Common Citizenship.*—In the great work which lies before the statesmen and peoples of the world for the extension of law and common citizenship and the prevention of war there are two parallel lines of advance.

One road lies through the development of what is known as International, but should more properly be called *Inter-State Law,* through the revival, on a firmer and broader foundation, of the Concert of Europe conceived by the Congress of Vienna just a hundred years ago—itself a revival, on a secular basis, of the great mediaeval ideal of an international Christendom, held together by Christian Law and Christian ideals. That ideal faded away for ever at the Reformation, which grouped Europe into independent sovereign States ruled by men responsible to no one outside their own borders. It will never be revived on an ecclesiastical basis. Can we hope for its revival on a basis of modern democracy, modern nationality, and modern educated public opinion ? Can Inter-State Law, hitherto a mere shadow of the majestic name it bears, almost a matter of convention and etiquette, with no permanent tribunal to interpret it, and no government to enforce it, be enthroned with the necessary powers to maintain justice between the peoples and governments of the world ?

Such a Law the statesmen of Great Britain and Russia sought to impose on Europe in 1815, to maintain a state of affairs which history has shown to have been intolerable to the European peoples. There are those who hope that the task can be resumed, on a better basis, at the next Congress.

" Shall we try again," writes Professor Gilbert Murray,[1] " to achieve Castlereagh's and Alexander's ideal of a permanent Concert, pledged to make collective war upon the peace-breaker ? Surely we must. We must, at all costs and in spite of all difficulties, because the alternative means such unspeakable failure. We must learn to agree, we civilised nations of Europe, or else we must perish. I believe that the chief council of wisdom here is to be sure to go far enough. We need a permanent Concert, perhaps a permanent Common Council, in which every awkward problem can be dealt with before it has time to grow dangerous, and in which outvoted minorities must accustom themselves to giving way."

Other utterances by public men, such as Mr. Roosevelt and our own Prime Minister, might be cited in the same sense ; but Professor Murray's has been chosen because he has had the courage to grasp the nettle. In his words the true position is quite clearly set forth. If Inter-State Law is to become a reality we must " be sure to go far enough." There is no half-way house between Law and no Law, between Government and no Government, between Responsibility and no Responsibility. If the new Concert is to be effective it must be able to compel the submission of all " awkward problems " and causes of quarrel to its permanent Tribunal at the Hague or elsewhere ; and it must be able to enforce the decision of its tribunal, employing for the purpose, if necessary, the armed forces of the signatory Powers as an international police. " Outvoted minorities must accustom themselves to giving way." It is a bland and easy phrase ; but it involves the whole question of world - government. " Men must accustom themselves not to demand an eye for an eye and a tooth for

[1] *Hibbert Journal*, Oct. 1914, p. 77.

a tooth," the earliest law-givers might have said, when the
State first intervened between individuals to make itself
responsible for public order. Peace between the Powers,
as between individuals, is, no doubt, a habit to which
cantankerous Powers "must accustom themselves." But
they will be sure to do so if there is a Law, armed with the
force to be their schoolmaster towards peaceable habits. In
other words, they will do so because they have surrendered
one of the most vital elements in the independent life of a
State—the right of conducting its own policy—to the jurisdiction of a higher Power. An Inter-State Concert, with
a Judiciary of its own and an Army and Navy under its
own orders, is, in fact, not an Inter-State Concert at all;
it is a new State: it is, in fact, the World-State. There
is no middle course between Law and no Law: and the
essence of Statehood, as we have seen, is a Common
Law.

Will this new State have the other attributes of Government—a Common Legislature and a Common Executive—
as well as a Common Judiciary? Let us go back to
Professor Murray's words. He speaks of "outvoted
minorities." Let us suppose the refractory country to be
Great Britain, outvoted on some question relating to sea-
power. Of whom will the outvoted minority consist? Of
the British members on the "Common Council" of the
Concert. But the question at once arises, what are the
credentials of these British members? Whom do they
represent? To whom are they responsible? If they are
the representatives of the British people and responsible
to the democracy which sent them, how can they be expected
to "accustom themselves to giving way"—perhaps to a
majority composed of the representatives of undemocratic
governments? Their responsibility is, not to the Concert,

but to their own Government and people. They are not
the minority members of a democratically-elected Council
of their own fellow-citizens. They are the minority
members of a heterogeneous Council towards which they
owe no allegiance and recognise no binding responsibility.
There is no half-way house between Citizenship and no
Citizenship, between Responsibility and no Responsibility.
No man and no community can serve two masters. When
the point of conflict arises men and nations have to make
the choice where their duty lies. Not the representatives
of Great Britain on the International Concert, but the
people of Great Britain themselves would have to decide
whether their real allegiance, as citizens, was due to the
World-State or to their own Commonwealth : they would
find themselves at the same awful parting of the ways which
confronted the people of the Southern States in 1861.
When at the outbreak of the Civil War General Lee was
offered by Lincoln the Commandership of the Northern
armies and refused it, to become the Commander-in-Chief
on the side of the South, he did so because " he believed,"
as he told Congress after the war, " that the act of Virginia
in withdrawing herself from the United States carried him
along with it as a citizen of Virginia, and that *her* laws and
acts were binding on him." In other words, unless the
proposed Common Council is to be made something more
than a Council of the delegates of sovereign States (as the
Southern States believed themselves to be till 1861), a
deadlock sooner or later is almost inevitable, and the
terrible and difficult question—so familiar to Americans and
recently to ourselves on the smaller stage of Ulster—of the
right of secession and the coercion of minorities will arise.
But if the Common Council is framed in accordance with a
Constitution which binds its representatives to accept its

decisions and obey its government, then the World-State, with a World-Executive, will already have come into being. There will be no more war, but only Rebellion and Treason.

Such is the real meaning of proposals to give a binding sanction to the decisions of an Inter-State Concert. Anything short of this—treaties and arbitration-agreements based upon inter-State arrangements without any executive to enforce them—may give relief for a time and pave the way for further progress, but can in itself provide no permanent security, no satisfactory justification for the neglect of defensive measures by the various sovereign governments on behalf of their peoples. Mr. Bryan, for the United States, has within the last eighteen months concluded twenty-six general arbitration treaties with different Governments, and may yet succeed in his ambition of signing treaties with all the remainder. Yet no one imagines that, when the immunity of the United States from attack is guaranteed by the promise of every Government in the world, America will rely for her defence upon those promises alone.

In discussing proposals for a European Council, then, we must be quite sure to face all that it means. But let us not reject Professor Murray's suggestion off-hand because of its inherent difficulties: for that men should be discussing such schemes at all marks a significant advance in our political thought. Only let us be quite clear as to what they presuppose. They presuppose the supremacy, in the collective mind of civilised mankind, of Law over Force, a definite supremacy of what may be called the civilian as against the military ideal, not in a majority of States, but in every State powerful enough to defy coercion. They presuppose a world map definitely settled on lines satisfactory to the national aspirations of the peoples. They presuppose a *status quo* which is not simply maintained, like that after 1815, because it is a legal fact and its disturbance would be inconvenient to the existing rulers, but because it is inherently equitable.[1] They presuppose a similar democratic basis of citizenship and representation among the component States. They presuppose, lastly, an educated public opinion incomparably less selfish, less ignorant, less unsteady, less materialistic, and less narrowly national than has been prevalent hitherto. Let us work and hope for these things : let us use our best efforts to remove misunderstandings and promote a sense of common responsibilities and common trusteeship for civilisation between the peoples of all the various sovereign States ; but meanwhile let us work also, with better hopes of immediate if less ambitious successes, along the other parallel road of advance.

The other road may seem, in this hour of dreams and disaster, of extremes of hope and disillusionment, a long and tedious track : it is the old slow high road of civilisation, not the short cut across the fields. It looks forward to abiding results, not through the mechanical co-operation of governments, but through the growth of an organic citizenship, through the education of the nations themselves to a sense of common duty and a common life. It looks forward, not to the definite establishment, in our day, of the World-State, but only to the definite refutation of the wicked theory of the mutual incompatibility of nations. It looks forward to the expression in the outward order of the

---

[1] The same applies to proposals for ensuring permanent peace in the industrial sphere. Neither capital nor labour will abide by " scraps of paper " if they do not feel the *status quo* (*i.e.* the conditions under which wage-contracts are made) to be equitable and inherently just.

world's government of what we may call " the Principle of the Commonwealth," of Lord Acton's great principle of the State composed of free nations, of the State as a living body which lives through the organic union and free activity of its several national members. And it finds its immediate field of action in the deepening and extension of the obligations of citizenship among the peoples of the great, free, just, peace-loving, supra-national Commonwealths whose patriotism has been built up, not by precept and doctrine, but on a firm foundation of older loyalties.

The principle of the Commonwealth is not a European principle : it is a world-principle. It does not proceed upon the expectation of a United States of Europe ; for all the Great Powers of Europe except Austria-Hungary (and some of the smaller, such as Holland, Belgium, and Portugal) are extra-European Powers also. Indeed if we contract our view, with Gladstone and Bismarck and the statesmen of the last generation, to European issues alone, we shall be ignoring the chief political problem of our age—the contact of races and nations with wide varieties of social experience and at different levels of civilisation. It is this great and insistent problem (call it the problem of East and West, or the problem of the colour-line) in all its difficult ramifications, political, social, and, above all, economic, which makes the development of the principle of the Commonwealth the most pressing political need of our age. For the problems arising out of the contact of races and nations can never be adjusted either by the wise action of individuals or by conflict and warfare ; they can only be solved by fair and deliberate statesmanship within the bosom of a single State, through the recognition by both parties of a higher claim than their own sectional interest—the claim of a common citizenship and the

interest of civilisation.[1] It is here, in the union and collaboration of diverse races and peoples, that the principle
of the Commonwealth finds its peculiar field of operation.
Without this principle, and without its expression, however
imperfect, in the British Empire, the world would be in
chaos to-day.

We cannot predict the political development of the
various Great Powers who between them control the
destinies of civilisation. We cannot estimate the degree
or the manner in which France, freed at last from nearer
preoccupations, will seek to embody in her vast dominion
the great civilising principles for which her republic stands.
We cannot foretell the issue of the conflict of ideas
which has swayed to and fro in Russia between the British
and the Prussian method of dealing with the problem of
nationality. Germany, Italy, Japan—here, too, we are
faced by enigmas. One other great Commonwealth remains
besides the British. Upon the United States already lies
the responsibility, voluntarily assumed and, except during
a time of internal crisis,[2] successfully discharged, of securing
peace from external foes for scores of millions of inhabitants
of the American continent. Yet with the progress of
events her responsibilities must yearly enlarge : for both
the immigrant nationalities within and the world-problems
without her borders seem to summon her to a deeper
education and to wider obligations.

But upon the vast, ramifying, and inchoate Commonwealth of Great Britain lies the heaviest responsibility.
It is a task unequally shared between those of her citizens
who are capable of discharging it. Her task within the

[1] The most recent example of this is the settlement of the very
difficult dispute between India and South Africa.

[2] French occupation of Mexico, 1862, during the American Civil
War, when the Monroe Doctrine was temporarily in abeyance.

Commonwealth is to maintain the common character and
ideals and to adjust the mutual relations of one quarter
of the human race. Her task without is to throw her
weight into the scales of peace, and to uphold and develop
the standard and validity of inter-State agreements. It
is a task which requires, even at this time of crisis, when,
by the common sentiment of her citizens, the real nature
and purpose of the Commonwealth have become clear to
us, the active thoughts of all political students. For to
bring home to all within her borders who bear rule and
responsibility, from the village headman in India and
Nigeria, the Basutu chief and the South Sea potentate,
to the public opinion of Great Britain and the self-governing
Dominions, the nature of the British Commonwealth, and
the character of its citizenship and ideals, and to study
how those ideals may be better expressed in its working
institutions and executive government—that is a task to
which the present crisis beckons the minds of British
citizens, a task which Britain owes not only to herself but
to mankind.

Note.—A friendly critic who saw this chapter in MS. remarked :
" I think the author has been very successful in ignoring some of the
shady methods by which the British Empire has been extended."
The criticism is not strictly relevant to the subject of the chapter, but
as it may occur to other readers it may be well to deal with it in a
brief note. I would answer :

(1) The " shady methods " of which he speaks were not the result
of British Imperialism, or of a desire for conquest on the part of the
British State. They were the result, melancholy but inevitable, of
the contact of individuals and races at different levels of development.
This contact between the stronger and the weaker (which can be
illustrated from what is said about the sandalwood traders in the
New Hebrides on p. 215 above) was the direct result of the explorations
of the sixteenth century, which threw the seas of the world open to
Western pioneers and traders. The extension of the authority of
Western *governments* (Spanish, Portuguese, Dutch, French, and
British), and the collisions between them, followed inevitably on the

activities of their citizens, as has been pointed out on p. 216 above. All the Western governments have made mistakes in dealing with this unfamiliar situation ; but the wise course for democratic public opinion, instead of railing at "Imperialism," would seem to be to familiarise itself with its problems and control its injurious tendencies.

(2) In any case, the mistakes of the past do not entitle us to wash our hands of responsibilities in the present. This war has shown that the non-self-governing parts of the Commonwealth are not, as our enemies supposed, a weakness to Great Britain in time of trouble, but a strength. In other words, whatever may have happened in the past, Great Britain has now won the consent of the ruled to the fact —not necessarily to the methods—of British rule. To use what is doubtless unduly constitutional language, we are now faced in India and elsewhere, not with a Revolutionary Movement, but with an Opposition. That is a great incentive to further development.

BOOKS

The Philosophy of Violence

Bernhardi, *Germany and the Next War* (2s.), has become familiar. But this is only one *application* of a doctrine which has found expression in many spheres, as, for example, in the writings of the French Syndicalists, who claim to be copying the *methods* of Capitalism, and the *principles* of Bergson's philosophy —with what justification must be left to the reader to determine. See G. Sorel, *Réflexions sur la Violence* (Paris, Marcel Rivière, 1910, 5 francs), and Sorel's other writings. "Bernhardi-ism" is, in fact, not a German product : it has been before the public for some years under the name of "militancy," in connection with various causes, though it has never been put into execution on so tremendous a scale as by the Prussian Government. Nor is its philosophical basis to be found only, if at all, in Nietzsche.

Kultur

The insistence on "Culture" as the main factor in the life and development of peoples is to be found in practically every German history, and in a great many non-German writers. It has received an additional vogue from the development of the study of *Sociology*, which naturally seeks out, in tracing the development of societies in the past, the elements which lend themselves to measurement and description, and these are inevitably, from the nature of the evidence, rather "cultural" than moral. It would be invidious to mention instances.

EDUCATION

For Dr. SADLER's articles see p. 119, above. See also PAULSEN, *German Education : Past and Present.* 1908. 5s. net.

THE PRINCIPLE OF THE COMMONWEALTH

The best philosophical book on the relations of advanced and backward races is *The Basis of Ascendancy : a Discussion of certain Principles of Public Policy involved in the Development of the Southern States*, by EDGAR GARDNER MURPHY (a clergyman living at Montgomery, Alabama) (1909, 6s. net). Though written with reference to the peculiar American problem, the book has a far wider significance. There is no good book which covers the ground either on India or the British Empire. E. R. BEVAN's little volume on *Indian Nationalism* (2s. 6d. net) may be mentioned. An article on *India and the Empire* in the *Round Table* for September 1912 is also worth mention (and worth reprinting).

THE GREAT SOCIETY

WALLAS, *The Great Society* (1914, 7s. 6d. net), and NORMAN ANGELL, *The Great Illusion* (1910, 2s. 6d. net), are the standard works— the former as a psychologist and a philosopher, the latter as a pamphleteer with a very acute vision within a limited field.

INTERNATIONAL LAW

See LINDSAY, *The War against War* (Oxford pamphlets, 2d.), a model of clear argument, so far as it goes. Also ALISON PHILLIPS, *The Confederation of Europe : A Study of the European Alliance, 1813–1823, as an Experiment in the International Organisation of Peace* (1914, 7s. 6d. net), the best book on the Congress of Vienna and the problems connected with it, especially on the subject of an International Tribunal and Universal Peace. The Prime Minister's speeches will be familiar. See also Mr. Roosevelt's pamphlet on the United States and the Hague Convention (Newnes, 2d.).

MONROE DOCTRINE

See an article by L. S. ROWE in the *Political Quarterly*, October 1914.